Writing Indian, Native Conversations

Writing Indian,

Native Conversations

John Lloyd Purdy

University of Nebraska Press
Lincoln and London

Library of Congress Cataloging-in-Publication Data

Purdy, John Lloyd.
  Writing Indian, native conversations / John Lloyd
  Purdy.
  p. cm. Includes bibliographical references and index.
  ISBN 978-0-8032-2287-8 (cloth : alk. paper)
  1. American fiction—Indian authors—History and
criticism. 2. Indians of North America—Intellectual
life. 3. Indians in literature. I. Title.
  PS53.I52P87 2009
  813.009'897—dc22   2009013675

Set in Minion Pro by Bob Reitz.
Designed by A. Shahan.

Contents

Introductions

There is a statement I kept coming across in ethnographies of Native American stories years ago while doing research: "No one ever did this to me before." Often it is the utterance of a monster, sometimes one about to get its comeuppance. It's a simple thing, but the line has stayed with me over the years because it seems that this is also the reaction many readers have when they first encounter the works of Native American authors. As I argued at one point long ago, reading the fiction of Native authors at their best is often a voyage of discovery, so to speak, where sudden revelations act as points of reference in a remapped landscape in which the issues of Native, Indigenous America are prominent. As I described it then, it is like a Mimbres bowl I saw in a museum entitled *Winged Beings*. I stared at it a long time, straining to see these beings, but as I gave up and started to move on to another display, they flew right at me. Sometimes all it takes is a slight shift in point of view, and the uneasiness of an encounter in new imaginative terrain becomes an aesthetic surprise. Something new has entered our vision.

Well, you say, isn't this always the case with good fiction, and I will answer, yes, of course, but in the works of Native authors reside some qualities not shared by the likes of Ernest Hemingway, or William Faulkner, or name your icon of the "old canon." But what exactly are these "qualities" that mark the canon? This is a long-standing bone of contention in scholarly circles and elsewhere, and that bone has been gnawed by some very impressive people as critics have tried time and time again to "define" this canon and thus argued about its parameters and sometimes its perimeters: what *is* a Native text and what is not; who *is* and who is not; and what does a truly Native aesthetic look like? The discussion continues as scholars mark out their "territory" and defend it with sometimes red-hot verbiage. (After all, "canon" is only one consonant removed from an implement of noise, heat, and devastation.)

Since 1978 and the publication of Charles Larson's *American Indian Fiction*, numerous books and articles have offered their authors' own readings of the canon and its definitive qualities. These came in increasing numbers after the 1970s as more scholars-educators studied works by Native artists and as the number of Native scholars increased. By 1995, when Robert Warrior published his *Tribal Secrets*, the discourse had expanded to include multiple generations of writers and scholars, and conditions were right for the reconsideration of the assumptions upon which much of the earlier criticism was based. Like Warrior's book, Jace Weaver's *That the People Might Live* (1997) and Craig Womack's *Red on Red* (1999) offered other ways of reading Native authors, including culturally specific criticism. However, this is what Michael Dorris argued in his seminal work, "Native American Literature in an Ethnohistorical Context," in 1979, and by the time David Treuer offered his own, ostensibly original, view in *Native American Fiction* (2006), the same year James H. Cox published *Muting White Noise*, we found ourselves back in critical terrain familiar to Larson: trying to define how this canon is distinct and where it is located within a wider aesthetic of Western literary history. Before I am lambasted for making such a claim, I will add that we are much richer for that thirty-year journey.

In 2003 Elvira Pulitano published *Toward a Native American Critical Theory*, a compendium, of sorts, of other attempts to define the critical canon and its reading, with her own readings of Native texts offered for added consideration. To say that this created a buzz in the community of Native scholars would be an understatement. I have heard the book condemned—and praised—*at the same conference*. In fact, the *American Indian Quarterly* published *six* reviews of the book in one issue, with equally conflicting responses. What no one seems to notice, however, is the operative word in the title of the book and what it implies: "toward" suggests a journey, a process, rather than *the* conclusive, definitive word on the canon, which is a criticism some readers level against the book.[1] Criticism is, or should be, an ongoing open discourse with as many voices and points of view as possible; if it is otherwise, the discourse is dead, and I have seen this happen in classes when students, confronted with essays critical of non-Native readings of works of literature, simply choose to avoid the dilemma by refusing to read any more of the literature. If the fiction produced by Native artists were produced for *only* Native communities or for *one* Native community (and there are instances where this is true), perhaps it would be otherwise. Since there are multiple reactions to any work of literature, there need to be multiple lines of inquiry to unpack its art. A recent issue of *Studies in American Indian Literatures*, in fact, holds a special section with some provocative titles in relation to this problem: "Pitfalls of Tribal Specificity," "Assessing Native Criticism," "A Relational Model for Native American Literary Criticism," and "Conceptualizing American Indian Literary Theory Today." The beat goes on.

The dangers of closing the dialogue persist. I believe this is one of the cautionary subtexts to be found in Louis Owens's wonderful "Coyote Story, or the Birth of a Critic" in *I Hear the Train*.

The multiplicity of voices is just what Paula Gunn Allen celebrates in the interview in chapter 1. As she takes joy in 1997 in the increased attention Native literatures were receiving after twenty years of critical discourse, she notes that criticism is not necessarily about "answers," not about one definitive reading of a work of art, but about the questions we ask of ourselves and, as scholars, for others about the world that the work describes. This is the benefit that the studies mentioned above offer: new and more informative questions to consider as we read Native fiction. In fact, I would argue, to present one's own reading as *the* definitive reading of any of the novels discussed in this book would more closely align the effort with the conventions of Western academic criticism than with an Indigenous mode of discourse. Thus, it is not my intention to challenge other critics' ways of reading the canon or to situate my readings as a counterpoint to theirs; instead, I offer other Native writers' and scholars' words *as context for my own readings*. The "theory" I offer is no more than a "provisional convenience," as Arnold Krupat noted of his own work at a conference years ago when he was challenged for "Westernizing" Native texts.

And, of course, debates such as this are not new. They descend from the first surprise of discovery when Columbus rowed toward shore trying to fit the people gazing out at him into his somewhat limited paradigm. However, for the purposes of contemporary fiction, the debates emerge from some interesting events and personalities. In fact, it could be argued that critical study of this literature began in 1977. This does not mean that a critical discourse did not exist prior to this year; on the contrary, for hundreds of years— from the publication of a sermon by Samson Occum in the 1770s at least—professional and amateur scholars have read the writings of authors who identified as "American Indian," and some of these recorded their reactions in essays and reviews and books. However, it was not until 1977 that a core group of scholars and writers convened to discuss this "field" of study (in the terms of the times) and where it was going. This event took place in Flagstaff, Arizona, and was funded by the National Endowment for the Humanities, the NEH. It provided a critical mass, pun intended, to the discourse and thus a locus for future events. I will refer back to this later, since it was a seminal event.

Coincidentally, my first foray into the study of Native American literatures took place in the same year under the tutelage of Montana Richards Walking Bull, the Native poet-scholar-professor. I will share some stories about her later, but, for the moment, suffice it to say that she opened up a new literary world for me. No one had ever done this to me before. As an English major I read and studied the primary works of the Western canon but from a New Critical point of view. After all, the canon's conventions, aesthetics, and culture were so ingrained in my consciousness that they were invisible. My rethinking of them began with Hal Borland's *When the Legends Die*, one of the works we read in Richards Walking Bull's course and that I haven't read since. The Native fiction I later read in graduate school, however, foregrounded cultural issues from the get-go. Surprise! Suddenly, literary conventions, aesthetics, and cultures became a relative study, and the world became more complex and wonderful. I have seen the same revelation strike home for countless readers and students over the years.

Despite those individuals who resisted the expansion of the canon during the culture wars of the 1980s and 1990s, this recognition is a beneficial thing and does not result in the wholesale dismissal of the "great works" of the Western literary canon, a contention that was posited by the National Association of Scholars in a full-page ad in the *New York Review of Books* during the 1989–90 academic year. The ad, a tour de force of illogic, was published while I was a Fulbright professor at the University of Mannheim, and in this context it is ironic that it came in the year when the Wall came down in Germany. At a moment of conciliation, unification, and liberation of global significance and, supposedly, a time of the ascendancy of democratic ideals, the ad called for homogeneous retrenchment. "Circle the wagons!" my German students responded, thinking they had found yet one more example of provincial, narrow thinking and the racist-sexist bias of Americans.

My German students were very discerning readers, and I hope I complicated their thinking, since they, too, were the recipients of some inherited paradigms. After all, Germany has its own James Fenimore Cooper in Karl May, whose romanticist depictions of Native Americans are equally pernicious and persistent, and his ideas played out in my classroom as contemporary Native authors resisted and complicated them time and time again in their works. However, as the students read these works, their initial reactions— "No one ever did this to me before"—naturally evolved into a line of inquiry much like that in critical circles in general at the time. They had their teeth into something that was new for them, and they tried to fit it into their understanding of literature and literary canons.

In one prose seminar, a course in Native literatures, there were several advanced students from the university as well as a PhD candidate from the University of Heidelberg, a short distance away, who wanted to include discussions of Native texts in her dissertation. In essence, I was discussing the course texts for three or more audiences: one that was in the class because of an interest in the subject matter (often thanks to the work of May) but that was not attempting a *Schein*, or credit for the course, and therefore not required to do a research project and receive a grade—a "general" audience of sorts; another one bent on an academic career and therefore reading with an eye for recognizable detail that would be useful in a paper; and one that would attempt to publish a dissertation or book that included Native texts and literary criticism. We needed a framework that suited all, and it came as I prepared a lecture on Native fiction, trying to provide a point of commonality for these diverse thinkers-readers, these diverse texts.

Definition is obviously the first task one encounters in any introductory (dis)course. Of course, we are concerned with writings by Native American authors, and thus a blood-quantum complication emerges immediately, but "definition" also implies other ways by which individual works form a canon, a distinct body of literature. In general, at that initial stage and point in time there were two interrelated ways to delineate the subject without falling immediately either into the biology issue or into a comparative analysis with other works of American literature (thus implying a nebulous mainstream standard of literary excellence), both of which persist in the works of some critics today. The first way was to examine, closely, several works to develop a feeling for recurrent characteristics or patterns: narrative motif, thematic focus, imagery, characters, structure, and so on. The second was to explore elements of tribal verbal arts in these contemporary writings, thus discovering the use of non-Western *and* Western literary traditions. In both cases the definition derives from within the text and canon, emphasizing its own techniques and standards, without imposing others from outside.

That statement should raise yet one more issue: we all come to a work of literature with a "lens," a critical-cultural orientation, so isn't this an "imposition" from the outside for a non-Native reader? Maybe. However, the fiction I am discussing leads to a disorientation, then a reorientation, in the terms mentioned above: surprise. The end effect of that process is that the lens becomes visible, and, I would suggest, this is true for non-Native *and* Native readers. Consider the hundreds of cultural lenses that exist for all people and thus the multiple responses from readers. If a work is clarified by only one lens, is it literature? Or does literature live in its ability to accommodate many lenses?

So one further consideration was born: how could either way of definition hope to encompass such variety? How does one approach Peter Blue Cloud's "Coyote Meets Raven" in a way that may also be applied to Linda Hogan's "New Shoes"? (Both works are in the wonderful Simon Ortiz anthology we were reading in the course.) The New Critical approach of close reading seemed to work well enough at first, but when we looked up from the individual piece of literature and to the canon, that approach led to diffusion rather than clarity, and a "tribal literary analysis" came to the difficult position of trying to establish literary "blood laws" to document the tribal identity and experience and objectives of the author, a tendency I noticed in many students that did not seem universally productive.

To accommodate such diverse pieces of literature we required a theory—one simple, specific, critical theory—that could facilitate reading not only for someone new to the canon but also for others with more experience in it, a theory that was not inhibitive, that could direct without becoming dogmatic, and that could be set aside when its work was done: something descriptive that did not become prescriptive. The texts must speak for themselves, after all, but one may certainly attune the ears of the listeners. Also, the canon grows over time, so what could help provide a sense of continuity without, again, becoming prescriptive?

I posited a four-part theory of elemental, structural traits of Native texts, and to demonstrate the diversity I used a simple graphic representation to visualize the range of each voice in the works we were reading. The graphic is no longer important here, although the theory itself may be. Although it was applied mostly to recent works of fiction, twentieth-century fiction, we also found it useful for examining poetry, autobiography, and even ethnographic texts. Although I crafted it long ago, I wish to return to this idea today in this collection of essays and interviews because so much has been written in the interim by way of "new" theories. In the chapters that follow I use this four-part frame to open a variety of critical approaches to some of the canon's central texts and authors. By way of introduction I will simply provide here a brief synopsis of my thinking on this, and it begins with the idea of someone walking into a bookstore and pulling a book marked "Indian" from a shelf.

When readers encounter this body of literature for the first time, they cannot help but ask what makes it "Indian." It is a simple, natural question, but it raises numerous layers of significant, complex issues, as noted above. At this stage of reading, however, it is sufficient to say that, more often than not, the text "tells" us it is Indian, that it is somehow distinct. No matter how this is done—by overt statement, by allusion to tribal attitudes or literatures, by the use of tribal structures or characters—it is accomplished.[2] Therefore, the texts employ *differentiation* by establishing themselves as works of Native literatures and, in many cases, as the consequences of a specific tribal literature, history, and culture.

There are a variety of ways to handle this, given the variety of backgrounds and talents of the authors. By evoking the term, however, one immediately focuses attention, time after time, upon the methods employed to achieve differentiation and therefore upon crucial elements of style, voice, and often tribal conventions of literary expression. Discussion of these, in turn, sensitizes the reader for future readings. In a word, spotting differentiation is spotting signification, the "signs" of culture, for good or ill, depending upon the writer.

Unfortunately, once a difference in cultural orientation is established, the reader must soon pose a potentially dangerous question: How does this tribal culture compare with my own? (Or, in the case of a shared culture between reader and writer, my own perception?) This query may be the effect desired by the author, but it is problematic, for it can lead to the dead-end debates of social Darwinism and popular concepts of "primitivism" if one is not careful to read closely. As in any work of literature, the question is how the author perceives and represents humanity, the strengths and weaknesses of people and cultures (either tribal or nontribal). Fortunately, Native American texts provide a degree of *investigation*, as characters act and react, events fold and unfold, images shape and reshape our perceptions. This investigation evokes the reader's sense of story, history, and cosmos and then engages it, and this interaction can be charted with critical tools. In fact, if the first stage lends itself to semiotics, this calls for audience-oriented criticism and also deconstruction. The use of value-laden binaries carries its own dangers, depending upon how these are inverted and reconciled.

The third theoretical stage of texts is *affirmation*. Tribal texts, especially modern written texts, are not usually self-deprecating. This does not mean that they are inaccurate or unconcerned with less-than-desirable issues and themes, that they are romanticized or sanitized; we have Cooper and May and their contemporary clones for that. Native American literatures explore social problems, despicable characters, and major blunders of tribal pasts as readily as they present heroics, victories, and power. But this literature explicates and reaffirms identity in community, moral centers at once tentative and supportive, threatened and durable. Urban or reservation based, contemporary texts assert this identification and thereby integration over alienation.

This will be difficult for some readers to accept because it presents a view of history largely at odds with popular misconceptions of tribal cultures. Why would authors affirm something that has been "lost"? Or, worse yet, something that should be lost? Such reactions occur at times, but the "doomed Indian" is an image easily addressed, if discussions of the first three stages are sufficient. The long-standing endurance of tribal verbal arts can be easily documented as well. By showing that a contemporary work of fiction—through overt statement or implication—also emphasizes this same sense of *continuation*, one provides a means of closure for one work while opening discussion for others, thus highlighting their relatedness. In brief, if readers doubt this fourth element of continuity, one can always point to the evidence in their hands.

While recent debates have considered a difference in works that argue either "survivance" or "victimry" (in the terms of Gerald Vizenor), these four elements are still relevant and useful. This is not a four-part prescriptive formula for writers but forms instead Krupat's "provisional conveniences" for readers. Granted, this is a simplified theory, but it is not simply arbitrary. It accounts for elemental traits to be found in fiction by Native writers, but, more importantly, it challenges introductory readers to look for the means of refuting it, thereby directing their intuitive compulsion for comparative analysis within the canon. The evidence they find to question the theory leads to crucial points of interpretation, to thematic and stylistic concerns worthy of exploration; critics have also enumerated and explicated these elements, so the readers' impulses are validated. Moreover, as one works through the canon, the growing awareness of diversity automatically works to shape and sharpen definition. For instance, when one discusses differentiation, one will isolate elements of landscape, language, literature, and cosmology that vary from tribe to tribe, writer to writer. This gives resonance to tribal authors' voices while it also provides for consideration of *why* an author would need to differentiate, investigate, and so on. Thus, social and historical contexts begin to emerge even if they are not overtly addressed in the text.

I developed this approach to fulfill a need, but I must emphasize that it is simply a useful tool for initiation and now, I believe, reconsideration; it helps initiate discussion and then direct future readings, although it may not necessarily resolve difficult analyses in all areas and genres of American Indian literatures. However, given the recent attempts to provide a "new" and "unique" critical theory, I would like to return to this old one and see what benefits may derive from it. As I consider some of the central works and authors of the canon, these four elements (differentiation, investigation, affirmation, and continuation) should prove useful: let's call them DIAC.

What follows is an exploration of how this theory applies to the canons of several prominent Native authors and to the works that one may be relatively certain most scholars of Native literatures have read. By walking through its structure in their books, one finds some intriguing aspects of them that authors use to mark their texts as Native and to investigate their personal visions of what that means. This study is not an attempt to be all-inclusive, by any measure. This would be impossible, given the numbers of Native writers and texts. Any collection is thus selective. However, it *does* attempt an historical framework, of sorts, moving from the 1970s. This, too, is difficult, since many of the writers discussed have careers that cut across several decades, and, as those decades reflect an alteration in the audience for this canon, they also reflect a changing discourse about the canon and a respondent revision in the artists' visions and texts. Since critics often, then, consider both canon and criticism to be linear, that they "evolve" over time, the following conversations have a few central questions. Is there a moment when returning to a critical approach termed "dated" may be useful for current circumstances and texts? Are there some elements of fiction in this canon that recur over time, and, if so, what can we learn by (re)considering them? And, finally, can we reread the classics and learn, once again? I would hope so.

Writing Indian, Native Conversations

1 | THE 1970s

The three authors discussed in this chapter—N. Scott Momaday, James Welch, and Leslie Marmon Silko—are prominent in contemporary Native American literatures. Certainly, during the last three decades of the twentieth century they garnered a great deal of critical attention. N. Scott Momaday is still the only Native author to have won the Pulitzer Prize, and the fact that he won it with his first novel is certainly remarkable and noteworthy. Moreover, this award helped open the door for publication by others, James Welch included, through the Harper and Row Native American series it helped initiate and the interest this in turn generated with other prominent presses. The first novels of these three authors are widely considered central to the canon, and many critical essays and books have been generated to discuss their merits since they were first published: Momaday's *House Made of Dawn* in 1968; Welch's *Winter in the Blood* in 1974, followed by *The Death of Jim Loney* in 1979; and Silko's *Ceremony* in 1977. By 1984 and the publication of Louise Erdrich's first novel, *Love Medicine* (the "next generation"), and critical studies such as Kenneth Lincoln's *Native American Renaissance* the year before, these earlier novels had achieved the status of "classics" and become part of, as Lincoln's title suggests, a new wave of literary production.

Keeping in mind that the publication of Silko's novel came in the same year as the NEH conference in Flagstaff that launched the Association for the Study of American Indian Literatures and all that subsequently happened to bring this canon into the curricula of universities and colleges, this would seem a fortuitous convergence of events. However, it is also notable that Silko was one of the participants at the conference, as was another woman writer from

Laguna Pueblo, Silko's home and the location of her first novel. Paula Gunn Allen's family has a long history at the pueblo, and one of her ancestors was a self-taught ethnologist; John M. Gunn published *Schat-chen: History and Narratives of the Queres Indians of Laguna and Acoma* in 1917.

After the conference Allen compiled a collection of works from other participants, and this became *Studies in American Indian Literature*, published in 1983. It was followed in 1986 by *The Sacred Hoop*, which extends the discussion of Native texts and cosmology originally presented in the former book. In other words, as the four novels noted above moved to define a critical center for the fiction canon, Allen and other scholars were attempting to articulate what made the canon distinct: what *differentiated* it from other canons.

In 1997, in preparation for a special issue of the association's journal, also entitled *Studies in American Indian Literatures* (SAIL), dedicated to the twentieth anniversary of the Flagstaff conference, I had the occasion to talk with Allen about the conference and those twenty years. The conversation took place at Château de la Brétesche in Brittany on June 25, immediately following the completion of a three-day symposium entitled "Theories of Representation in American Indian Literatures: European and North American Perspectives." The symposium brought together European and American scholars, both Native and non-Native, to share research topics and approaches, and the discussions that ensued were enjoyably intense and wide-ranging. Since much of the symposium brought historical contexts to bear in the discussion of Native texts, it seemed an appropriate moment to discuss the last twenty years with her.

John Purdy (JP): It's interesting, this morning, to be talking about the last twenty years, and that's one of the fun things about doing this issue of SAIL. It's been twenty years since Flagstaff, and as you were saying this morning, there's a lot that's happened in twenty years.

Paula Gunn Allen (PGA): Tremendous, so much . . . It's hard to know what the group . . . the first meetings were so funny. You'd go to MLA [the Modern Language Association's annual conference], and there'd be this nice group of English professors or American lit professors, whatever. The first one I went to was, it must have been '73, Michael Dorris and myself and one other person, I forget who it was, and the people in the audience were asking, no, making these comments like, "Well, I know an Indian and he told me that the Indian way is blahda blahda blahda blahda." And then, by the time I went to the last MLA I went to, which was a couple of years ago in San Francisco, the level of the discussion is like the level here, at this symposium. It was just so far beyond what we could even dream of doing then. It's ah . . . I'm on the eve of retiring and I feel completely comfortable, in terms of my responsibility to the community, because my job has been to work in the literary field, and that's my contribution to our people, and I feel completely comfortable. It's not a problem. There's enough people out there doing enough variety of things, with really some solid approaches, that are useful to the Native people as well as to the literary community. So it's perfectly all right; I can quit, and others can do it as well.

I started doing criticism because nobody could read my work. Nobody could read Momaday's or anybody's, and so I started writing about it because there was no other way to get a readership. Quite selfishly for myself, although I never made any money from it. It was a bit disgusting that everybody else's [non-Native writers'] work was being studied . . .

JP: Well, that's kind of interesting, because if one thinks of all the works people refer to most often, many of them are yours. Not just fiction or poetry but the criticism. *The Sacred Hoop*, the early ones, *Studies in American Indian Literature*. Those are two prominent things that came perfectly spaced in these twenty years . . .

PGA: Actually, they are the first ones out of my [creative] work, and the novel came between *Studies* and *The Sacred Hoop*. But since I began as a poet and a novelist, and then I did these other things because they needed to be done—and I do enjoy it, I really enjoy it—I feel overshadowed, like I should have stayed with poetry, like Joy [Harjo] or Linda [Hogan] or Jim Welch or so many others, and stayed as a creative artist, but then I tend to have a discursive mind as well as the other kind, so when I stop to think about it I realize, yeah, I couldn't have done that.

JP: Well, it's been an interesting time, a few decades of talking about the literature and then the different critical approaches that have come along, some of which have evolved, some of which haven't, over the past twenty years but also the books, the novels, the poetry, the drama itself. I mean, my god, it is truly phenomenal.

PGA: But there was nothing then, and now there's everything, like I said earlier. I can't even keep up with it all . . .

JP: None of us can . . .

PGA: For a while there I could do Native American Literature [a course]; it was so hurried to try to do it in one semester, particularly the contemporary literature, meaning from [William] Apess forward, but it could be done. There just wasn't that much in print. By 1982 I was at UCLA on a grant, and my idea was to do a comprehensive anthology of Native American women's poetry. After I counted two hundred American Indian women in print I gave up. I thought, It just can't be done. By then you couldn't do American Indian poetry and do it justice, there were just too many poets, let alone American Indian women's poetry. But in '77 you could have done it, and you could have at least given a wide representation of much of the poetry that was in print. Can you imagine that?! Since then it's very hard to deal with just one person's work. Isn't that wonderful? It's so exciting for me.

So then I went to fiction, the novel, and I specialized in that for quite a while, and finally short fiction started getting published. There was only a Richard Seaver book, *The Man to Send Rain Clouds* [edited by Kenneth Rosen], until the late '80s. And after [*Spider Woman's Granddaughters: Traditional Tales and Contemporary Writing by Native American Women*] came out I was amazed, it was received so well. I couldn't believe it. I just didn't think people read short story collections, never mind Native American women's short story collections. And that was reviewed in the *New York Times* and in the *Chronicle*, it was a "Pick of the Month" and of the year, and one thing and another, and it was just delightful, because the works are so splendid. Oh my, it was a delight to be asked to edit. So now there are so many fiction anthologies that I can't even deal with them all either.

JP: That's what's amazing about these last twenty years, too, is certain points in that history where something like *Granddaughters* comes along and, it's so successful that it opens some doors, and then it's progressive because each work that's produced just demonstrates again and again the power of the works that are being produced . . .

PGA: Without Momaday and *House Made of Dawn* and the Pulitzer Prize none of us would be here, because it made people in publishing and the academy more willing to pay attention than they had ever been. Our big problem now is to get ourselves out of that minority literature "The Oppressed People Garden," which I find entirely irrelevant. It's not multicultural literature. I've taught Asian American literature, meaning Korean American, Chinese American, Japanese American, Vietnamese American, and I've taught Chicana American, Hispanic, Latina, and I've taught black American, Caribbean, et cetera. Our situation, the Native people's situation, is *quite* different. We don't belong in ethnic studies any more than English does, and English is, from my point of view as an Americanist, an ethnicity. And English literature should be studied in comparative literature. And American literature should be a discipline, certainly growing from England and France, Germany, Spain, Denmark, and the Native traditions, particularly because those helped form the American canon. Those are our backgrounds. And then we'd be doing it the way it ought to be done. And someday I hope that it will be.

But certainly we [Native writers] make no more sense [being studied] with African American literature than we make with "New World" American literatures. It's not sensible to put us into that category. Are we oppressed? Well, yes, we are, but no, we're not, because we still live on our own land, and we still live with our own gods, and we still live with our own ceremonies, and so people have moved, or were forcibly moved, but they took themselves with themselves. That was actually common, like with the Sioux, who eventually emerged out on the plains as the Lakota. But they took themselves with themselves on that entire, long, that centuries-long journey. So it's not that they've lost that Native tradition; they just moved. And they have re-moved. I mean, if you look at the oral traditions, which is what we must look to if we are going to do accurate and responsible criticism, we can see that these things actually happened. We see that abduction narratives were a very important part of Native American traditions, if it was the Shoshonis or Laguna or whatever, we find these abduction narratives. And contemporary Native cultures don't have any slave narratives. What they did was they took the abduction narrative and shifted it to contemporary situations so that all that happens is that the oral tradition gets reframed, but it's the same story. It's just got a different setting. Different costumes, same story.

JP: That's interesting. One of the things people have been discussing in academics for at least twenty years, if not longer, . . . is, well, we get into the binaries again, don't we? Should there be a Native American literatures course, or should it be studied in the "American canon"?[1] So that has always been a debate, but to take a topical approach like "what we have carried with us" or abduction stories, and then we could look at various cultures . . .

PGA: And then you could do it without creating the dimensional problems we've been having, because it's not binary, it's not either/or, and the thing is, I would like to call the university a "multiversity." The university means there's only one god, there's only one way to do things, and to me that is directly counter to the American experience. That's fine for the English or the French or whoever, and in discussion they say they don't like that [to be grouped together], but then why do they do it to us? Why can't we have many literatures, all of which are American? African American literature is not African. It really isn't. It's American literature informed by the experiences here and African oral traditions, which were brought over from various African nations.

JP: Well, that makes a lot of sense. If we're ever going to be able to have a true discourse, we have to get rid of those simplistic determinations. The thing is, and it's always been kind of fascinating to me, that the geographical space we call the United States has always been multicultured. What has happened is there has been a construction and perpetuation of a myth of a unicultural experience.

PGA: Well, you know, I think it's Christian. You can only have one god, one holy and apostolic church. Okay, so imbedded in Western thought for two thousand years, or fifteen hundred years at least, is the idea of one king, one emperor, one people. But that's not true. And even the motto *E pluribus unum*, out of many one, but really what we have is out of many, many. And it's wonderful, 'cause that's the reality. Have you ever heard of one anything? You can't just have one leaf, you've got to have the whole tree.

JP: If you have only one thing, it dies off.

PGA: Gone. That's right. Everything has to be community, and it has to be multiple-community literature. That's what it has to be. There's no reason why we can't develop a contemporary Native American stance that enables us to generate political strategies that will apply. Not the same ones for everyone, but the appropriate ones for the case that you're examining. I don't see why, especially with computers and all. I think the issue is about status.

JP: Right back to what we were talking about earlier.

PGA: You have got to have "the right one," because once you have mastered "the right one" you can become the elite, and what worries them is they won't be the elite anymore, and then what would they do for meaning? Well, they might have to get a life, and we can't have that.

But just in terms of, well, from Flagstaff to now—that I can say these things, that I can even think these things is such an enormous leap. There're so many approaches, there're so many writers, there're so many critical studies, which I find all delightful.

JP: It is exciting, the way it should be.

PGA: Even when they're wrong, they dream up excellent ways of saying why and in what ways they succeed and in what ways they fail, which we couldn't do then. All we could do was stand there and say, "No, no, no," because we didn't know that kind of [critical] language and those kinds of critical strategies to work from.

We've come all this way, to a point where Mary Churchill can develop a *Cherokee* critical approach. It's just staggering. Like Henry Louis Gates did with *The Signifying Monkey*, and certainly for me that was a model of thinking, thinking, Look. He did it. He's got an Africanist model that is mediated by what they call "New World" experience.

So by the time you get to popular thought, yes, you have Esu-Elegbara, but you have something very unique, very American and that is peculiar to African experience in the United States as opposed to the Caribbean, as opposed to Brazil, I suppose, or wherever. But it's distinctly not just African. And you could take the critic as the man at the crossroads, the one who interprets what the gods said to the speaker, the writer, the poet, duh dah duh da duh da (the expression). You have the code—I can't remember their name for the code [alphabet of Mawu?]—but there's an actual code, and the critic is the one who knows the code, and she decodes it. Just as the case in the Esu-Elegbara figure decodes what's coming through the channel, the transmedium. So you begin to see that the critic fits into a tradition that's entirely whole. It's not about appropriating, it's about interpreting.

JP: As long as the critic doesn't keep the code [secret].

PGA: Well, that's the thing. You have to know the code well, and then you can share it. Instead, if you don't know it well, of course you hide it because you don't want anyone to know how ignorant you are.

JP: Good point.

PGA: No, I agree the code has to be there for all.

JP: Along those lines, then, since we began this by talking about the last twenty years, what do you see happening next?

PGA: I don't know.

JP: Part of the fun of it, huh?

PGA: Yeah, because I truly do believe that when White Buffalo Calf was born, that when the Blue Star Kachina returned, that's what they called the Hale-Bopp Comet, that's Quetzalcoatl, it's actually a whole new game.

But if things stay going in the many directions in which they are going, certainly in publication, our voice will be heard more and more strongly, because readers love it. Far more than publishers, and far more than the academy, just readers, out there, really relate to it. Because I think that Native stories and novels and poetry speak to something that's peculiarly with America. It catches American readers, because we're all trying to figure who we are and what we're doing here. Canadian Native writers don't write that way. There's very different stuff going on up there, and south of the United States, they're writing about other kinds of things, but all American, U.S. folks are sitting around going "Who the hell are we? Where do we come from? And isn't this difficult?" We're trying to negotiate too many traditions, too many ways of understanding. And that's what Native writers are dealing with.

Among all the writers, that is why we've got to get out of ethnic literature, because the strategies for understanding it don't work for understanding Native literatures. Very little of our literature is the literature of protest, of oppression. Very little of it. Most of it is the literature of the spirit or the literature of ritual. Almost all of it is, call it political voice and drama, is always informed by the presence of this knowledge that there is always this other world with which we are always engaged. It isn't over there somewhere; it's in our presence and our midst, and we are in its presence and its midst. You can't get a text if you don't get that as a principle. You can't do that with African American literature or Chinese American literature or so on. Though I do . . . and I find all kinds of things in their works that their own critics aren't finding, because they all have a tendency to stay connected to the spirit world. Women's literature often does, too, unless it's pretending that it isn't X or Y. In which case it turns out to be something else entirely.

JP: Are you back to the genetic model [which we discussed during our final symposium meeting]?

PGA: I'm back to the genetic model of X and Y. Well, what's interesting about that is all zygotes are X, and for some reason, and nobody has talked about why (but maybe it's a mutation), one leg of the X gets dropped as the zygote becomes an [female] embryo. Okay, so then what gets lost is that socialization capacity.

For a long time feminists talked about women networking, but I know an awful lot of women who do no such thing. And so I couldn't understand . . . I knew there was something to it. It doesn't matter where I go. I sit down, and we start talking about babies and shopping and hairdos, and we're fine. All the woman needs are the culture she comes from and to share all this. And then there's the boy culture, the football and the sports, et cetera. Men tend not to communicate. All the studies show it, and they just don't, and that's their way. And then women are at them all the time, "But you don't talk, but you won't share." But then this study came out, and it was published in *Nature* magazine in June 1997 . . . It explained to me the difference between the male and the female, and I think it's significant.

Certainly in a Native world you have strongly gendered traditions, and you can't really say "Kiowa is," you have to say Kiowa male or Kiowa female, because they really are different, and that's very important in oral traditions, and it continues to inform the literature. Look at the treatment of women in Welch and Momaday and so on compared to the treatment of women in Allen or Hogan what have you. It's not that we sit around and think, Well, let's see, the woman's tradition is . . . You just grow up, being informed of these things, and nobody says, "That's the Indian way." It's just part of what you learn from your folks. They seldom identify it in any way, so you just think, That's how reality is—at least, that is how your reality is, at least, that is how your reality works. It's going back to this genetic code for how we understand reality. There's a male code and there's a female code. Neither one is better or more important, obviously, or they wouldn't both be here, would they? And the truth is probably more complex than that. There's probably, like, nine genders. I was just reading about the Eskimos—they didn't say Inuit—a very contemporary documentary on the number of genders that these people experience within their communities. And if you look at the genders we recognize, there's male, female, homosexual male, bisexual male, lesbians who go both ways, estrogen conscious, but also in another valence, then there's the true hermaphrodite, and there's probably variations within there, like there's people with fundamental heterosexual feelings who have strong homosexual pulls, and that's probably pretty common. In each case there's the male partner and the female partner. There's people with XXY chromosomes and XYY chromosomes, and all of this is going to have an effect not just on gender but on consciousness. But the tribal people pay attention to this, and the modern people try to eradicate these differences.

JP: Uni—

PGA: Exactly, there's only one way. Instead of saying there are many ways and we need them all, unless this were true, we wouldn't all be here. It seems to me fairly straightforward.

And that goes for criticism too. Back to your question: what will happen, if we're lucky, is that American scholars will continue to work the way most of us are working, which is to open it up. Open it up.[2] As chaos theory . . . and there's some new stuff that I can't remember the name of, change theory or something like that, and I haven't had time to research it, but something called the principle of mediocrity, which is the idea of the golden mean or the median: anything that is will tend toward balance, will tend toward the median, which opens up everything. You don't have to find the extremes, because what will happen is that the patterns will keep reiterating, but that also means varying. So we will always come back to what it was, but it will always go away from what it was.

JP: Well, that kind of fits in with what you were talking about this morning, especially with the image of the swirling water. It's [the worldviews of Natives and non-Natives] fundamentally a very minor shift in one's point of view, but it's a world apart.

PGA: You're right. It turns out to be major, and all you have to do is shift your eyes a little bit, and suddenly you realize that wider pattern: it's the tree pattern, it's the hill pattern, it's the grass pattern, it's the literature discussion pattern, is the . . . is the . . . is the . . . and they are all singing to each other, you know, which is of course what we say. It was a dance, sweetheart. There's Joy Harjo. And that's exactly why it works. "Something sacred is going on in the universe," Momaday says. Or "Grandson, this earth is fragile." And we're all saying the same thing. I'm saying chaos, Mandelbrot set, Julius [Ruis] set, pay attention here, look at fractals. Because in this way we can explain not only our literature, but now everybody, once we develop these processes appropriately, we'll be able to give a fair shake to anybody's book, to take the book itself on its merits, where it comes from, rather than trying to make it an issue like the canonical blah blah blah. Well, who cares? What is it? Not, what is it like?

JP: Yeah, that's a good point. It has to go that way, doesn't it? If it doesn't, we're in deep trouble.

PGA: It just terrifies me.

JP: It's going to be just that much more fragmentary and divisive.

PGA: Balkanized, as they like to say in the States. Fragmented. Bricolage! [Earlier in the day there was a long discussion about the implications of this French term.]

JP: Bricolage! Let's talk about your bricolage.

PGA: I'll tell you about my bricolage; I huffed and I puffed and I couldn't blow it down.

JP: Wonderful . . . wonderful. So what's on for you next? What about writing?

PGA: I've been working on a book called *The Seven Generations*. It's supposed to be a book about Native spiritual systems. A sort of "how to be an Indian without even really trying." Everything you ever wanted to know about being an Indian but were afraid to ask. But I really mean that in the sense of what I mentioned in the talk today. There's this mythic sense and there is this way of perceiving, and that the dances are somehow connected to that, so you can't just get a drum and sit around and chant and feel good and call yourself enlightened. That's not how it is. The idea is to work out a text that will help people who are searching. This is not a literary text; it's not meant for literature people. In fact, I see this conference as my last literary thing that I'm doing in Native literature, perhaps in any literature, because I want to move away from it. My own calling has always been of the spirit, and I just want to do that before I get too old and can't. So that's happening. I've got a book of essays that Beacon has picked up and will be coming out within a year [*Off the Reservation*]. All my essays until now.

JP: A collection of your essays.

PGA: Everything. Stuff that was not in *The Sacred Hoop* but that predates it and a number of things that I've written since. I don't know the title yet. I think I'm going to argue for *Pocahontas Perplexed: An Indian Woman's View of Life, Literature, and Philosophy*. The publishers want it to be *A Native American's View of . . .*, and I don't like that. I want, you know, just one person. It's just me, what I think. I'm saying these things. I know what I think; that's my responsibility. I'm not supposed to know what other people think.

I just had a book of poetry published called *Life Is a Fatal Disease*. West End Press brought it out. Nice book, Albuquerque. And I did a book called *As Long as the Rivers Flow* with Pat Smith. It's nine biographies for young people. Scholastic picked it up.

JP: Scholastic just did something by Tiffany Midge, too, and some other people are under contract. Looks like this is going in the direction it needs to go in, that audience.

PGA: Absolutely, to get over these stupid images [of Native people] like the ones we were talking about yesterday.

Let's see, what else? Oh, *Song of the Turtle* came out, so that collection is complete. But I would like to write several more volumes: *Son of Turtle, Turtle Island*, and *Turtle Soup*. And *The Revenge of Turtle . . .*

JP: And *Turtle XIII*.

PGA: And *Turtle XIII*, yes. In some other life, perhaps.

JP: About that anthology, when you talked about that anthology this morning, you said you conceived of it not as most editors or publishers do—as a collection of distinct and discreet units—but as a novel. That was wonderful!

PGA: It goes back to the Flagstaff conference when [Carter] Revard said, "Yes, but is it Indian to write novels?" And I spent years thinking about that, and I thought, Yes, actually, it is. We have something that would fit what folklorists call cycles; so there's the old woman cycle, the trickster cycle, or the warrior cycle, on and on, the deer dance cycle. Well, those are long, involved narratives that go quite a long time. Well, a novel is a long, involved narrative that goes on a long time. But in truth you can see that certain thematic concerns, preoccupations, will arise and then get reiterated and explored and deepened and then they'll get dropped and later they will be picked back up. So, in essence, our cycles are doing the same thing. Probably, novels developed out of the same kind of thing.

JP: Yes, like you said, very event structured, but they are strung together by certain concerns . . .

PGA: Yeah, there's a narrative coherence or thematic units . . .

So, then, given that, if you take a whole bunch of stories that are about Native female supernaturals, like my *Grandmothers of the Light*, why . . . what happened—and I didn't know this would happen—was all these different Native nations were telling the same story.

[Here the tape ended. Once it was replaced and the recorder was ready, we moved back into a discussion of criticism.]

JP: You were saying that that's what Aristotle did, he looked at the text rather than trying to impose something on it.

PGA: That's what I was taught in criticism class.

JP: Well, so was I. People look down on the New Critical approach and brand it as something outdated and insignificant, but actually it's all in how you use it. Isn't it?

PGA: I'm a firm defender of the New Critical approach. I just don't think there's anything else you can do. All the rest is extra. If you can't do that one, then you can't do the others.

JP: It goes back to that coding we were talking about, too. All of a sudden you have a language there that you don't want to share or open up for other people. I've always considered some of the things happening today, especially in Native literary criticism, as an ex post facto prophecy. In other words, this is what it's going to be, and if it doesn't fit this pattern or this mold, then it is something else. Very prescriptive.

PGA: Even the scientists do that, and they're not supposed to. I read Francis Bacon and I know what they're supposed to do as scientists. But they have this wonderful thing called the null set. What you do, basically, is erect an hypothesis based upon what your important, high-status predecessors have done and then compel the data to conform to it. If it doesn't, then you throw it into the null set. Isn't that cute?

JP: Right. We need more null sets.

PGA: Yeah. I don't like that, kid. Let's throw it in the trash. Instead of saying that's going on for a reason, I wonder why? Maybe it's my approach, my methodology, a variety of things, but there it is, let's examine it. But if I understand Bacon, he said we are to look at what is there, examine it, and then, perhaps, come up with some comments that will lead us to the next plane of exploration. Something was said today, something about answers. And I wanted to say, No no no! That's not the point. It's not about answers; it's about good questions.

JP: Good questions, yes.

PGA: One exploration leads to another—that's fractal.

JP: Right. Answers are conclusive; questions open up possibilities.

PGA: Answers stop discussion, close out possibilities. Questions open them and encourage conversation.

JP: 'Course, lots of people just want the answers.

PGA: My students, for instance. "Just give me the answers so I can get an A."

JP: I was talking about *Green Grass, Running Water* yesterday, and in the beginning [Thomas] King has the classroom with Mary Rowlandson and anthropologists in it, asking, "Is this going to be on the test? Do we have to remember this?"

PGA: It's like the doctor who says, "I could really practice medicine here if it weren't for the patients."

JP: But that's what it's all about, isn't it? The students. That's what keeps us going.

PGA: Yeah. So often I have good students. I'm lucky that way. They're always teaching me things I would have never thought. That's my idea of how to teach.

JP: It blows them away when you say that, though. It's funny, you take twenty-five undergraduates and drop a text on them you've used before, and they'll see things you've never seen, even after reading it a dozen times.

PGA: And they'll see stuff, and they're always taken aback, because they are so used to professors who already know everything— or who don't but won't ever admit it. Not to undergraduates at least.

JP: And the joy continues.

PGA: The story goes on.

And indeed it has. However, let's go back to the beginning, of sorts, for the twenty-year advancements experienced in the 1970s and 1980s. Although I wish to revisit some earlier critical studies of three early novels by these three authors, I would also like to note that older novels found new footing in the 1970s as well. Elsewhere I argue that many of the "ethnic" (in terms of the 1970s) literary resurrections of the decade can be traced to the baby boom generation (whose attributes are examined later in this book) and its growing fascination with Natives, but these reclaimings of "lost" works were also the result of the growing number of writers who identified ethnically and who were looking for literary roots (see my "The Babyboom Generation"). After all, this was the decade that saw the republication of D'Arcy McNickle's (Métis [Cree and French]) novel *The Surrounded* (1936, 1978), Zora Neale Hurston's *Their Eyes Were Watching God* (1937, 1969, 1978), and John Okada's *No-No Boy* (1954, 1976), to name a few. I do not, by any means, wish to imply that these books are simply ethnic manifestos and that was why they were recovered. On the contrary, they are still in print, and this requires an audience that recognizes and appreciates their literary merit; it just took that audience forty years to mature.

However, it was the original publication of Momaday's *House Made of Dawn* that brought Native fiction into its own in the latter half of the twentieth century. It had ancillary effects, too, of launching the careers of other writers, Allen included, who once said that the book had literally saved her life. This is a lot to ask of a novel, but it also praises the power of fiction to enlighten our world and lives, providing direction and meaning and moral lessons.

N. SCOTT MOMADAY: *House Made of Dawn*

There has been a great deal of criticism written about N. Scott Momaday's novel. This is understandable, since Momaday won the Pulitzer. The novel also came at an opportune time historically. The advent of the baby boom generation and its exploration of culture certainly proved fertile ground for his prose, and a few years later the Flagstaff conference worked to direct that interest in college classrooms. It is no wonder, then, that the critical approaches to his book also chart the evolution of the scholarly study of contemporary written Native literatures in recent times.

At first, critics attempted to "validate" Momaday's accomplishment by examining the modernist conventions and traditions apparent in his novel: the "fragmented narrative," its structure, and so on. Others considered *House* a new and unique literary phenomenon and therefore tried to classify it as such by assessing its degree of "authenticity." This means simply that scholars matched textual references to Jemez Pueblo, Navajo, and Kiowa stories and ceremonialism, for example, to those found in ethnographic sources in their attempts to mark its difference from other literary texts produced in the United States by non-Native authors. Today, scholars apply contemporary Western critical theory—by Bakhtin, Todorov, and others—to Momaday's text in their own attempt to understand his art.

While these approaches are useful to open the text to non-Native academic readers, there are many others that may bear fruit as well. It seems that in their rush to canonize Momaday's text critics tended to overspecify his stance, his narrative point of view, by suggesting that he could, or would, attempt to adopt a Pueblo or Navajo perspective, for example. Although Momaday lived at Jemez Pueblo and on the Navajo Reservation with his parents, and although he focuses his first novel on the life of a Pueblo veteran, Momaday was and is an outsider to these cultures, one "looking in" from an uninitiated point of view. "Authenticity," then, is not the key issue here, for his rendering of Pueblo and Navajo lifeways and points of view is his and his alone.

However, Momaday's "inward gaze" was amazingly accurate, at least for Jemez Pueblo, where many people were upset by the "revelations" about their culture to be found in *House*. Interestingly, Allen leveled similar charges against Leslie Marmon Silko when she published her own powerful first novel, *Ceremony*, a few years later. What these early detractors never seemed to understand, though, is that Silko and Momaday do not reveal any culturally specific details that cannot be found readily elsewhere: in the publications of the Bureau of American Ethnology or, in Momaday's case, in Elsie Clews Parsons's 1925 book, *The Pueblo of Jemez*. Furthermore, despite its evocation of specific Native cultures and communities, Momaday's novel is a cross-cultural statement that has significance for all people, not just Native Americans. Jemez, Navajo, Kiowa, Hispanic, and Anglo beliefs exhibit great diversity and difference. These cultures are not the same, and Momaday knows this, as is evident in the novel itself. However, they do share certain basic human concerns, and it is in these that he finds his audience's reactions. The novel is fiction, after all, a linguistic construction aimed at the imaginations of a diverse readership.

Perhaps the greatest accomplishment of the novel is that it was both an immediately popular and critical success and ahead of its time. By this I mean that the novel anticipates what happened much later in writings by other Native authors, and it thus could be discussed in many of the same ways recent scholarship has engaged the work of Louise Erdrich, Thomas King, Louis Owens, and Gerald Vizenor, to name a few. In the works of these mixed-blood authors we find astute explorations of a diversity of cultures as well as characters who make use of points of common ground—points of commonality—between those cultures while keeping cultural distinctiveness, the novel's sense of *differentiation*, alive as they negotiate between their senses of self and an audience's point of view.

Momaday accomplished this in his first novel as well, although much has been written to suggest that it proffers solely a Pueblo message of exclusion: that Jemez culture will survive only in its steadfast isolation from others. In literary critical terms this idea is prescriptive and essentialist, for it requires that the culture be static, unchanging, and thus "dead." Momaday's novel is after something else, a realistic portrayal of how cultures meet and exchange and grow. Much as his second novel, *The Ancient Child*, finds a mythic point of convergence for very diverse cultures in the bear stories of northern Europe (such as *Beowulf*) and those of the northern plains in the United States (for a concise handling of this motif see Rekow), *House* locates Abel's struggle within the universal confrontation between fundamental absolutes: good versus evil. While the resolution to this conflict is culturally and geographically specific and influenced by numerous historical events unique to Jemez Pueblo, it is also one immensely comprehensible and therefore relevant to readers across time and cultures. While not wholly the first successful attempt by a Native American author to accomplish this delicate balance of appealing to a multicultural audience while remaining true to the specific cultures he or she is representing, Momaday is certainly the first to obtain such a degree of success.

The novel is centered on Abel's illness, and numerous critics have discussed its symptoms and its cure (see Scarberry-Garcia; Nelson; Jaskoski). Drawing upon an ethnographic reading of the novel, Susan Scarberry has amply argued that Abel and his brother, Vidal, exhibit striking similarities to characters in southwestern oral traditions, including the Stricken Twins of the Navajo healing tradition. Helen Jaskoski has extended this parallel to include a pairing of Abel's grandfather Francisco and the Catholic priest, Father Olguin, as twin figures. Both Scarberry and Robert Nelson have explored the ethnographic basis for the figures of the snake and the eagle in the novel as they examine what is wrong with the protagonist. Besides the external ethnographic texts that critics have employed to understand Momaday's vision, however, there are stories and events residing within the text itself that establish a cultural matrix out of which we may search for meaning and by so doing come to recognize Momaday's points of shared experience as well as the differences among peoples with distinctive cosmological orientations. In other words, Abel's illness—much like that of Tayo in Silko's *Ceremony*—is part of a larger one: his story is an extension and reenactment of others that precede it. If we recognize this connection and pattern, we also can understand both the cause of his illness and its cure, and as we search, we engage in Momaday's *investigation* of Pueblo beliefs.

One of these stories appears very early in the novel as one of the numerous memories with which we are bombarded as Abel sits in the hills above the pueblo to await the dawn the morning after his return from the army and World War II. It is in this initial collage of seemingly disjointed "flashbacks" that Momaday locates the nature of Abel's illness, its historical analog, and its potential cures. In each instance these focus on the "holy" in conjunction with the "evil."

The story of the Bahkyush people is one of survival against the foreign illness that arrived with Europeans. Decimated by the new diseases introduced by the colonizers, the remaining members of Pecos Pueblo migrate and are adopted by the people of "Walatowa," Momaday's fictionalization of Jemez Pueblo. The old story of their survival parallels Abel's own. As Momaday notes, the Bahkyush "gave themselves up to despair and were then at the mercy of the first alien wind" (14). However, the survivors who move to Walatowa carry four important objects: "a sacred flute; the bull and horse masks of Pecos; and the little wooden statue of their patroness, María de los Angeles, whom they called Porcingula" (16). They have made a "journey along the edge of oblivion," and this is exactly what Abel's story reenacts in modern times (16). Their survival as a people rests upon the fact that they carry the crucial ceremonial core of their culture with them; the evil of their dispossession is mitigated by the holy things they save, and one element of this is derived from their adopting and adapting an aspect of Catholicism: the agent of the "alien wind."[3] Moreover, they maintain a primary ceremonial group, the Eagle Watchers Society. All of these elements of culture are adopted into the ceremonial life of Walatowa, and through such exchanges cultures change, learn, grow, and survive.

There are several things we may surmise from these early memories that are evoked by Abel's attempt to reintegrate into the life of the pueblo. His problem stems from a pull in the opposite direction, away from his community and toward alienation.[4] This is exhibited by the ways he behaves and also by his most recent experiences: his departure for the army, which heightened his sense of exclusivity. He became "centered upon himself in the onset of loneliness and fear" (23). Like the Bahkyush before him, he gives into despair and therefore has no control over his own destiny, his own future. We exert control through our actions, of course, and this is the point of connectedness that Momaday's novel investigates: how do we react when we are confronted either with events of highly spiritual significance or with danger and adversity? Abel's story demonstrates a wide array of reactions to circumstance. In this way it is the story of his search for appropriate behavior and thus a very moral narrative. Despite his intimate knowledge of the community, Abel feels like an outsider, and the extent to which he acts independently from his community's behavioral practices becomes painfully apparent in the central memory in this section: the eagle hunt.

Abel is invited to participate after he reports that he has seen two eagles mating while playing with a deadly rattlesnake: "It was an awful, holy sight, full of magic and meaning" (15). The conjunction of "awful" and "holy" is significant. In an earlier sense the first term meant "full of awe" and was often applied to events of religious significance. In its contemporary sense, however, it connotes fear and/ or disgust, both of which are symptoms of Abel's subsequent illness. (Later, he both fears and loathes the albino, whom he murders.) However, the fact that he observes the eagles and then is invited on the hunt itself suggests that he is initially aligned with the Bahkyush; the Eagle Watchers Society, the group to whom he reports and the one charged with the hunt, is theirs, after all. Also, their near extinction has turned them into "medicine men" who have "a keener sense of humility than their benefactors [the people of Walatowa], and paradoxically a greater sense of pride" and who have "been fash-

ioned into seers and soothsayers. They had acquired a tragic sense," and thus they became "rainmakers and eagle hunters" (16). These are qualities that Abel achieves. Moreover, the running of the Pecos Bull is theirs, and it is a ceremony in which his grandfather—his closest male relative—has participated all his life. Within the context of the novel, then, as readers attempt to piece together an understandable narrative from the barrage of memories first presented, Abel is continually related to the Bahkyush people and their ceremonial practices and thus their tragic history as well as their resulting power to determine their future.[5]

Centered upon himself, however, Abel does not behave in a manner that perpetuates that power. When the hunt is successful and he has captured a magnificent eagle with which the Bahkyush might perform their ceremony, he circumvents the process by sneaking away from the hunters and strangling the bird. In a sense this unilateral act terminates a series of potentially fortunate events but also risks subverting the possibility for a successful performance of their faith. This is not appropriate behavior, as illustrated in the context of the novel, and it marks his movement away from their way of life. In fact, it is, chronologically, the first in a series of events in which his subsequent actions exhibit very similar attitudes. There are three others I will discuss: the ritual of the "chicken pull," the killing of the albino, and the attack upon the Los Angeles police officer, known as *culebra*, for which Abel is severely beaten and left for dead on a beach, on the "edge of oblivion." Here, he has a vision, and it is one that saves him. He then turns toward Walatowa, much as the survivors of the Bahkyush did, and participates in a ceremonial run that underscores his newfound understanding of the nature of evil and the ways to engage it.[6]

The chicken pull is a part of the larger celebration of the Feast of Santiago, in which Porcingula features prominently. Her statue is brought into the ceremonial space for the pueblo, the "Middle," where the chicken pull takes place. Therefore, since she is the "patroness" of the Bahkyush, it is once again significant that Abel should participate and, since he has returned home from the war only days previous to the feast, a logical step for his reintegration.[7] However, when his turn comes to ride his horse at top speed through the Middle, lean over in his saddle, and try to pull the rooster from the hole in which it is buried to its neck, "he made a poor showing, full of caution and gesture" (42). The albino, on the other hand, participates fully and is rewarded when he plucks the chicken from the earth. In a completion of the ritual he corners Abel and flails him with the chicken until its blood has returned to the earth, thus ensuring future abundance. As in the eagle hunt, Abel has not performed well, and this means that he has not fully given himself to his role, his place in his community and culture, a commitment Francisco exemplifies.

That night his poor behavior takes a deadly turn. In what has been variously described as a murder of retaliation for his humiliation at the hands of the albino during the chicken pull, as a symbolic act of revenge against "the white man," and as the act of a frustrated veteran, Abel kills the albino. However, the scene is full of an implied duplicity, one evocative of a conspiratorial overtone. The two men spend the night drinking in a local bar: "The two spoke low to each other, carefully, as if the meaning of what they said was strange and infallible" (81). "And then they were ready, the two of them" (82). They go outside, where, in a description dense with language suggesting ritual, Momaday depicts Abel murdering the albino. Later, as Abel remembers the trial that follows, we are told that he thought he was killing someone evil, a witch. Therefore, his actions would seem appropriate, if he was intent upon ridding the pueblo of an evil influence. But they are not. Once again, he has misbehaved, and Momaday gives even the reader who has no knowledge of Jemez ceremonial life or cosmology the information necessary to interpret the inadequate and dangerous nature of Abel's actions. As Abel plunges the knife into his adversary, the albino takes hold of him, and his "white hands still lay upon him as if in benediction. . . . The white hands laid hold of Abel and drew him close, and the terrible strength of the hands was brought to bear *only in proportion as Abel resisted* them" (83, emphasis mine). The relevance of this passage becomes apparent when it is connected to other events.

Only a few pages earlier Momaday constructs a scene in which the albino is also central and in which his nature is clearly delineated. Old Francisco is busy hoeing his cornfield, and, as he becomes physically tired, his awareness of his surroundings becomes more acute. His "aged body let go of the mind, and he was suddenly conscious of some alien presence close at hand. . . . He was too old to be afraid. His acknowledgment of the unknown was nothing more than a dull, intrinsic sadness, a vague desire to weep, *for evil had long since found him out and knew who he was*" (66, emphasis mine). When he "lets go" of his physical concerns, his awareness dawns, but this does not mean he is powerless to engage the evil that lurks around him. "He set a blessing upon the corn and took up his hoe" (66). The evil he senses is the albino, but Francisco does not confront this evil directly or alone, as Abel does when he kills the albino; instead, Francisco engages it through ritual.

The albino is continuously described in snakelike terms. His tongue darts from his mouth, he hisses his words, his skin is dry and scaly. He has his counterpart in *culebra*, the snake, the corrupt Los Angeles police officer who preys upon the poor and disadvantaged of the city: those whose despair makes them easy targets for this alien wind. When Abel is relocated to the city after his parole from prison, where he serves his sentence for the albino's murder, he is confronted once again by evil incarnate. The cop demands money and then strikes a blow at Abel's outstretched hands. Therefore, it is not money he wants from the poor; it is power over their ability to move freely and to perform actions shaped by their senses of self. Later, it is strongly suggested that Abel, drunk and in an angry mood, goes in search of *culebra*; much like the confrontation with the albino earlier, Abel intends to retaliate, avenge, and destroy in his quest for power over his own life. Once again, he is unsuccessful, and the danger of such an undertaking becomes apparent. He awakes on the beach, his hands broken and his body beaten. At this moment, at the nadir of his existence and as far from his place, his "Middle," as the land will allow, he has a vision, and it is a vision about the true nature of evil in the world and the ways that he must encounter it if he is to survive.

The scene in which his vision takes place is carefully crafted. The phrase "something was going on" is repeated as Abel transforms from someone who awakes nearly dead to one who moves about and observes events in a place other than the beach on which he was left to die. He sees old men running, "full of tranquillity, certitude" (103). And then, it is suggested, he cries, for he has an epiphany that relates directly to his own situation, and almost every word in the scene is significant for understanding the nature of his vision.

> The runners after evil ran as water runs, deep in the channel, in the way of least resistance, no resistance. His skin crawled with excitement; he was overcome with longing and loneliness, for suddenly he saw the crucial sense in their going, of old men in white leggings running after evil in the night. They were whole and indispensable in what they did; everything in creation referred to them. Because of them, perspective, proportion, design in the universe. Meaning because of them. They ran with great dignity and calm, not in the hope of anything, but hopelessly; *neither in fear nor hatred nor despair of evil*, but simply in recognition and with respect. Evil was. Evil was abroad in the night; they must venture out to the confrontation; they must reckon dues and divide the world. (103, emphasis mine)

As presented, this ceremony is central to the culture Momaday constructs, as ceremonies to address evil are central to most cultures. Because of these men's dedication, a cosmological orientation— "perspective, proportion, design"—is perpetuated, and the people survive. Harmony—a balance between evil and good—and thus the world are maintained.

Abel then reflects upon the nature of his illness, one that this new perspective—allowed through his vision—will cure. One does not confront evil alone or with the hope of destroying it but through an awareness of evil's existence and the basis of its power. In his own confrontations with the albino and *culebra* he has, in fact, given them power over him; there is, in a sense, a destructive collusion, for through his actions he creates a series of events that circumvents his attempts to reintegrate and to exert control over his own future. If one balances evil through ceremonial, communal actions, however, evil remains powerless, impotent. In *Other Destinies* Louis Owens notes:

> While southwestern Native American cultures may also see the world as divided and balanced [between good and evil], the vital difference is one of teleology: to the Calvinist (and colonial American) mind the world is a millenarian battleground where Satan must, and inevitably will, be defeated, whereas to the Indian mind that balance constitutes a wholeness that must be precariously maintained through ritual and ceremony. (105)

The distinctions between fundamental worldviews about good and evil, however, are not that clearly drawn in the novel. It could be argued that in Christian belief individual humans cannot "kill" Satan, only his emissaries (and hence the Salem witch trials and Abel's murder of the albino) and that only by recognizing his influence and addressing it through acts of devotion may humans escape his power. In other words, if viewed from a philosophical distance, the cultural distinctions here may not be polar opposites. In the context of the novel it is more important that Abel recognize how evil is empowered, and this recognition comes about through his habitation of a landscape where European and Pueblo cultures intersect. It does not come about due to his participation in the inner workings of Walatowa ceremonialism. Thus, Momaday's cross-cultural call may be for people to acknowledge the ways they participate in evil and to practice their ceremonies as originally intended. At the very least, this is what Abel's story exemplifies.

Interestingly, his visionary perspective about the nature of evil is given to us very early in the novel, in the central memory in the sequence after his return home. It is the "humility" the Bahkyush have learned through their own encounters with death. It is also apparent in the description of the mating eagles, who have in their talons a deadly snake but who do not concern themselves with its venom and engage, instead, in their mating ritual. The snake is therefore powerless, since the eagles do not fear it. It is, literally, "out of its element." They drop it, and it dies.

There is another memory that follows in the sequence that pertains to this idea as well. During the war Abel is knocked unconscious during a mortar attack. He awakes to find himself in the direct path of an enemy tank. What do you do in such a deadly situation, when the dark machinery of the world rises up to "eclipse" the sun and threaten your life? In this early record of the event we know, simply, that he survives; it is later, only a few pages after his vision takes place on the beach, that we are shown how. He rises, dances around, and makes obscene gestures toward the tank; he acts the clown of Pueblo ceremonials. The machine responds by firing its machine guns at him at close range, but to no avail. Abel walks slowly off the field of battle, unconcerned about the danger and thus victorious (116–17). He has confronted evil and prevailed, and there is a lesson in each of these events about the ability of our perspective to determine an outcome.

This philosophy—that by directly confronting and trying to destroy evil we in fact empower it—can be found in numerous cultures and their stories as well as in contemporary literatures. In any event, the confrontation model Momaday constructs is from a pueblo, even though its idea that enlightened inaction disempowers evil may be recognizable cross-culturally. This is Momaday's accomplishment. By the end of the novel we can recognize that, as he runs in the dawn, Abel is once more realigning with his people's ceremonial practices and that this cure provides the *reaffirmation* of those practices in modern times. As a young man, his efforts will insure their *continuation* into the next generation.

A close, New Critical reading of the novel helps underscore details that critics have used to extend the discussion of Momaday's accomplishments. After all, a close reading initiates most readers' more elaborate reflections upon the stories it provides. For non-Native readers this is particularly true. As James Ruppert has pointed out, this constitutes mediation between a reader's interpretative devices and the author's attempts to expand them. In the 1970s Native authors faced the need to develop a reading market while defining their own sense of belonging within the literary landscape of the time; as

James Welch once put it, he wanted to be considered an American writer and not simply an American Indian writer.[8] That discourse would evolve over the next few decades, however.

For new readers to Native fiction there are resources for understanding in the novels themselves, and sometimes this includes the ways subsequent works by the same author extend our initial reactions to our "first read." Later I will look at James Welch's first novel, *Winter in the Blood*, in relation to a later novel by the same author, *Fools Crow*. The latter is an historical novel set at a moment in time Welch found foundational for contemporary Blackfeet society and his own sense of self as originally explored in *Winter*. Since *Fools Crow* was published in 1985, I wish to look at these two novels together as a means of extending the discussion of texts from the 1970s into the next decade and the qualities of differentiation, investigation, affirmation, and continuation as they evolved: their DIAC.

For the moment, however, let us consider Welch's second novel, published in 1979, and his exploration of one strand of the heritage from his family: the Gros Ventre. The critical acclaim of *Winter* and his early collection of poetry, *Riding the Earthboy 40*, shaped early critical reactions to the novel. It may usually be the case that powerful first novels inhibit the writing of a second (hence the long wait for a second novel from Ralph Ellison), but in Welch's case this was not true, although early critics used the first novel as a comparative measure of the second, as Ellison feared. Their responses are telling. However, a close reading of it once again allows for an understanding of the author's attempts—overtly or covertly—to provide something "new" for a general readership.

JAMES WELCH: *The Death of Jim Loney*

Readers and critics alike were quick to point to the bleak ending of *The Death of Jim Loney* and bewail Loney's victim status and thus his representation of the loss of Native cultures, so at first this novel seems a perfect candidate to refute the DIAC structure, a text from the closing days of the 1970s. However, a close reading suggests what few critics have acknowledged: Loney's lonely stand as the creative act that Welch himself has called it. And of these few, only Kathleen

Sands has carefully drawn the connections between Loney's actions and his Gros Ventre heritage.

In "*The Death of Jim Loney*: Indian or Not?" Sands traces Loney's final hours and argues convincingly that his actions after Pretty Weasel's death are contemporary manifestations of those of a warrior in the Gros Ventre tradition. He gets a shotgun from his father (as the young warrior would get arms from his), tells him where he is going (which amounts to a public declaration), and prepares to meet his enemy—the police and the world they represent—in a place of his own choosing. "Like an ancient warrior, he [Loney] takes a position from which there is no retreat, and waits for the attack, even taunting his enemy and revealing his position" (Sands 8). Sands's insights are interesting, and they fit clearly into the progression with which Welch has structured his novel. Despite Loney's seeming isolation and alienation from his mother's people and their ways, he is a man with a vision, and the novel depicts—as do oral literatures—the ways by which his vision is translated into action in a world that has changed vastly from that of his ancestors. From the outset, then, and on an overt level Loney marks himself as Native, but I would argue that it is in the subtext that the senses of affirmation and continuation for the novel, bleak as they may be, are to be found.

Although Welch purposefully shrouds Loney's affinity for his people, their land, and its beings, his connections to them are continually suggested by two seemingly unrelated devices: Loney's physical appearance and his memories of specific places in the landscape. Throughout the novel Loney is described in wolflike terms by various characters. An old Cree woman at the local airport sees his face as "wolfish." Loney's sister, Kate, echoes that description when she arrives at the same airport. His friend Pretty Weasel describes Loney's face as looking like a "hungry and predictable" mongrel (82). And his lover, Rhea, as she opens her door for Loney on his last visit after Pretty Weasel's death, sees "Loney's thin face in the moonlit night. His nose and cheekbones were silver and his eyes were dark caves" (151). His close identification with an animal is heightened by Loney's revelation, quite early in the book, that he believes his mother was a member of the Westwolf family. These associations are important because they imply an inherited relationship between Loney and the land beyond Harlem—the world "out there," as Loney's mother tells him in a dream—and therefore with the traditions that have always enlightened the Gros Ventre's perception of their world.

Although the wolf may have a set of negative connotations for the "white" characters in the novel, including Kate and Pretty Weasel, we immediately begin to wonder if the same is true for the Gros Ventre. Interestingly, the Wolf Society is one of the two traditional soldier, or warrior, societies and, as such, it has a respected place in the ceremonial life of the people; its members may gain knowledge and personal power through kinship with the wolf or through an intimate relationship with other power beings established by a vision quest. As the narrative progresses, Loney's almost instinctual relationship with traditional sources of power in the Gros Ventre world emerge from his behaviors, including those Sands explores.

All the major characters, with the exception of Loney, want either to leave northern Montana or, like Pretty Weasel, to transform the land into some personal image of what they think it should be. Loney, however, wants only to understand who he is, and although he realizes that memory, the past, is usually the way to one's identity, his memories seem to be dead ends. They are confused, incomplete, and chaotic; they have no central frame of reference to control them, no interpretative framework that, one would assume, comes from the Gros Ventre cosmology. However, as he thinks about his past he continually encounters memories not just of people but of other beings and the land itself. They are intertwined somehow, and he tries to separate them. He believes that his memories of people hold the key to his present state, but gradually we see that the landscape itself and certain animals who inhabit it are more a part of Loney's identity than he realizes: they are points of reference for his identity.

Just as Welch obscures the connection between Loney's movements and those of a traditional Gros Ventre warrior, he makes subtle connections through Loney's memories of Snake Butte (where he imagines his own face among the pictographs) and the Little Rockies but most of all through the place he chooses to die. Mission Peak in the Little Rockies was at one time a source of key ingredients for the Feather Pipe ceremony given to the people by Bha'a, sometimes called Thunderbird or Ruler of Storms. Bha'a also is said to inhabit the crags of mountain peaks, and the final scene of Welch's novel is set in the crags of Mission Canyon. But there is further evidence to suggest that Bha'a has an influence on Loney's behavior.

Very early in the novel Loney tries to think, to unravel his memories and identity, and alone, sleepless, and beyond drunk in his kitchen in the early morning he has a vision. In several ways his isolation is reminiscent of the isolation practiced by the seekers of visions and power in the Blackfoot and Gros Ventre traditions. Like them, Loney's fasting, crying, smoking of tobacco, and watchful waiting have the result of providing him with the altered perception necessary to communicate with forces in the world unavailable to most people:

> And again, as he had that night after the football game, he saw things strangely, yet clearly. The candle, the wine bottle, the letter before him, all burned clearly in his eyes and they had no reality in his mind. It was as though there were no connection between his eyes and his brain. And he saw the smoke ring go out away from his face and he saw the bird in flight. Like the trembling, the bird was not new. It came every night now. It was a large bird and dark. It was neither graceful nor clumsy, and yet it was both. Sometimes the powerful wings beat the air with the monotony of grace; at other times, it seemed that the strokes were out of tune, as though the bird had lost its one natural ability and was destined to eventually lose the air. But it stayed up and Loney watched it until it reached into the darkness beyond the small candlelight. (20)

After the bird disappears Loney reacts in the only way he knows how at this point in his life; he drinks a toast to "his" bird. Something is happening to Loney; a significant event has occurred, but we are left as puzzled as Loney when he tries to interpret the event, to judge its significance and the appropriate way to react to it. The vision could be attributed to the wine (the bird is a drunken hallucination), but if we posit that Loney's actions shadow those of a traditional vision quest, then another interpretation becomes available. Sands's reading and the questions it asks generate further questions and readings.

Loney later states that he has never seen a bird like his before in the surrounding country. The dark bird, however, bears a number of similarities to Bha'a, one of the most powerful beings in the world of the Gros Ventre. Like Coyote, or Sinchlep, of the Salish and Na'pi of the Blackfoot, he is the most powerful agent of the "Supreme Being," and as such his influence is far-reaching. He is most commonly associated with summer thunderstorms, and in this connection a ceremony and a story have evolved around him. The Feather Pipe—one of the two most powerful pipes in Gros Ventre ceremonialism—is said to have been given by Bha'a to a boy who was unlike any of the other children in his village. Although there are different versions of the story, they resonate with Loney's. The boy who receives the pipe does not play with the other children but instead stays to himself; he is told in a dream that he is going to be given something, so he moves his lodge away from the others in the village; and he is visited by Bha'a, who takes the boy's lodge and everything he owns but leaves him with the pipe (Flannery 446). Isolation, alienation, and vision are directly connected in the story to the power gift of Bha'a; the loss of material possessions and human companionship results in the gift of something immensely more valuable for individual and community alike. One wonders.

Like the boy, Jim Loney seems to develop a personal relationship with a very powerful force. Quite often, this type of relationship—between a guardian or Helper and a person—emerges from a vision, may last a lifetime, and is present year-round. There are veiled parallels between Loney's actions and those of a vision quest, but there are also similarities between the boy in the story and Loney to account for his unwitting acquisition of a guardian. Moreover, there seems to be ample precedent: "While supernatural power was not explicitly sought from Bha'a he might occasionally on his own initiative have pity on a man and give him power to be a great warrior and even to make storms" (Flannery 12). And Loney cries for pity.

The actions that occur after the vision strengthen the identification of the bird with Bha'a and Loney's association with him. As

Sands demonstrates, Loney becomes a warrior after he is given a shotgun, as he foresaw in his vision, but he also becomes a maker of storms. When Loney walks to Rhea's later, she comments on the severity of the wind. Loney replies, "'I think I might have something to do with it" (28). The possibility that he might be affecting the weather is never explored, at least overtly, but this slight and seemingly inconsequential statement says a great deal about Loney's vision of the bird, the image of which remains with him. As he stares into Rhea's fireplace he sees it again, and either it or his memory of it arises to direct his actions throughout the remainder of the novel. The story ends, as does Loney's life, with a reference to his vision; the sense of complicity lingers, as does the sense that any distinction between Loney's vision of the bird and Loney himself has disappeared: "And he fell, and as he was falling he felt a harsh wind where there was none and the last thing he saw were the beating wings of a dark bird as it climbed to a distant place."

Loney's death may be, and has been, interpreted as a bleak statement about the plight and supposed fate of Native cultures. However, as is so often the case in contemporary Native American novels, we may also see in it an affirmation of the traditional relationship between a place and a people and an age-old way of perceiving the world through an understanding of the stories and traditions that speak of that relationship. Jim Loney takes control of his own life by responding instinctively to the forces that are told of in Gros Ventre literature, and although society at large may take Loney's death as suicide and therefore a terminal act of desperation, we must consider the clearly deliberate and controlled ways that he works it. As Sands amply demonstrates, these are more than simple acts of an individual tired of his existence. Welch once told Bill Bevis: "He [Loney] does orchestrate his own death . . . He creates it, he creates a lot of events to put himself on top of that ledge in the end . . . he knows how his death will occur. And to me, that is a creative act and I think all creative acts are basically positive" ("Dialogue" 176). Creative acts spring from knowledge and insight, and these are the gifts that may be derived from a guardian like Bha'a. Others have gone before Loney, and yet the power exists today, despite these warriors' creative ends. It is not a sense of continuation as we see in *House* by any stretch, but the novel's subtext conveys a sense that connections can be made and thus provides a cautionary tale about the need to understand what best to do with this knowledge, now and in the future.

Although many recent critics have moved away from such "ethno-graphic" or "anthropological" readings of Native fiction, this is as much due to the evolving nature of the literature itself as the viability of such readings to enlighten. Besides, new readers often look initially and naturally for elements of differentiation. These are still noticeable, to varying degrees, in the fiction produced today as they were in the 1970s. Depending upon an author's proximity to a tribal identity and vision of the past in relation to the future, elements of tribal lifeways are proportional. Moreover, since "great literature" is often said to hold a variety of layers for interpretation and therefore new delights for those returning to it several times, I would suggest that this is a characteristic of many Native novels; when we reread, we discover new layers of signification, and thus our appreciation of the complexity and multiple dimensions of our aesthetic experience is heightened. Surprise. This is certainly the case with Leslie Silko's first novel and the ways we "read" the central story of Tayo, who, like Abel in *House*, returns home to the pueblo from World War II disoriented and ill. The novel differentiates itself from the outset, and the investigation that follows is tied directly to Tayo's quest and cure.

LESLIE MARMON SILKO: *Ceremony*

Tayo is an intriguing and complex character, and, thanks to Silko's abilities as a storyteller, his story is engaging. As we read of his search for a cure, we sympathize with his plight, and when Tayo defies the witch, Emo, and the evil forces he represents at book's end, we see once more Abel's lesson affirmed. Like Tayo, we come to recognize the responsibilities he has to his world but also that meeting these responsibilities results in his gaining the power to survive the con-frontation through his awareness of appropriate action, or inaction in this case. Like Laguna oral literature, *Ceremony* is concerned with entertainment and enduring cultural values, and when Silko writes of a man trying to come to grips with a chaotic world seemingly bent on self-destruction, she does what past Laguna storytellers have done: clarify the changes in the world and dramatize how old ways may be adapted to accommodate those changes. This reaffirms those values in modern times and into the future: DIAC.

Tayo's story emerges from a long-standing literary tradition that continues to define and enlighten the sources of power found in the Laguna landscape and to provide knowledge of the ways that these sources may be utilized. As Tayo moves through his narrative, his awareness of the relationship between his experiences and those told of in the stories of his people grows, and he in turn moves from being an isolated, ill individual to a powerful, competent representative of his people. In a word, he becomes a hero.

Silko's use of traditional stories as bases for her fiction is easily demonstrated. We need only look to her short works such as "Yellow Woman" to see how she acknowledges the relevance of the old stories to an understanding of the present. In this story a woman is carried away, figuratively and literally, by a man she meets near the stream on the outskirts of Laguna, and throughout the story she continually asks herself if the man is actually a mountain Ka't'sina and if she is a modern incarnation of Kochininako, or Yellow Woman. Silko never overtly answers the question, but the reader does, and the mere fact that another, updated version of the stories of Yellow Woman is being "told" is answer enough. Yellow Woman, the perennial heroine, lives through Silko's story.

Tayo shares a similar life in that Silko conscientiously tells the stories that relate to Tayo's life and from which his story emerges. When she tells of Hummingbird's and Fly's endeavors to set the world right and bring the rains back, she establishes the ways that individuals can act for the people and work transformations through correctly ordered actions and perseverance. And when she tells of Sun Man's confrontation with the Evil Gambler, Kaup'a'ta, she provides both the genesis of the plot for Tayo's narrative and a hint at his genealogy as a fictional character.

Sun Man climbs a mountain to rescue the rain clouds from

Kaup'a'ta. He is successful because Spiderwoman tells him what the Gambler will do so that he can anticipate events and react accordingly, thus turning the Gambler's evil back on himself. Obviously, these characters have contemporary counterparts in Silko's tale; *Ceremony* has its own hero, who climbs the mountain and who with the aid of mysterious beings—Ts'eh and the hunter—is able to bring the rains and turn evil into its own defeat. If there is doubt that the character Emo is evil, we need only remember the scene in which Silko describes him playing with the teeth of a dead Japanese officer. He rolls them like dice; he is quite literally gambling for Tayo's life, and he nearly wins. If there is any doubt about Tayo's character, we need only reexamine the stages in his story that speak of his identity as well as the ways by which he comes to understand what is happening in his world and how to react to the changes he sees taking place. His strength comes from his awareness that his story is very similar to those he heard from Uncle Josiah when he was a child.

The earliest event in Tayo's life is quite revealing. As Silko carefully notes, Tayo was four when his mother, Laura, left him with her kin—Josiah, her grandmother, and Auntie. Four is a number often used in sacred contexts, and this is Tayo's age when his memory begins. He lives with the family from that point on, but Auntie (Laura's older sister) will not let Tayo forget his mysterious parentage or his mother's behavior. After Laura's death Auntie periodically draws Tayo aside to tell him stories about Laura that at first seem to be delivered with the sole malicious intent of tormenting and humbling the boy by emphasizing his isolation and his inferiority to Auntie's son, Rocky. On one such occasion, however, Silko provides an added dimension to Auntie's burden as the self-proclaimed mediator between her family's actions and its place in the fabric of the community. The event takes an interesting turn from the Christian morality that would seem to be Auntie's prime concern:

> "One morning," she [Auntie] said, "before you were born, I got up to go outside, right before sunrise. I knew she [Laura] had been out all night because I never heard her come in. Anyway, I thought I would walk down toward the river. I just had a feeling,

you know. I stood on that sandrock, above the big curve in the river, and there she was, coming down the trail on the other side. . . . I am only telling you this because she was your mother, and you have to understand. . . . Right as the sun came up, she walked under that big cottonwood tree, and I could see her clearly: she had no clothes on. Nothing. She was completely naked except for her high-heel shoes." (73)

Readers might interpret this passage as proof of Auntie's narrow nature as well as Laura's wild abandon. The younger sister could be viewed as another lost soul, an Indian going "bad," or the older as a reincarnation of the evil stepmother from Western folklore traditions. However, there is another possibility; by fulfilling her role as an older sister and family matriarch, Auntie helps—in her own way—her adopted child understand his character by emphasizing certain qualities of the scene she witnessed long ago.

In the first place, she notes that the event took place *before* Tayo was born. Likewise, she is very specific about *where* it took place— "on that sandrock, above the big curve in the river"—as well as when—at dawn. The earliest events in Tayo's life story are tied to water and to a specific place and time, all of which are associated with the Ka't'sina. As Silko and Elsie Clews Parsons (*Pueblo Indian Religion* 176) both note, the Ka't'sina of Laguna are traditionally connected with water, either rainfall or the river. Like Yellow Woman, Laura has gone to the river, where meetings between humans and Ka't'sina have been known to take place, as in "Yellow Woman." Moreover, Auntie tells Tayo the exact place on the river, the same place, Silko suggests later, where the Laguna people wait for the arrival of the Ka't'sina during a ceremony. Also, she sees Laura at dawn, a time associated once again with Ka't'sina (Parsons, *Pueblo Indian Religion* 179). In brief, Silko implies that her protagonist may in fact be directly related to and therefore aided by Ka't'sina; his mysterious conception and birth conform to those of other heroes in the Laguna tradition, once again as in the short story.

This connection becomes clearer after Tayo visits Betonie. With Betonie's help Tayo initiates a journey that begins with a search for the spotted cattle on Mount Taylor, a place once again bearing numerous sacred associations with the Ka't'sina (Boas 38). This is where he meets Ts'eh; since their meeting follows immediately after Silko's telling of the Gambler story, the reader begins to draw parallels between the actions presented in it and those of the main narrative. Given Tayo's obscure parentage, the similarities are cause for wonder. Before Tayo begins climbing the mountain, however, he spends the night with the mysterious Ts'eh, and this act has a profound effect on his ability to complete his quest. Like the meetings between the Mountain Ka't'sina and Yellow Woman, theirs happens near a river, and it provides him with a powerful accomplice; interestingly, their lovemaking is described in terms appropriate to Tayo's developing character: "It was the edge of a steep riverbank crumbling under the downpour until suddenly it all broke loose and collapsed into itself" (188). The drought is nearing an end, and this is a direct result of Tayo's dawning knowledge of appropriate action, as his movements the next morning indicate.

In her seminal article "An Act of Attention: Event Structure in *Ceremony*" Elaine Jahner focuses on Tayo's greeting of the dawn to support her contention that the novel's structure is based upon events that mark a pattern of convergence and then emergence. Her insight is intriguing, for such a pattern exists in Laguna oral tradition and ceremonialism. Stories tell of the people converging in a previous world and then emerging into this one (which is only one event in a long history of transformations), and when a ceremony is to begin, the people converge by societies, then emerge into public celebration. As Jahner points out, the major events in Tayo's story are those points where "time, place and story" intersect ("Act" 44). These are times when Tayo makes crucial associations between his own experiences and those of his predecessors, and Jahner's definition suggests that an event is significant when it marks the convergence of the story of an individual with the perceptions and lifeways of his people as related in their oral literature. Such moments lead to insight and knowledge and in turn to appropriate action.

On the morning Tayo begins his climb he sings to the dawn. He also notes the "damp and cold" quality of the air. His actions and the conditions of his world mark a vast change from those described at the opening of the book, when he was passive and inert in the hot, dry air of the drought. Things are changing, and Tayo is at the cutting edge of a transition. Significantly, he breathes deeply; breathing in Laguna ritualism is an act of blessing (Parsons, *Pueblo Indian Religion* 421). The effects on Tayo are obvious: "Being alive was all right then; he had not breathed like that for a long time" (189). Since his visit to Betonie and his night with Ts'eh, his cure has taken the form of a journey, a series of instances in which he perceives his own experience through the knowledge gained from Laguna oral literature.

As Tayo waters his horse in the dawn, Silko provides another important connection between Tayo's story and Sun Man's:

Before the dawn, southeast of the village, the bells would announce their approach, the sound shimmering across the sand hills, followed by the clacking of turtleshell rattles—all these sounds gathering with the dawn. Coming closer to the river, faintly at first, faint as the pale yellow light emerging across the southeast horizon, the sounds gathering intensity from the swelling colors of the dawn. *And at the moment the sun appeared over the edge of the horizon, they suddenly appeared on the riverbank, the Ka't'sina approaching the river crossing.* (189, emphasis mine)

Tayo rises to sing his song, and by this point in her narrative Silko has given her readers enough evidence to make crucial associations that will allow them to share in the event by recognizing its significance to Tayo's developing character. Again, water and the dawn are connected with his actions, but readers also relate Tayo's memory of a ceremonial place by the river where the Ka't'sina appear at dawn with qualities of the earlier story Auntie tells about Laura. Strange forces are at work in the narrative and in the minds of Silko's readers, for whom Tayo's song becomes an appropriate observance of an ancient relationship between his people and forces in their cosmology. As Tayo rides into the mountains he looks at his world differently; his story now has purpose and direction through his renewed knowledge of the powers that have aided, or challenged, past heroes in their quests, and Silko's investigation of these beliefs makes its transition into their reaffirmation.

Tayo's experiences on the mountain are confrontational, like those of Sun Man in the story Silko tells; however, rather than confront the Evil Gambler at this point, Tayo confronts himself. Although he recognizes the sacred associations between this place and his people, he is hampered by his fear of the white rancher, Floyd Lee. Lee "owns" the mountain now and has the forces of law and order on his side, but there is another, Laguna order that predates Lee's by generations and survives despite expensive fences and other physical boundaries. Tayo's fear is so great that it threatens to turn him from his journey, but as a hero in the ancient tradition he finds the courage to continue with the aid of another character who, like Ts'eh, appears somewhat mysteriously to play a crucial role in Tayo's development.

As he mysteriously falls to the earth under a pine tree, Tayo has a vision. First he goes through a transformation, becoming "insubstantial" and therefore free from the fear of the riders Lee employs to guard his property. Then Tayo sees a mountain lion:

> The mountain lion came out from a grove of oak trees in the middle of the clearing. He did not walk or leap or run; his motions were like the shimmering of tall grass in the wind. . . . Relentless motion was the lion's greatest beauty, moving like mountain clouds with the wind, changing substance and color in rhythm with the contours of the mountain peaks: dark as lava rock, and suddenly as bright as a field of snow. When the mountain lion stopped in front of him, it was not hesitation, but a chance for the moonlight to catch up with him. (204)

The lion's actions speak of his fitness to his surroundings; there is no hesitation on his part as he moves freely and confidently in "rhythm" or harmony with his world. And Tayo recognizes the importance of the meeting. He, too, needs confidence in the old ways of moving with ancient powers to help him face the Floyd Lees of the modern world. He must fulfill his responsibilities, so he immediately rises to his knees to address the being before him: "mountain lion becoming what you are with each breath, your substance changing with the earth and the sky" (204). Tayo learns a valuable lesson about the nature of change, and when the lion leaves, he pours pollen into the tracks in devotion to "Mountain lion, the hunter. Mountain lion, the hunter's helper" (205). For a non-Native reader, this is a curious act but one that is obviously full of significance, and as readers attempt to fit it into the progression of Tayo's journey, Silko gives it significance by connecting it to subsequent events on the mountain.

First, Tayo finds his cattle. Has the hunter's helper responded to Tayo's actions? Then, Tayo is captured, but Lee's fence riders are drawn away from their prisoner by the lure of the mountain lion. The mountain lion's presence quite literally saves Tayo. Next, as Tayo moves down the mountain, a storm approaches, so he seeks shelter in a scrub-oak grove: "He lay in a shallow depression and heaped piles of dry leaves over himself until he felt warm again" (212). This event seems insignificant compared to those preceding it, but it is the final step in a process—a sequence of events or actions—that finalizes Tayo's transformation from a fearful, ineffectual individual into a traditional Laguna hero capable of confronting the evil forces at work in his world and prevailing.

There is another published version of the story of the Evil Gambler that provides further connections between past narratives and Tayo's. In John M. Gunn's *Schat-chen: History, Traditions and Narratives of the Queres Indians of Laguna and Acoma*, it is Pais-chun-ni-moot, or Sun Youth, who undertakes the journey to the Evil Gambler's mountain stronghold to end the drought that threatens the people, and he is the offspring of the Sun and Yellow Woman. Pais-chun-ni-moot first climbs a mountain to meet his father, who then takes him to the people, who, in turn, ask the boy to perform four tasks to prove his birthright. For the last they place him in a room full of lions, "and the lions fawned upon him" (163). Then the people perform the initial ceremony to celebrate Sun's child:

And when the sun saw that the people were convinced, he ordered them to go to the mountains and gather leaves. These they brought and made from them a bed for the youth; and they warmed him in the leaves until he was made in the image of his father.

Then the people cried, "Behold Pais-chun-ni-moot! He will go to the mountain where Kai-na-ni [Gambler] dwells and release our people." (163)

Silko constructs a similar process, taking Tayo through a like transformation from a lost and wandering individual to a character who can perceive the significance of events and the forces that move people and who can respond accordingly. This knowledge provides him with the power to succeed in his final confrontation with the witch, Emo, to release his people.

Subsequent events progressively enhance the mythical implications of Tayo's story. As he walks off the mountain through the storm the following morning, Tayo realizes that he and the mountain lion have been saved by the falling snow, which Silko immediately associates with the lion: "The snowflakes were swirling in tall chimneys of wind, filling his tracks like pollen sprinkled in the mountain lion's footprints" (215). Almost immediately, he is joined by a mysterious man carrying a deer. The man is dressed in traditional clothing: rabbit fur and, for a cap, a fur that "looked like mountain lion skin" (216). As the two men continue down the mountain, the hunter sings. The first song Tayo hears is from Laguna, but the man sings songs from other pueblos where, interestingly enough, Mountain Lion is also a powerful figure in literature and ceremony. When the two arrive at the cabin, the accumulating snow threatens to break the branches of a tree near the house, and the hunter makes a simple statement connecting the storm to Ts'eh: "The tree . . . you [Ts'eh] better fold up the blanket before the snow storm breaks the branches" (218). Ts'eh goes into the bedroom, where the "black storm-patterned blanket was spread open across the gray flagstone" (218). The storm ends when she folds it; she has brought the two men home safely after their successful trips onto the mountain.

By this point in the narrative we can accept the possibility that Ts'eh's blanket may bring snow, and we can grant that Tayo walks with the same hunter we have already met on the mountain, because we, too, have made the same story associations that transform Tayo from a man lost in the fog into an effective hero. Like characters in other Laguna stories, Tayo gains personal relationships with powerful beings in his world (beings similar to those Silko carefully describes in the traditional narratives she reproduces), and we know he will counterbalance the influences of Emo and his cronies. Like his predecessors, the heroes of Laguna literature, Tayo is affirmed as a responsive and therefore powerful human being who leads the way for his people as they try to react to vast changes in their land.

A contemporary Laguna storyteller has written an imaginative narrative that has its bases in the narratives of her people—in the characters, landscape, motivations, and, most of all, desire to provide continuity between the past and the present. However, her narrative goes beyond what has already been told to address an audience that her ancient, and contemporary, oral counterparts would never reach. When Tayo moves in the imagination of a nontribal person, he brings to life the possibility that one person may work a massive transformation in the world and bring about sweeping, beneficial change through close attention to forces in the world that respond to considerate and responsive actions. Silko brings the stories to life today and demonstrates their global significance. Through the implication that story itself provides a means of perpetuation and accommodation, she also underscores the possibility that these values will continue long into the future.

These prominent novels from the 1970s that became a central core of the canon deployed similar structures for DIAC, despite their topics' and authors' varying tribal affiliations. There is no doubt for the reader that they are "Indian" in origin and orientation. Moreover, they share a similar message, one of "survivance" in the borrowed French word used by Gerald Vizenor later: the resilience of cultural attitudes and values in the present and into the future. The novels of the 1980s reiterated and, in places, extended these ideas.

2 | THE 1980s

The 1980s saw a growing interest in Native literatures. Besides the authors discussed in the first chapter, others who had been equally prominent in Native writers' circles—some for decades—found new readers for their work. It would be difficult to name them all, unfortunately. By the late 1980s Dan Littlefield and James Parrins gave up their attempt to provide a bibliography of all the publications by Native writers from 1924 to 1985, as they had done earlier with 1772–1924; the job was too massive and unwieldy.

Fiction writers bloomed in the 1980s. For instance, Gerald Vizenor had published his first novel in 1978, the postapocalyptic *Darkness in Saint Louis Bearheart*, and in the 1980s he flourished. By 1982, when Alan Velie published his critical study of Native fiction, Vizenor had been added to the "core" group (see Velie). And "new" writers appeared on the scene, most notably Louise Erdrich, whose popularity and critical acclaim helped move the canon along as Momaday's work had helped in the 1970s. Her first novel was published in 1984, and *Love Medicine* remains a classic in the canon. Still others, such as Joseph Bruchac, continued to publish as well as open new venues for young authors; Bruchac managed and edited the Greenfield Review Press, publishing "new" voices in the canon.

Momaday, Silko, and Welch continued their careers as well, moving into new terrain with works that blurred the definitions of traditional genres and conventions, Momaday with *The Way to Rainy Mountain*, Welch with the historical novel *Fools Crow*, and Silko with *Storyteller*. Others, Bruchac included, began to write for a young audience; he also edited and published the influential poetry anthology *Songs from This Earth on Turtle's Back: Contemporary American Indian Poetry* (1983), so fiction was not the only genre feeding this urge.

There were several fiction anthologies that helped bring Native authors to the fore as well. One from the 1970s is of note for our purposes here: Kenneth Rosen's short fiction anthology *The Man to Send Rain Clouds: Contemporary Stories by American Indians* (1974), which showcased the early works of Silko, Simon Ortiz, and Anna Lee Walters, to name a few of its contributors. By the early 1980s the number had increased. Geary Hobson's expansive multigenre collection *The Remembered Earth: An Anthology of Contemporary Native American Literature* (1979) attempted an all-inclusive geographical coverage, thus highlighting the obvious: the large number of Native nations and thus the wide variety in artistic voices and visions. This was followed by Ortiz's own *Earth Power Coming: Short Fiction in Native American Literature* (1983). I should note here that Hobson's title comes from Momaday's classic essay (and its various incarnations) "An American Land Ethic" and Ortiz's from the last novel by D'Arcy McNickle, *Wind from an Enemy Sky*, published in 1978. The canon was growing, and its authors were becoming self-reflective. Within a few years, in 1992, Bruchac, Hobson, and others would arrange a conference of Native writers—"Returning the Gift"—that brought hundreds of writers and scholars together for days of discussion about their work, the canon, the future. The fifteen years since the Flagstaff conference had produced a central core of authors and texts as well as a critical discourse about them. Concurrent with these developments, a growing global discourse developed among Indigenous writers, artists, and activists.

I had occasion to speak with Simon Ortiz about these trends. Together with Blake Hausman, a colleague, we reflected upon the expanding nature of the canon. I have admired Simon's writings for as long as I have known that "Native American literatures" exist. When Montana Richards Walking Bull first opened the door for me, Simon was there. While it was not the first of his poems that caught me, "My Father's Song" remains a favorite. His fiction in Rosen's anthology also still works for me (and one of his stories in it was selected for my own anthology in this new millennium), and for years I introduced students to his *Earth Power Coming*.

In our time together we talked of many things: the future of contemporary Native literatures, the worldwide issues that face us all, the past. However, what continues to impress me about our visits— and what marks this poet, writer, man—is the obvious commitment to the world that he exudes. I know several people he has mentored, or supported, or encouraged, or put into contact with others who could assist them.

Simon Ortiz (SO): For a long a time I've been interested in the African connection with Native literature as a decolonizing strategy. My own interest goes back to the late '60s, when I began to read Chinua Achebe and *Cry, the Beloved Country* by Alan Paton. Ngũgĩ wa Thiong'o used to be James Ngugi, didn't he? Kenyan. Achebe is from Nigeria.

When I was at the University of Iowa in 1968 there was a guy I'll always remember. His name was Peter Palangyo. Tanzanian. He was quite a person, an intellectual, a writer. He was the cultural minister after he went back home to Tanzania. In the International Writing Program at the university there were numbers of people from other countries, but there were only two Americans, me and Emory Evans Jr. Having come out of the Watts Writing Workshop, Emory was an African American, a tall, lanky guy, Emory Evans. A great poet, a great poet. Had this wonderful laugh that would just fill up the room [laughs]. He was just a kid, actually, about twenty, twenty-one. He had been through the Watts riot and all that. Others in the International Writing Program were from Europe and Africa. And China, a couple people from the Philippines, and South America. And I remember a Chilean poet, Juan Palazuelos.

John Purdy (JP): Juan Palazuelos? Chilean.

Blake Hausman (BH): It seems to me that so much African literature is at the center of the decolonizing impulse in literature today. It seems that colonized people around the world could benefit from more . . .

SO: Self-assertion. Self-assertion as a style and decision of identity is necessary for Indigenous peoples of the Americas. And they can look toward Africa for example. I think one of the things about Native American intellectualism and writing is that we have often been caught in a real dilemma, sort of a forced choice about what to do in terms of the language to use. So we end up very early on, starting five hundred years ago, going along with the colonizer, the Spanish conquistador first and then other Europeans. As a means of survival we were forced to acquiesce. Yet it's a choice that people did make.

And so to some degree repercussions of that continue, which really undermines our sense of wholeness. Not that there isn't a way in which one can still be whole and express oneself in terms of one's integrity—cultural, spiritual, or physical integrity—with this other language. But it's got to be a real choice; it's got to be a real choice. To some degree you know, obviously, we use the language of colonization, the language of domination, in an appropriate manner. But it is still not a complete choice because we find ourselves regarding our Native or Indigenous languages as secondary. In South America, Mexico, Central America, we find ourselves speaking Spanish. Here in the United States, English.

JP: Or in Africa, French . . .

SO: Or British English. Or in Brazil, Portuguese. It's a dilemma.

BH: Ngũgĩ has approached it by writing in Gikuyu and English. What do you think about that? You mentioned something about risks [earlier] . . .

SO: Ngũgĩ's friend and associate at NYU, Tim Weiss, and I talked about the possibility of getting together with Ngũgĩ, for him and me to talk. I want to learn from him. What are the principles, the theories, and the practices that make it possible for him to believe in the use of an Indigenous language? It's much more of an assertive method to use an Indigenous language such as Gikuyu or any other Indigenous language as the main mode of communication for the conveyance of knowledge. I really think it's possible to use an Indigenous language so that it is truly a language of choice for you, but still you can use another language or other languages. For example, though I don't have any real research to back this up, I think that Native peoples in the

Americas were multilingual before the Europeans came. They spoke not only their home language, that is, say, Acoma—let's just go with the people at home. We spoke our own home language, but we also spoke neighboring languages such as Navajo. By the time the Spaniards came, Navajos had become a part of the general cultural world of Acoma, so Navajo was spoken. That was a fairly recent language.

Before that there were other Pueblo languages. Zuni Pueblo is to the west, fairly close to Acoma. It has an entirely different language, yet I believe people were familiar with and knew how to speak the Zuni language. To the east are the Tiwa speakers of Isleta and Sandia, just north and south of Albuquerque, wholly different languages. And then not too far away are the people of Jemez Pueblo, another different language. And then there were people of the plains farther to the east who certainly interfaced with Pueblo peoples.

So there were a number of languages. When the Spaniards came and brought a language different from any of the others, I think that the people were already multilingual.[1] European people used language as the device to control and to dominate, certainly as a means of control and imposing their power. I think today there is no real reason not to use your own language, that is, the language of your choice. Meaning that if I decide to use my own Native language—that is, Acoma, or Keres, which is the language that Acoma speaks—I'll use that as a choice, a decision, but also if I want to use English or Spanish or any other language, Navajo or Zuni.

JP: German.

SO: German, yeah. I should be able to do that. As long as it is a decision that is made as a matter of ethics, that it's the right thing for me.

BH: Critics may look at Ngũgĩ and say, "That's wonderful; you're writing in your native tongue, but the majority of people in your homeland can't understand it." It seems like quite a paradox to be able to exercise that choice, an act of reclamation, if you will. But I wonder what you think of some of the tensions involved in using an Indigenous language. You have such a larger audience when you work in English or a European language.

SO: We make that choice. Or we are forced into making that choice because of the larger context. The larger context of the world surrounds us, and obviously choices are made, choices determined by the surroundings. Political choices are kind of choices of convenience. In other words, since not many people speak Gikuyu here in Bellingham, or Acoma, or in Lummi, the Indian community and reservation where I was today, then we end up making the choice and decision to speak the language that everyone understands. Meaning that right now, the present society we are surrounded by and we live within speaks and understands English—and so we go along with English, not that that's a better choice and not because it's a wise choice but that it is a choice of convenience. It's what we manage things by.

Someone asked me a question yesterday about the Internet as another form of language, another form of communication. As long as the Internet doesn't become a language of control that takes me over, I think that it can be helpful and useful. But I think the tendency is to become dependent upon it, and we have no choice except to live by it.

JP: It becomes the default language.

SO: Yeah. In the same way, in some sense. Let's look at the political economy. We end up using dollars and cents because we either lack the imagination or the will or the power to not use dollars and cents. We end up going along with the system as it is. We know it's not the best system in the world. We know in a deep innate sense that it's not and that we're somehow working against ourselves when we use the default.

In terms of literature we really can speak truly for ourselves and have a sense of authenticity, honesty, and integrity. It's not as if we don't have a sense of that choice, a decision we can't make. I bring up the question to myself and to others: What happens when we don't conscientiously use the English language? And go along with it just because it's convenient? In answer to myself I said that when I use *nuu yuh Aacquemeh hano ka-dzeh-nih*—Acoma people's language—it feels more tangible in a palpable way. It's not abstract. When I speak English sometimes I find myself in the Western cultural world of abstraction. I don't know whether this is a conflict or not, but abstraction and objectification, treating ideas like things or objects. I find it quite convenient to objectify when I'm in that mode of Western cultural thought. When I am speaking in the Acoma language, it seems to be less so, less abstract, unless I'm just fooling myself somehow. I am less abstract when I am speaking in the Native language. But perhaps I don't really know because I haven't fully thought it out—because in some way there is a sort of abstraction that may come from a defensive position, when you are only speaking in a very specific dimension and only thinking for a specific purpose.

JP: Well, do you think it could be just second-language use? I wonder about that, too, because when you speak in your native language, whether it be Acoma or English or whatever, and then you speak in another language, the process of speaking has a different significance than it does when you're speaking the language that you're born and raised in as a native speaker.

SO: If you mean a different process, you believe in it in a different way? Or do you believe it's somehow much more tangible or weighty?

JP: No, I think it's that the act of utterance itself becomes the focus rather than the thing that you're saying, because of the translation difference. So if I'm a native English speaker and I go to Germany, for instance, and I'm conversing with someone in German, all of a sudden there's a subtle shift in the dynamics of language itself.

SO: When I have found myself translating, I don't feel comfortable translating mechanically or technically, because I felt like I was objectifying my thoughts. And I don't want to objectify my thoughts. In other words, this sort of relates to what I was saying about making it abstract. Nothing should be abstract, because some abstractions are intended to be manipulative, and you're abstracting only to create diversion and to create a different sense other than what you intend. Do you speak other languages?

BH: I speak Spanish and Russian, and I've stared at the Cherokee syllabary many times, though I think I may need to go to Oklahoma and stay for a while to pick it up. But there is something in the process of translating your ideas . . .

SO: You know I wanted to read the Yiddish writer Isaac Bashevis Singer in Yiddish and study his ideas, discussions, and conversations about language. When a native speaker speaks in his own language and in his own cultural mode, he is his own cultural real self. He is probably more real then, unless I'm just saying this because it's what I want to believe. Singer was much more real when he wrote in his native Yiddish than when he was working with translators, although I've never heard him say that.

How about that other guy? Conrad?

JP: Joseph Conrad?

SO: He was Polish, but he wrote in English. A great English writer.

JP: There are a number of them. Nabokov, Russian and English. That kind of takes me back to what you were saying earlier about that possibility for cross-pollination, working with people or peoples or authors from other continents who have faced colonial issues as well. When we were talking about it earlier, it was only directional in one way, in a sense. Well . . . it would be nice to work with them, to find out what they've experienced, but also what you could learn from them. But the other possibility is that they could learn a lot from that exchange as well.

SO: That's the other motivation for wanting to talk with Ngũgĩ. To know the agenda or the reasons for insisting on your own language. It has to do with what your experience has been under colonization, your experience of colonialism. We Native people in the Americas have not really faced our use of Spanish and English. We use them, but we have not really looked at our use. I even have the feeling, maybe more of a sentiment, that we have arrived at our use of English too easily. In other words, we have had not a big experience with English and Spanish, but we use them quite well. What does that mean? Does it mean that we have let our Native spirit, our Native soul, our Native culture, our Native identity go too easily? I hate to think of it, but that's one of the explanations.

BH: I'm sure that people have asked you this before, but when you write something in your Native language, how do you hope that younger people, on the reservation or in cities, wherever, would react to that?

SO: That they be encouraged. That they be encouraged to write in their own Native languages. Although, of course, representations of Native language are for the most part phonetic and using alphabets of Western cultural languages such as English, using the symbols and script, using equivalent sounds represented by visual symbols. The devising or development of a written Native language has not taken place. Although Sequoia, the Cherokee, to some degree did that, developed a syllabary that has been useful and is an example.

I do have some reservations about writing. It has reference to why some Indian people do not want to teach the writing of their Native language or do not want to allow the writing of their Native language. Oral language—compared to written language—is much more immediate and intimate; that's the only way language and culture can actually be lived. Not represented but actually lived. Representation is like photography. Take a photograph of this cup of coffee; it's just a picture, it's not the coffee. Language is the same way; you can't "write" the language down; that's a representation of it, a photograph of it. Actual language is what you and I are talking—words, sounds, body and facial and eye language. We are involved in and participating in the act of language.

Language and literature are a form of participation. Story, I think, is participatory. There's not just one way of telling a story. Story is a manifestation of flexibility.

BH: Like the end of *Ceremony*, when Grandmother says, "It seems like I already heard these stories before . . . only thing is, the names sound different."

SO: People, of course, have imagination and different kinds of insight and may still be tied to something consistent, but yet they're different. And that kind of difference is a kind of love. You don't let something go, you keep it. Although it's different, it is still useful and helpful to you. Songs, I think, are good examples. Songs that evoke emotion. They may be different, but they are rich and full and deep and have a dimension of emotion that conveys feeling.

BH: Every time I read one of your poems, there is so much emotion that I feel a connection to it. This is sort of a big shift of topic here, but not really. I'm taking a poetry seminar right now, and among the many things we're reading is language poetry—English fragmented, fractured, so many ideas taken out, verbs taken out, to the point where the finished poem is, at least has the appearance of being, void of emotion, void of narrative. There is no "I" in the poem. It raises interesting issues about how you ask the reader to interact with a poem, and it even has music in it somehow. But often I feel a huge distance between myself and the poem. I just wonder what your take on that approach to modern poetics was, because personally I identify with your work much more than that.

SO: Sometimes I find that I'm not very well schooled in formal poetics. I've read a lot, but I think I've not been a very good scholar of what I've read. I read because I like the appeal of being immersed in ideas. It's like jumping into a pool of ideas. I feel that maybe I'm more into the sensation of those ideas rather than following any analytical string of thought. My reading is this and that . . . all over the place.

I'm a student of poetics because I like poetry [laughter]. I'm not a very good critic either. When I first began to read poetry as poetry I read Beat poetry because it seemed to be very ordinary, very common, very approachable, very accessible. It was something that I could identify with without having a formal, scholarly, or analytical, or critical, approach. It was something very tangible, something that I could relate to in a very immediate, nonabstract way. Of course, I was also very impressionable when I was in high school. That was in the late 1950s, when the Beats were people like Ginsberg, Ferlenghetti, Gregory Corso, Jack Kerouac.

JP: Like yesterday, when you talked about Black Mountain in North Carolina, and Robert Creeley.

SO: Yeah. They seemed to me something that were not removed from my own world. It was all right to be all right, it was all right to be who you were, and I think there's a real freedom in that. And yet there were also specific things, like Zen Buddhism. I was reading Eastern philosophy that I associated with my own Native culture. I mean, there's some Native American similarities with Buddhism. I also liked Dostoyevsky. Of all the Russian authors, Dostoyevsky was my favorite. And also Chekhov. I'm not sure why. It wasn't a real highly developed intellectual reasoning, I think.

BH: Something that was tangible.

SO: Chekhov is very tangible. He was a dramatist. I like not his plays so much but rather his stories. I think as far as American literature went I know I really liked some of the same kind of style. Like Steinbeck, some of Hemingway. Sherwood Anderson. Of course, this probably had something to do with the kind of high school literature classes that I had. I like literature, but I don't know why [laughter]. Probably in retrospect, if somebody did analyze why, they would come up with something I would agree with [more laughter].

JP: There's always that chance.

SO: You know who I liked years and years ago? I haven't read him for a long time. Saul Bellow. But I wonder why? And I liked Norman Mailer too. You read him?

JP: Yeah, sure. But it'll be curious to look ahead maybe fifty years or more. Have someone sitting around with an up-and-coming young writer, or somebody who's doing very well, some Anglo guy, and say, Who are your influences? Have him say, Scott Momaday, or Jim Welch, or Simon Ortiz, or Louise Erdrich, or Leslie Silko.

SO: I had a kind of strange sort of reading upbringing. My father read some, and also my mother, but I would not say that they were literary people at all, not in the classical or "literary" sense. My dad used to like Zane Grey and Louis L'Amour. I remember my mother reading Pearl Buck to me. And who was the guy who wrote *Shangri La* [*Lost Horizon*]?

JP: Hilton?

SO: Yeah. James Hilton, I remember being fascinated. I was in grade school then.

JP: Well, you may not agree with the elements of the story, but they were stories.

SO: Oh yeah.

JP: Stories that kept you going.

SO: I haven't talked to Leslie Silko or Louise Erdrich or James Welch or Scott Momaday about this, but I wonder how similar we may be in our reading backgrounds. I was kind of a strange kid. I read a lot, but I don't know why, I just wanted to know. I just wanted to know.

Part of it was being conscious of myself as an Indian, so I may have been deliberately making a choice of trying to attain something. If I felt like I was being looked at disparagingly, that is, in a demeaning way, as an Indian, I think that I may have selected literature accordingly, literature I liked and identified with. Not that I didn't like it; I mean, I loved reading. I still do. But that may have been part of my subconscious decision or choice that I read in high school someone like Blake or Shakespeare. I remember I checked out books like *Rise and Fall of the Roman Empire*, not your typical high school fare. And I think that it became a part of my aesthetic development. I don't think it's a matter of choice of developing one's mind; you go where your interests are.

JP: So you find somebody who's writing who shares an interest with you, and that's part of the attraction?

SO: Yeah, I think. Or you like something that someone else likes. And you sort of admire that person—so you go with that. Or you identify with someone you admire and respect.

JP: Rudolfo Anaya was here a few years back, and I'll never forget.

For his reading he said, "Everyone's always asking me to read from *Bless Me, Ultima*. That's an old book. I've read from it a thousand times. I want to read you a poem I've never read." And it was a poem about Walt Whitman coming to New Mexico [laughter]. He said, "I like Walt Whitman. Why not? So I wrote a poem about Walt Whitman coming to New Mexico." That's the way literature works. I mean, we all share stories and find someone who has a similar interest and a different story. It's good to share in that somehow.

SO: There was an old guy, I think he may have passed away by now, Sabine—I'll always remember his stories. A Chicano, he used to teach Spanish at the University of New Mexico. He'd say, "Simon, my friend, you and I, we are the only storytellers left" [spoken in dialect, laughter]. I got a kick out of that.

Native American literature is a way—for those who write it, Native writers themselves—for us to insist on our validity. Because in some ways Native literature is still not accepted. That may have to do with the choice of language. We use English, obviously, as the language of dominant culture, and we go along with the dominant culture. But I think we have to be conscious of our reasons for using English and to be aware of its pitfalls. If we're not, we're simply going along with it, pitfalls and all. I know that some of my fellow Native writers may disagree with me.

BH: It's a matter of your consciousness of your language.

SO: There are a few writers who insist on Native language use. Rex Lee Jim is one. And Irvin Morris. And Ray Young Bear, from Iowa. Let me ask you a question.

BH: Okay.

SO: You said you had looked at Cherokee—why?

BH: Why?

SO: Do you want to speak it or just understand it?

BH: Both, I think. I suppose that as a Jewish Cherokee who can't speak Hebrew or Cherokee I sometimes feel dislocated. And as a young writer I think there is much I can learn from the old stories in their native tongue. Every time I look at a newspaper or something that comes from Tahlequah, the tribe puts so much emphasis on maintaining culture through language. To teach the language, to maintain culture through language. I feel like I should be doing something that I could justify as helpful or constructive in some way, and one way I can do that is learning to speak the language, so maybe that's what I ought to do. People in my family have worked to sustain the vitality of Indian people in many ways, on reservations, in the courts, the government, academia. I look at my cousins and myself and our place in time, and I think that it's important. I don't know, I'm not quite sure how to explain it.

SO: I'll tell you a story. Years ago, in 1970 or so, I had gone to Oklahoma. This is on that trip that I took to look for Indians. I went to Tahlequah and met a couple of Cherokee guys. We'd become friends. The guys told me, "You know, we're Cherokees. But do you want to meet a real Cherokee?" I said, "Well, sure." They said, "Let's go see ol' Smitty." I said, "Okay. Where does he live?" They said, "Oh, he lives over there, behind those hills." They pointed over toward the Ozark hills, northeast Oklahoma. Kind of over to the Missouri-Arkansas border.

So we go out that way a day later or so. I don't know how many miles we went, quite a ways up into those hills. Soon the road gave out onto just this dirt track. And then we stopped. At a little house. Nobody seemed to be around, and we just sat in the car drinking beer and stuff. Pretty soon the door of the house opened, the guys got out of the car, and they talked to a woman. The guys came back and said, "He's not here right now; he'll be back in a while I guess." So we sat some more, waiting. Waiting.

Pretty soon from around the back of the house comes this older guy, maybe seventy something. He was a nondescript older Indian man. He spoke Cherokee, nothing but Cherokee, at least that's what I thought then. And they—the guys and he— all spoke Cherokee, and of course I don't speak Cherokee. The impression I got was that he—ol' Smitty—was this real authentic Cherokee man who didn't speak English, who only spoke Cherokee!

Well, after maybe an hour or so, it turns out he *did* speak English. But he only spoke English when he was assured that you were going to approach him as a Cherokee man. We talked. He was a nice guy, good sense of humor, a storyteller. I think if he had only spoken Cherokee I would have thought he was just being stubborn or he didn't want me to be associated with him. And when it turns out he spoke English, he was even more Cherokee to me.

JP: Well, then, we're back to the issue of choice, right? Like we're talking about with the writing . . .

But at this moment we found that we were late for Simon's reading, and we had no choice but to defer the conversation until later.

In a subsequent letter Simon noted that his last story was cut short. His story of ol' Smitty continues: "He was an elderly fiddle maker who young white people from Tulsa and Oklahoma City came to seek out, I guess. They seemed to regard him as some kind of folk figure, an exotic throwback or something, an Indian artifact more or less, and that's the way they saw him or preferred to see him! And he spoke only in Cherokee to them, never English. Although he spoke English! Which he spoke with me after he decided-understood I wasn't going to treat him like he was some throwback Cherokee artifact."

As Simon suggests, all utterance involves making choices, and this is quite true of writing in both the literary *and* the critical genres. In the context of this discussion the choices in fiction writing come in relation to that sense of Indigenous self-differentiation and the author's sense of the reader to whom he or she is writing. As noted in the opening of this chapter, as the popularity and critical acclaim of Native writers generated more exposure for their works and as the "culture wars" of the 1980s were engaged, the choices and options increased as well; writers used Native languages, discussed Indigenous consciousness, championed causes with rhetoric.[2] Some moved into new (for them) genres and media: into children's literature, film, and popular genres such as the historical novel. James Welch was one author who chose to explore the use of this genre in reinscribing colonial history while exploring imaginatively that history from his own Indigenous point of view. However, he did so by building on techniques learned in the 1970s with the publication of his first novel. Looking at the two together can underscore the ways that differentiation, investigation, affirmation, and continuation (DIAC) were presented in the two decades. As Simon also said, "Story, I think, is participatory." One way of reading Native fiction—as several critics explored throughout the 1980s—is to look at the ways we participate in these four activities.

JAMES WELCH: *Fools Crow* and *Winter in the Blood*

Fools Crow was published in 1986, and it is important to say at the outset that it is an imaginative gaze back into a psychology related to, but also slightly different from, that of the Blackfeet (Pikuni) in the 1980s. In this way it utilizes but complicates the historical novel genre, a genre that has historically appropriated Native cultures and revised them to fit a convention of romantic depictions, as with Cooper, and perpetuate the idea that Manifest Destiny was just that: destiny. As Welch calls us into this psychology he asks us to participate in the investigation of its efficacy, then and now.

For some authors such as Welch, participatory involvement in DIAC is accomplished through the narrative interaction between culture and motion. I will come back to this later, but for the moment I will add that the reasons for this are deceptively simple and suggest a number of intriguing, complex associations between fiction and autobiography, community and individual, art and life, people and place. Some Native authors employ, in various ways and to varying degrees, verbal literary traditions that reflect long-standing associations with specific landscapes, just as we saw in Welch's second novel and in Momaday's and Silko's first. As in Native verbal art, the written often emphasizes singular qualities of motion in the actions of individuals or groups in specific real-world places and primal situations; action development is tantamount to character development. It is this emphasis on the detailed descriptions of motion in relation to setting that is so apparent in writings by Native Americans. In fact, as Geary Hobson notes, when nontribal people attempt to write

"Indian" books or understand Native ways, they "often overlook the importance of the everyday occurrences, the prosaic and undramatic elements of small things conducted in almost unnoticeable ritual" (103). Native writers make visible this ritual for us, and when we see it—surprise—we are participating in the story in some fundamental ways. This ritualized narration is their domain, their donnée, and it is immensely provocative. In fact, if one does not recognize this dimension to the story and participate in its investigation, one can make some monumental blunders in one's reading, as we see in numerous reviews of Native novels.[3]

Until the publication of his historical novel, *Fools Crow*, though, Welch did not make overt use of tribal stories by reproducing them in the context of his own writing, for which others are noted. In *The Death of Jim Loney*, after all, by exploring stories and ethnographic materials one sees how deeply they are insinuated into the narrative. Elements of Blackfeet or Gros Ventre stories and literary conventions are to be found in all his novels, and the central, unifying element in each is the concept of motion as described from a tribal point of view, suggesting a fundamental differentiation between a Blackfoot novel and a non-Native novel.

Each of Welch's early novels demonstrates how a people find identity in terms of a landscape's character and how they express, reaffirm, and perpetuate their senses of self in relation to it through their actions therein. For his protagonists, resolution to their problems is directly proportional to their understanding of the things their people have learned from an intimate interaction with place but also their willingness to allow that knowledge to direct their movements or actions. *Fools Crow* explores the roots of this tribal knowledge while qualifying a very dark point in tribal history through a compelling, detailed investigation of a Native worldview in which animals converse with people and visions and dreams convey the unknowable. Like the stories one finds in ethnographies such as *Blackfoot Lodge Tales* by George Bird Grinnell, *Mythology of the Blackfoot Indians* by Clark Wissler and D. C. Duvall, and, more significantly, Percy Bullchild's expansive *The Sun Came Down: The History of the World as My Blackfeet Elders Told It*, Welch's book focuses narrative attention on primal times or, more accurately, on very primal actions that have come to define ways of moving appropriately and effectively. If we understand this definition in the context of *Fools Crow*, we may recognize it in the fiction of other Indian authors as well.

Like characters in traditional verbal arts, Welch's characters interpret, interact, and move within their world in very personal ways: through dreams, journeys, and vision quests. Moreover, the knowledge Pikuni individuals gain through these processes is valued by its potential benefit for their people. Useful knowledge is then encompassed in narratives that align the audience imaginatively through the detailed motions they describe and the attitudes about actions they convey; in these we are asked to participate through rescripted acts of the imagination derivative from but ultimately reconfigured by Welch's co-opting of the popular novel genre. Like older Pikuni stories, *Fools Crow* dramatizes human movements illustrative of one's accountability to the landscape, one's people, and the future. In this we find a comment upon U.S. history, a message for contemporary (Native) Americans, and, perhaps, a hope for the country's future.

Fools Crow differentiates itself from the opening words, developing from the beginning a style and tone that resonate with previous historical fictions in which Natives are to be found. Its setting also aligns with the convention of, as Sherman Alexie puts it in his classic poem "How to Write the Great American Indian Novel," "a horse culture." However, the bulk of the novel is devoted to investigating what Pikuni culture was in the later 1800s, and much of this is carried by the characters' movements, in two basic senses of the word. First, it explores the relationship between movements of individuals as directed by a sense of self and those of a people as directed by a sense of community. Second, it explains the relationship between actions and movements, between the mundane performance of "the everyday occurrences, the prosaic and undramatic elements of small things," and the epic, such as the journey or vision quest. Ultimately, the explorations define appropriate action or movement and the ways one may acquire the knowledge that facilitates that definition.

The setting of the novel is important in this context as well; its actions take place at a point in Pikuni history when the community at large was torn between only two apparent courses of action, violent resistance or resignation, with the life of the people hanging in the balance. At a time so crucial, even seemingly insignificant actions may irrevocably shape the future. However, as we shall see in Welch's canon, when a binary such as this is presented, we are faced with a real but limiting set of choices; a wise person will be attuned to other options.

Interestingly, the novel opens with the protagonist, White Man's Dog, ruminating upon his life and future. In the very first words the main character struggles to define himself as an individual. As he betrays his doubts, weaknesses, and aspirations he also reveals the ways to address them in the context of his culture. Immediately, he is offered the chance to direct his own future, to turn thoughts into actions and dreams into reality, through his participation on a horse raid against the Crow: the novel's first journey. The search for identity becomes a group effort, and in this communal context one's actions reveal and develop one's character.

Welch describes this raid in great detail, for the specifics chart more than a simple removal from one place in the land to another; they describe how either an individual or a group must carefully consider and control movements in light of the complex interplay of forces that bear directly upon their success and their lives. In a presentation strongly suggestive of Blackfeet verbal tradition, Welch has Fast Horse recount a dream he had and then has us participate in a dream with White Man's Dog. The former shares, too freely, his dream with the group and loses its power, while the latter keeps his secret and lives to regret his silence, which suggests that there must be another, beneficial alternative somewhere in between. Welch also notes the exact places where things are seen or things happen because place and event coincide to provide crucial information to help Yellow Kidney, the leader, determine if they should alter their movements, return to camp, or go on. The isolated, significant movements found on this journey are echoed elsewhere by the actions of individuals in other settings and on other journeys, for they, too, must be directed by similar considerations. Appropriate behavior is described as the result of smart reading (of circumstances using all available evidence) followed by deliberate, coordinated action: mind and body in balance, a philosophical pragmatism. Welch systematically explores the ways that choices would and perhaps should be made and actions initiated: the primal, universal necessity of choice to which Ortiz speaks.

An elaborate example appears later in the novel. The horse raid on the Crow has disastrous results for Yellow Kidney, who is captured and mutilated by Bull Shield, the Crow warrior. To avenge Yellow Kidney, White Man's Dog and hundreds of warriors from the bands of the Pikuni return to the Crow encampment, and this journey also has its signs, which the attuned reader now sees:

> Just after midday of the fourth sleep, a strange event took place. The party had ridden down a shallow coulee just north of the Elk River, keeping above a brush line that marked the course of a dry creek. The grass around them had turned golden in the late summer sun. The yellow-wings jumped and buzzed in the air before the horses. Fox Eyes [the leader] had decided to await the return of the wolves [scouts] at the mouth of the coulee. From there they could see the valley of the Elk River and remain unseen. The scouts would by now have located the camp of Bull Shield. On their return a strategy could be determined.
>
> White Man's Dog was worried about his horse. Although he didn't limp, there was something wrong with his gait, as though he were favoring a leg. White Man's Dog pulled out of the dusty stream of riders and got down. The sun was warm on his back as he felt the horse's legs and bent the fetlocks to look at the hooves. He could find nothing wrong and decided it must have been his nerves. He stretched his back and looked up to the southwest. The Day Star was a brilliant pin of light in the orange sky. He hadn't noticed how bright it was this day. . . . He shielded his eyes and peeked between his fingers. The sun had ceased to glow and a chunk of it was missing. He had not seen this happen before. . . . Again he peered at the sun, and this time he didn't have to shield

his eyes. It had become a dark ball with just a rim of glowing gold. His horse had gentled some and he released the ear and stared at the hole which had replaced Sun Chief. . . . White Man's Dog was too frightened to pray or even to think. (142)

The ways Welch chooses to describe a full eclipse of the sun emphasize a major assertion in this novel: natural occurrences are intimately related to human actions, and the internal and external worlds are intricately intertwined for this character, who gives motion and form to an ancient cosmology.

First, Welch is very careful to note exactly where the eclipse transpires and the logistics of the Pikuni's communal movement against the Crow. The Pikuni use the character of the terrain to dictate a route that will protect them from being discovered and enable them to avoid places where an ambush may be hidden. This is logical movement. Welch also notes when the eclipse happens, midday on the fourth sleep; the number four has ritual significance for the Pikuni as well as other Native peoples on the continent. Time and place and actions accounted for, Welch then isolates White Man's Dog, whose horse's movements have become unnatural. He is sensitive, insightful, and attentive and thus receptive to events. These qualities, investigated for a contemporary audience, define in the personalized terms of an individual how myth and present might interact. In its transcendence of the historical novel genre in these places the book moves into tribal realism.

Welch has his character note the power of Day Star, despite the time of day and year. In the Pikuni mythos Welch presents, Morning Star is Sun Chief's son, for Welch has already told a brief version of the story of Morning Star, Feather Woman (So-at-sa-ki), and Star Boy (Poia). Once this story is added to our interpretative repertoire, the eclipse suggests more than merely a natural phenomenon, and suggestion enhances participatory urge. The old story ties the people directly to a supranatural force who was once intimate with a Pikuni woman, resulting in their most powerful ceremonial, and who exerts his influence in the lives of the people, especially in times of danger. With the eclipse, Day Star is in ascension, so his influence is strengthened. White Man's Dog feels that strength in the battle, from which he emerges a "new man," a leader with a new name: Fools Crow. The eclipse is a message, a forewarning about the near future of the raiding party but also of the coming upset to the balance of forces in the Pikuni world brought by the Napikwans, the European Americans. It is Fools Crow's lot to find a way of mediating this change without following one of the initial courses of action: to fight or to accept.

White Man's Dog has never seen an eclipse before, so his shock is quite understandable. It derives from a lack of experience, yet his next reaction provides Welch's revelation of one source of knowledge and its uses: "White Man's Dog remembered his grandfather telling of a similar event. That time, when Sun hid his face, the people trembled and cried. A few days later, Emonissi, the great head chief of the Siksikas, was thrown from his horse and trampled by the black horns [buffalo]" (143). The stories of past events and connections enlighten present courses of action and decision making—and possibly the future—for someone who knows them. Fox Eyes dies in the raid on the Crow rather than turn back because of the sign.

Welch handles these passages very subtly, balancing the Euro-rational, scientific explanations of his modern readers against a system of logic, a teleology, based upon tribal imperatives, a system derived from eons of involvement with a specific landscape intricately tied directly to the larger yet very similar system of the cosmos. But there are even more explicit statements of these imperatives in the stories of individuals.

The story of White Man's Dog/Fools Crow is a constant refrain to the stories of others and therefore to the larger narrative about the Pikuni as they faced trying times and looked for a way to survive as a people. Welch compares Fools Crow's actions with those of Running Fisher (his younger brother) and Fast Horse (his friend). Then, by telling the stories of the Beaver Medicine bundle, So-at-sa-ki, and Poia, he gives his readers the means to judge whose actions are appropriate, much as Silko does with the interplay with Tayo's story and Laguna literature in *Ceremony*. Through the juxtaposition of past and present actions, between the old and the new stories, Welch differentiates and investigates the ways to move that will insure the stability, the survivance of a culture, in the terms of Anishinaabe writer Gerald Vizenor.

Running Fisher's reactions to the eclipse are unique; although he participates in the raid on Bull Shield's camp, he is incapacitated by his fear. He cannot address it and still function as a member of his collective. When the others attack the village, confident in their power to direct their fate, he rides on the outskirts of the encampment, firing his gun into the air and then retreating with the first wave of Pikuni to withdraw. He insures his own survival by withholding himself from the movements of the party and thus jeopardizes their communal endeavor. Much like Abel in the chicken pull in Momaday's *House Made of Dawn*, Running Fisher's movements are full of "caution and gesture" (42).

We may sympathize with his reservations, but Welch does not let us condone his actions. Due to his easy discarding of his people's faith in their power and his refusal to throw himself into the battle along with his comrades, Running Fisher becomes a despicable character: he later seduces his father's youngest wife, thus violating a familial and social trust. However, Welch provides another model of action. White Man's Dog has also felt longings for the same woman but overcomes them by calling upon his faith in his intimate relationship with his landscape, and his "helper" teaches him in a dream how to act. He controls his actions and therefore the future; Running Fisher is at the mercy of forces beyond his control. The message is clear.

Like Running Fisher, Fast Horse is moved by self-interest rather than the community. He wants to be powerful and respected, but he also wants shortcuts and easy, direct roads to success. During the early horse raid against the Crow he acts foolishly, forgetting all he has been taught about appropriate movement. He shouts into the Crow camp after he has taken a horse from it, thus alerting the Crow and directly initiating Yellow Kidney's capture. By this act of senseless self-expression, Fast Horse limits his future options. He dooms himself to repeat similar acts later because the immediate rewards of individualism are hollow, transitory, and unsatisfying. One must constantly reconstruct and reexperience them, but ultimately they isolate one from the greater, lasting concerns of community and cosmos. Fast Horse does not fulfill his obligation to Cold Maker (the spirit of winter) as he promised and wanders instead with a small band of alienated individuals, killing, raping, and becoming as cold and distant as winter itself.

With the two journeys against the Crow, Welch demonstrates the crucial connections between the movements of individuals and those of a people. Both must be initiated and directed by a sense of selfless devotion to the best interests of the larger self: the community and its homeland. If this sense is subverted by the immediate and transitory concerns of the individual, ill results follow; power is lost. Also, journey is defined as a series of movements during which continual choices must be made to insure success and survival. These decisions are made by drawing upon several potential sources of information. One of these is literature, the stories that possess past knowledge. If this is insufficient, one must look for new ways directly from one's surroundings through dream, vision, or helper. If one is attentive, if one moves attuned to one's environment, knowledge will come. These fundamental assumptions about the relationships between place and people provide the system of logic upon which the actions described in *Fools Crow* are based, from those of Yellow Kidney to those of Poia, Mikapi, Boss Ribs, Fools Crow, and So-at-sa-ki. The power of self-determination derives from this knowledge, but, as their stories suggest, it is power held in common for the people, not for the individual.

This communal responsibility extends to the other beings with whom the Pikuni share the land. While Fools Crow and his wife, Red Paint, hunt alone in the Backbone of the World (the Rocky Mountains), he is approached by Crow, an animal mentor, who not only tells him the number and sexes of the people killed in Bull Shield's camp—information obviously inaccessible to the Pikuni—but also enlists his aid in removing a major threat to the animals of the mountains. A wild white man is killing animals merely for the sake of killing. He must be stopped, but the animals are powerless to kill him, so Crow and Fools Crow conspire to ambush him. Crow sings to the white man in his sleep and directs him to Fools Crow's camp, using Red Paint as bait. It works, and the senseless destruction ceases through the willingness of one individual to risk all to bring balance back to the world.

The final journey of the novel illustrates the potential inherent in a system of logic based upon an intimate sensitivity to one's environment. In a dream Fools Crow's dream helper, Nitsokan, calls him to a journey. He knows it will be very difficult and demanding and that his resolve will be tested again and again, as in the quests found in Blackfeet verbal arts. Welch replicates a tribal literary tradition in his novel to similar effect and for a similar purpose.

Fools Crow's movements, initiated and motivated by his dedication to his people and their needs, take him beyond the limitations of time and space, and although he goes through the land of his people, he recognizes from the very first that this journey is different from the earlier ones Welch describes:

> As he scanned the snowy short-grass plains stretching away to the blue mountains of the Backbone, he began to be afraid. He knew this country well, knew all the buttes and mountains, the creeks and rivers; yet this day he felt strange, and when he looked at familiar landmarks he saw them as a stranger would, in a different place, in another time. He was grateful when the sun broke above a cloudbank to the east. He was grateful that Sun Chief would watch over him one more day. (317)

His actions result in a transcendence, a removal of all barriers as the physical landscape accommodates his movements, his journey. He rides all night and day for three days through hostile territory and yet remains unseen. And when he arrives at his destination, he enters an unknown place in this familiar land that is at once physical and mythical: a "green sanctuary between earth and sky" (360). He also moves beyond linear time into a timeless realm where the future is as easily accessible as the present. In this state Fools Crow finds perspective and therefore the knowledge that will dictate his actions in the future and offer an alternative to either violent resistance or resignation.

Fools Crow's vision of the colonized future, obviously, comes to pass: smallpox kills many, the soldiers come to attack Heavy Runner's camp, and so on. But the final scene he is granted is the most important. Throughout his stay in So-at-sa-ki's sanctuary he hears the laughter of children. Then, as he kneels above the hide, scanning the wide range of his people's lands as if looking through a hole in the sky above them as So-at-sa-ki had so long before, he sees a modern schoolhouse. Unfortunately, the children laughing are Napikwans, and as they play Fools Crow recognizes a small group of Pikuni children standing apart; in pants and dresses, hair cut short, shoes on their feet, they stand apart.

At first this appears to be a bleak image of the Pikuni future, a life of disempowered victimry. Much will be lost as things change. However, the children in Fools Crow's vision still stand as a group, a community, and their standing apart from the white children's "games" may, in fact, be a saving grace. The choice is theirs, for the conscious, deliberate, and continual reidentification with the knowledge contained in tribal narratives can reaffirm tribal identity and therefore provide both continuity and flexibility, just as Ortiz suggests, despite the outward appearance of loss and assimilation. It allows them to accommodate change while remaining in control of their own future through tribal autonomy. The final scenes of the book underscore the ways that much may be saved through a resistance to what others thought of as the "inevitable" demise of Indigenous cultures.

The book ends, significantly, with the Thunder Pipe ceremony. Spring has come to the land, the Pikuni are still alive, and they still perform their obligations to the other beings of their cosmos. As they dance and sing, they move in unison, sharing a primary belief in and exercise of their power as a people. Welch presents his unqualified vision of the effects this has on them. As he dances, Fools Crow thinks of So-at-sa-ki: "He knew that she was here, someplace, watching him, watching the procession, and he saw her smile in the blue light and he smiled. For even though he was, like Feather Woman, burdened with the knowledge of his people, their lives and the lives of their children, he knew they would survive, for they were the chosen ones" (390).

As they feast that night, their children play in the rain: "They were Pikunis and they played hard" (390). Unlike the white children in the fenced school yard, they move freely in the open with the rain. Moreover, through the ceremonies—through communal movements that mark them as a people, and a powerful, chosen people at that— the Pikuni survive. Their ways to gain the knowledge of how to move to insure self-determination remain, and if their actions continue to be motivated by a concern for the community and in ways dictated by their homeland, both will endure.

This may appear very romantic for someone who has given us two previous novels with bleak endings. Also, since it is set in the past, *Fools Crow* seems to have little in common with *Winter in the Blood* and *The Death of Jim Loney*. However, there are some very clear parallels and enlightening qualifications if we consider the ways Welch's characters and narratives move.

In *Winter*, years earlier, the difference between European American and Blackfeet ways of moving in this land is clearly drawn with the central, structuring device of the novel: the Highline (Highway 2), "the straight ribbon of black through the heart of a tan land" (39). The highway is an imposition upon the natural and traditional landscape of northern Montana; it is an artificial surface rolling from east to west across the plains, through the hills, over the rivers. It is a surface built upon the dominant culture's belief that science, geometry, and technology are absolute and universal. In a word, it is the metaphor for Manifest Destiny as well as the material manifestation of Fools Crow's vision.

The antithesis of this, of course, is a logic shaped by the contours of a particular landscape and the associations that it holds for the Indigenous cultures who inhabit it. One builds dams on sacred lands; the other moves to celebrate and protect them. As *Fools Crow* describes, people traveled this terrain for many generations by using literary "maps" that reflect more than simply the most direct or easiest roads, and, using these guides, every destination, physical or mythical, had a way. Once there was a freedom of movement that defied the limitations of Western reason and logic, time and space, one that expanded the limits of story.

However, the modern life Welch depicts along the Highline and in particular in the towns that dot its path is restrictive: an invisible snare baited with apparently limitless freedom of movement. The life along its black surface and in its dark bars is a never-ending cycle of hopeless wandering that takes its inmates only to another distant yet identical point on its way. It generates perpetual motion that takes people nowhere, and, as the airplane man learns, it is virtually impossible to escape its clutches. There is no power of self-determination here, only self-flagellation. As Ortiz notes above, it is easy, and characters "end up going along with the system as it is." As Welch once told Bill Bevis, this is the life that he saw as he grew up in northern Montana, the stories that he saw repeated again and again:

> You know there are all kinds of problems in living up there. It's very isolated country. Distances are great. There isn't much to do. . . . Basically what people do—not only Indians but white people, too—they drink a lot. They drink too much. They get in their cars and go out and kill themselves. Families break up. . . . I've chosen to write about these two guys [the protagonists in *Winter* and *Loney*] who sort of have self-limiting worlds, who don't try very hard to rise above what they are, because they interest me. I've seen people like this all my life. (Bevis, "Dialogue" 166–69)

In both novels, Welch carefully constructs that mood of hopelessness, ties it to *self*-limitation, and then qualifies it in ways strongly suggestive of his vision of the past depicted in *Fools Crow*, thus reaffirming cultural values and attitudes in contemporary times for his readers.

A sense of loss, of lost power and direction, permeates his early novels, but the hopelessness it fosters is based in what Welch offers as an unacceptable view of life in which one's choices of movement appear limited, in which one seems not to have any choice in or power over one's movements, one's future. However, his early novels and his readers move from this fatalistic worldview to one founded upon a belief in self-determination, from a European to a Native American sense of empowerment. Surprise.

The fatalistic is repeated throughout *Winter* in several brief and sometimes seemingly insignificant images: the almost invisible movements Hobson notes. These begin with the opening scene, in which the protagonist stops along the highway as he returns from town. He has been in a fight, and lost, and he stops to relieve himself on the site of a dilapidated ranch belonging to yet another lost family, the Earthboys. It is also near the place where his father, First Raise, was found frozen to death in a barrow pit on the highway shoulder. Death, despair, and immobility set the book's mood, and this sense of loss and deterioration is reinforced again and again: by a tadpole sinking into a watering trough, a dog shot simply because it is moving, a bug helplessly floating down an irrigation ditch, a dying grandmother. Each, however, is carefully balanced with the implication of purpose and power, a way to move deliberately and in productive ways. Once again, as in *Fools Crow*, resignation and rebellion are equally destructive. As Welch calls us on a journey through this land in quest of alternatives, he systematically investigates the nature of contemporary Blackfoot experience, including those hidden elements of culture that are a residual of Fools Crow's understanding.

Everything bad that happens to the unnamed protagonist happens on the Highline, in particular, the deaths of his brother, Mose, and his father, First Raise. This is also where he is beaten—time and time again—physically, spiritually. But why? The Highline is immensely attractive, but it offers only two choices, east or west, an either/or fallacy of existence, just as the elevator operator in Havre exists only "to take people up and down, whichever way they want to go" (121).[4] This is the nonchoice tendered to Native individuals and cultures since the first encounter with the Europeans: either assimilate— become a servant of the "dominant" culture—or die with the others who refuse "progress." Welch's characters search for another method of existing. Ironically, they can find it only if they first recognize the artificial nature of the limitations placed upon their freedom of movement when they are attracted to the "good life," the fast lifestyle of the road. The Highline goes only two ways—"up" for those who will make sacrifices to it and "down" for the rest—but there are other paths through the tan land.

In fact, the Highline is strongly suggestive of some roads found in Blackfeet verbal arts: in particular, the way taken by Kut-o-Yis, who is sometimes called Blood Clot or Smoking Star. As Bullchild notes, Kut-o-Yis is sent by Sun Chief to rid the Blackfeet world of cruel monsters who threaten the survival of the people. Interestingly, these monsters vary greatly in form and action, but they share some basic qualities. They inhabit places where the people must live or pass: near a piskun for the running of buffalo, on a path near a river, or near a place where they camp. The monsters also share a basic evil: they limit freedom of movement either directly, by control-ling a path, or indirectly, by controlling the essentials of life such as food. They are also destroyed in similar ways. Kut-o-Yis allows them to perform the actions through which they have dominated the people because he recognizes that their predictability is, in fact, their weakness, a limitation to their power. He anticipates and turns their actions against them. He uses the evil son-in-law's arrogant anger to kill him; he impales the wrestler on her own flint; he feeds the woman on the slide to her accomplice, the giant fish; he is consumed by the man-eater four times, only to return from his bones each time, to kill the monster on the fourth resurrection. In each case he recognizes the inflexibility suggested by the monster's actions and exploits its inherent limitation. Each time he sets the people free. This is, as we have seen, a view of "evil" closely aligned with those given by Momaday and Silko in the previous decade, an element of an Indigenous cosmology that differentiates it—for these authors at least—from those that immigrated from Europe.

Today, the people must travel the Highline. It is unavoidable, given the economics of recent times, and the effects, as Welch tells Bevis, are sometimes disastrous. However, they are not without the resources to deal with its influence. Once his protagonists move away from the towns and the Highline, they are given the chance to learn to move deliberately. On the protagonist's rides to Yellow Calf's in *Winter* he learns of other alternatives to assimilation or death: his grandfather and grandmother survived in a very hostile environment and isolated from their people. The protagonist finds his future in an understanding of the past with its connections to the tan land, not on the Highline, and he also finds the confidence he needs to recapture his Cree girlfriend. He is, for the first time in the book, taking control of his own future and strategically planning his movements based upon his sense of place: he will buy her a few drinks and use the attractions of that lifeway to his own advantage. He will defeat the monster on its own terms in its own terrain, using its attractions for his own benefit.

And so does Loney, as Welch suggests: "He creates it [his death], he creates a lot of events to put himself on top of that ledge in the end . . . he knows how his death will occur. And to me, that is a creative act and I think all creative acts are basically positive" (Bevis, "Dialogue" 176). This act takes place beyond the roads and towns that have played central, dismal roles in his life.

Like Fox Eyes in *Fools Crow*, Loney dies on his own terms. The movement between life and death, like movement between any two places or realms of experience, may be handled appropriately, even by someone like Loney who has been isolated from the tribal knowledge and worldview that have enlightened the movements of other generations. The intimate connection between a people and a landscape remains, even though one member may lack the knowledge of how to perform responsibly his obligation to that relationship. However, Loney's actions are directed to a positive effect; the final words of the book describe his transformation in terms of his prophetic dream of the dark bird. There is a sense of fulfillment in his death. There is a sense of affirmation and implied continuation into the next generations with the story but also the continued attachments to the homeland.

I suggest that the actions created are one of the central sites of differentiation, and these actions vary from writer to writer. This fundamental building block of narrative provided the participatory, imaginative landscape upon which Native authors had characters and readers interact; since audiences and critics in the 1980s were looking for that sense of differentiation (what "made" the text Native or not), it is a landscape of highly charged potential, and many writers found it a productive one.

One of the writers to appear in the 1980s, Louise Erdrich (in early collaboration with her partner, Michael Dorris), has come to exemplify the "new generation" of writers who made their presence known in the canon. However, she and Silko are close in age as well as artistic talent. Interestingly, Silko's later novels moved away from the Laguna Pueblo of *Ceremony* and thus the sharp definition of that homeland: her second novel is set in Tucson, Mexico, and in between, and her *Gardens in the Dunes* (her own foray into the historical novel) moves from the Colorado River valley, across the continent, and through Europe. Erdrich's canon, however, as it evolved in the 1980s and 1990s, is focused squarely upon a geographical location in proximity to the Turtle Mountain Reservation of her youth, and, much as in the canon of William Faulkner, this place is given a deep, complex history in which several characters figure prominently. Perhaps this is one explanation for her devoted readers, who read with this history in mind. While Erdrich did not make consistent and overt use of tribal traditions and stories—crafting ceremonies and storytelling sessions, for example—in her early works, she did weave a fabric throughout her canon that has strands of these, and they develop renewed life with each telling. Her first novel clearly marks, clearly differentiates, the place and culture that became central to her canon.

LOUISE ERDRICH: *Love Medicine* and the Early Tetralogy

Since its publication in 1984, Erdrich's first novel has been reprinted several times, including a 1993 edition that reintroduces four chapters supposedly excised from the originally published version. In other words, the book continues to attract new readers as well as those who thirst for more of the story, and the novel certainly reveals the strength of Erdrich's gift for storytelling, for involving readers in lives less than glamorous and hardly alluring but that, nonetheless, are compelling and notable. Her characters often reveal the transcendent qualities of human nature. She has a talented eye, so it is small wonder her popularity has grown with each successive work.

One of the attractive characteristics of *Love Medicine* is its subtle complexity; it offers a diversity of perceptions through a multilayered narrative in which each character's story is centered in a relatively small, seemingly loose-knit community of characters and events, one that is marked very early on as Native. Much like the novels of modernists such as Faulkner (who was one influence upon her art and to whom she is often compared), *Love Medicine* evolves through each successive telling of events and builds toward understanding by requiring the reader to adopt a participatory role and thereby invest in the lives and events it portrays. As Ortiz argues above, this participation is central. This process is enhanced by Erdrich's use of first-person narratives that engage us directly in the discourse. We are spoken to sometimes like amateur ethnographers and at other times like familiar confidants; we are asked to respond; we are required to build connections and patterns; and we are satisfied when our efforts at making the story work out are rewarded. Unlike Faulkner, however, Erdrich describes "life on the rez," the funnel end of colonialism in the United States of America, and the ways she does so entice non–Native American readers into a network of history and a present largely foreign to them. An analysis of how this is accomplished reveals the intricate nature of her DIAC as well as ways Native fiction moved in the 1980s.

The novel revolves around four characters: June, Marie, Nector, and Lulu. The latter three comprise a "love triangle" that is explicated through a nonlinear, fragmented narrative of events that covers fifty years. It begins with Marie Lazarre, who, at fourteen, climbs the hill above town to join the Catholic convent and become a saint. (I will return to this later.) She returns down the same hill a short while later, wounded, triumphant, and remorseful, only to stumble into Nector Kashpaw and, almost inexplicably, become his wife, despite his infatuation with Lulu Nanapush. With Marie's forceful direction, Nector becomes a "success" and even tribal chairman, while in later years he carries on a relationship with his first love. Lulu, like a primal force characterized in mythical narratives, gives birth to sons from several fathers, spreading compassion and love throughout the landscape. As the novel opens, in 1981, Nector is in his dotage, and Marie and Lulu are moving toward a time in their lives when, no longer driven by their concerns for self-image, mutual understanding emerges. Their triangle has touched the lives and stories of all the other characters, the extended families the two women share.

However, it is June who is the heart of the novel, a referential center for all the other characters, and it is she to whom we are first introduced. Her section of the first chapter is told in third-person past tense, which in effect removes her own "voice" (and vision) from the novel. It is also very brief, yet it effectively smoothes the ground for all that is to follow and all that is to become significant. In fact, one means of highlighting the effect of the novel is to read these few opening pages immediately after finishing the last page. For instance, the closing line of the novel—"So there was nothing to do but cross the water, and bring her home"—takes on added dimension from the ideas and images presented in June's section, for she is as much the antecedent to the pronoun "her" as the car Lipsha (her son) is driving over the bridge on his return home to the reservation.

The first pages seem to describe a bleak, rootless, unsatisfying life. In fact, they conform to but engage dramatically the long-held stereotypes of American Indians found in popular literature written by non-Native writers from Samuel Purchas to Henry David Thoreau to Ken Kesey. More specifically, Erdrich directly confronts those stereotypes of Native women as "loose" drunks whose ill fates are foregone conclusions. In fact, early reviewers clearly demonstrate how pervasive these images have become; for one, June is simply "a drunken prostitute," worthy of mention, it seems, but not of understanding or contextualizing (see Alabaster; Lyons). Thus, the popular media perform: no surprise. To Erdrich's credit, she does not avoid the fundamental issues behind such easy generalizations or the materialistic bias upon which racist stereotypes are based. She opens her first novel with this all-too-familiar image of poverty, yet she does not allow readers to wallow in the comfort of moralistic judgments from a distance: we cannot dismiss with easy categorization.

We come to learn that June is simply looking for love, as she has all her life, to heal the hurt and loss she suffered when her mother died, leaving June alone in the bush to fend for herself. June survives, and from this experience comes pain as well as strength. In the opening pages, near the end of her life, she is not the helpless pawn of fate or poverty or men as much as she is, somehow, a proud, deliberate force who initiates and directs the actions described. In effect, Erdrich devotes the remainder of the text to shaking the assumptions upon which ethnocentric and egocentric pronouncements—based upon false information and emerging through privilege—are made, and this provides the investigation of Anishinaabe life and culture in contemporary times. This is no small task.

Like many other contemporary Native novels, *Love Medicine* begins with a homecoming, what Bill Bevis has termed a "Homing In." However, unlike Abel in Momaday's *House Made of Dawn*, June's return is subtly veiled, for she does not return "physically." Instead, she comes home as vivid, warm, unshakable memories for all the characters who speak to us after, or, more pointedly, she comes home a character in the stories they tell, the oral literary canon they all share that tells them who they are in relation to others. She dies; at least, we are told that she is brought home and buried, although, like Albertine (June's "niece" who is away at school and whose own homecoming provides us with the initial first-person narrative), we do not "witness" the act: it is not made an event in the novel. Although it may seem inconsequential, this is a significant point, for it establishes June as a disembodied, silent, yet palpable presence—a nebulous yet powerful point of reference—throughout the stories and lives of other characters. That she returns later in their stories in other novels speaks to her conceptualization as a transcendent, almost mythical character. Furthermore, it draws attention to the details of the brief description of June's final moments, where Erdrich presents not June's death but this transcendence (for lack of a better term). This, of course, should undermine the reader's ability to consider her death a justifiable punishment for a "freewheeling" lifestyle. Life and death, particularly on reservations, are not that simple.

Two sections of the text—"Scales" and "The Red Convertible"— were published as short stories before the idea of the novel materialized. When she was asked to submit an entry for the Nelson Algren Award, Erdrich evidently wrote "The World's Greatest Fishermen" in response, and not only did it win, but it also provided the impetus to bring these three together (Coltelli 43). In other words, her first chapter, for which June's section acts as a preface, is a kingpin for the book. Late in the chapter we learn that June's son King has a hat with an inscription that reads "The World's Greatest Fisherman," so the slight yet crucial revision for the chapter's title poses an interesting tease. Readers face several possibilities for relating to the title: that the plurality, as opposed to singularity, is significant; perhaps that the Anishinaabe (Chippewa), about whom Erdrich writes, are implied; that the evocation of Christ, the "Fisher of Men," is poignant; that the concept of fishing is in some way relevant, perhaps even metaphoric or symbolic. All these possibilities are explored throughout the text, beginning with June's section.

In the opening sentence Erdrich establishes two critical points. First, she tells us that June is "killing time" before she returns home. Although isolated and alone in a North Dakota boomtown, she still possesses an attachment to a place and family that "home" implies: a plurality. Erdrich also sets June's "time of death." The events described—June's meeting of an Anglo oil worker (in a later novel revealed to be a mixed-blood), their day of drinking, their abortive sexual encounter in his pickup that night—begin on the eve of Easter Sunday. She dies, therefore, at a time synonymous with resurrection, and this initial connection is strengthened by the final lines of the chapter.

Rather than walk back to town after she leaves Andy passed out in his truck, June makes a decisive turn away from the road and toward her home on the reservation. Erdrich carefully emphasizes that June "did not lose her sense of direction. . . . The heavy winds couldn't blow her off course. She continued" (7).[5] She moves through the gathering snowstorm, stepping lightly upon the dry spots of the prairie, avoiding "the slush and rotten, gray banks" as she focuses on home and family, on "Uncle Eli's warm, man-smelling kitchen." She moves deliberately, freely, and almost joyfully, swinging her purse: "Even when her heart clenched and her skin turned crackling cold it didn't matter, because the pure and naked part of her went on. . . . The snow fell deeper that Easter than it had in forty years, but June walked over it like water and came home" (7). Her death is described in terms of movement, continuance, and a return rather than as an end. Moreover, this line is echoed in the concluding sentence of the novel, where Lipsha also crosses the water "and bring[s] her home." With two lines Erdrich establishes a circular structure but, more importantly, an implication of continuance and endurance, tied to home, that provide a precarious counterbalance to the images of loss, disintegration, and assimilation that some readers may initially discern. This is not Faulkner's Yoknapatawpha County.

June's section is reflective of later sections and other works in the ways Erdrich toys with quick interpretations. Given all the obvious Christian references here, we might feel the urge to consider June a "Christ-like" figure, one who has been sacrificed to the sins of history. This dramatic revision of the "drunken prostitute" image may be a useful line of inquiry at first, but it makes her, oddly enough, a much too simple character, the text too didactic. Another possibility exists, one that marks Erdrich's ability to work the points where cultures and traditions, European American and Anishinaabe, engage. Her text rests upon the reader's ability to winnow kernels of truth from the confusion of human experience and to interpret events and characters based upon a complex social fabric evoked through the life stories of a very few characters. To accomplish this she employs repetition of key images and phrases.

The first section provides several of the central, recurrent motifs that string the disparate narratives together like the beads on June's only childhood possession, a rosary: the metaphors and allusions from Christian belief; those dealing with water and fishing; the heart as repository of humanity, in particular the ability for love; the important, attractive power of home and family. These, of course, are universally recognizable to a widely diverse audience and are therefore useful to engage readers in terms of Western written literary conventions, but Erdrich extends their application by using them so consistently that they become intertwined with very basic definitions of self and ethnicity: in this instance, what it is to be Native. She presents the ways that cultures borrow from one another and thus change while maintaining a singular sense of identity. Surprise. As she revalues the Anishinaabe points of differentiation, she reaffirms them.

In an interview with Joseph Bruchac, Erdrich once commented

upon the powers of this exchange: "That's one of the strengths of Indian culture, that you can pick and choose and keep and discard" ("Whatever" 79). As she notes in another interview, many family trees on the reservation and in the novel possess "a lot of French, but in particular the French and the Indian had been so blended by that time, it's a new culture" (Coltelli 45). Rather than dwell upon loss, upon victimization, Erdrich underscores the ways people are empowered, even in the most destructive of situations, such as colonialism.

Each of the storytellers in the novel defines himself or herself as "Indian" and, more specifically, by family in an elaborate social structure; even Marie's constant reference to her "white" appearance is referential to the local community. Yet each speaker also utilizes the same Christian metaphors or allusions: even Lulu, the seemingly least "Christian" of the characters, refers to angels when she describes her lovemaking (277). In short, the novel takes us into the lives of mediators, characters who must find satisfying existences through negotiation. The effects of colonialism are apparent in all aspects of their lives (in religious, economic, and social interactions), and in each realm the teachings of the church, the government, the schools can clash with basic instincts and emotions that appear to form Erdrich's sense of the enduring core of Anishinaabe culture. The insistence upon singular salvation (or the ancillary damnation, a "personal hell" [53]) or upon personal financial success or upon individual academic achievement places undue stress on social systems comprised of individuals whose primary concern is with the welfare and health of their families within a community: their survivance, its continuance.

In the novel this stress is revealed through several conflicts. Lulu's overt sexuality is condemned by some, yet she is, indeed, the embodiment of love and compassion: "I was in love with the whole world and all that lived in its rainy arms" (276). As tribal chairman, Nector signs the papers to force Lulu out of her home to make way for a factory that will make toy tomahawks, but she realizes that the economic scheme is ultimately doomed, a mockery of tribal values (283). Although called a hardened criminal by the larger society, Lulu's son,

Gerry, possesses admirable, positive human qualities—compassion, an unshakable sense of justice, an ability to love wholeheartedly, a sense of humor. All these qualities are related to his mysterious powers, which are directly equated to his heritage as a "Nanapush man"—all Nanapush men have an "odd thing with our hearts" (366). The tensions within the community emerge from the pulls people feel between personal achievement and social well-being.

However, there are points at which cultures touch—at least ideally—by possessing similar fundamentals. These are the points at which a borrowing or sharing may occur, or at least at which that potential is heightened, and these are the "hinge" points of the novel, the points of convergence that act as bridges (yet another recurrent motif) for readers into Erdrich's rendering of the Anishinaabe worldview. For instance, the image of a "Fisher of Men" is molded into an apt metaphor used by several of Erdrich's characters. Before their removal to the west, Lulu tells us, the "Chippewas had started way off on the other side of the five great lakes" (282). Water and beings of the water figure prominently in Anishinaabe culture, whether the Turtle Mountain Band, about whom Erdrich writes, or those of the Minnesota lake lands, so the preponderance of fishing metaphors and similes is understandable, although its significance goes much deeper than mere "local color." Erdrich's husband, Michael Dorris (Modoc), verified this when he talked about the novel he had a hand in shaping:

> Maybe native tribal culture has changed like all cultures, and *Love Medicine* is a story about a contemporary group of people that are in some ways indistinguishable from other rural North Dakota people who are not rich, but in other ways they are very much unique, very much who they were; they have the same kind of symbols that inspired Chippewas in the past, the water and the water god, and they have the kind of family connection which has always been the core of the tribe. (Coltelli 45)

This uniqueness emerges as we recognize the ways Erdrich's characters express their perceptions of their place, much like we see in the works of James Welch along the Highline.

Although the underwater being Lipsha tells us about, Missepeshu or Misshipeshu, does not become a central character until the third novel of Erdrich's canon, *Tracks*, in *Love Medicine* he plays, like June, a significant role without appearing onstage. As Lipsha expresses it:

> Now there's your God of the Old Testament and there is Chippewa Gods as well. Indian Gods, good and bad, like tricky Nanabozho or the water monster, Missepeshu, who lives over in Matchiman-ito. That water monster was the last God I ever heard to appear. It had a weakness for young girls and grabbed one of the Pillagers off her rowboat. She got to shore all right, but only after this monster had his way with her. She's an old lady now. Old Lady Pillager. She still doesn't like to see her family fish that lake. (236)

The landscape Erdrich paints has several mythical beings, some good, some bad, some local, some imported. While the Christian god is a contentious sociological force through the presence of the church, in particular the nuns, the Indigenous powers still inhabit their place and intervene in human lives. Misshipeshu, it seems, is also perceived as a fisher of people, one whose presence has been reported recently and felt personally, and this presence is maintained through language, through story.

Furthermore, when Lipsha describes his view of Nector's mental incapacity, he does not rely upon Western psychological interpretations; he speaks metaphorically and pointedly for the man who became the apparent embodiment of the "modern Indian" but who is still moved by forces ancient and local: Nector "was fishing in the middle of Matchimanito. And there was big thoughts on his line, and he kept throwing them back for even bigger ones that would explain to him, say, the meaning of how we got here and why we have to leave so soon" (234). When Lipsha describes Nector's death, he does so in the same terms: "He was still fishing in the middle of Matchimanito. Big thoughts was on his line and he had half a case of beer in the boat. He waved at me, grinned, and then the bobber went under" (250). Once again, death is described as a continuation, not an end, and its meaning in the scheme of things is not found in church or convent but in the intersection of a place and a people.

Throughout *Love Medicine* readers are confronted with the potential inherent in the landscape that surrounds the lives of the families, a potential that consistently qualifies the intervention of Christianity and provides a point of differentiation for those characters who identify as possessing or being related to those who possess an Indigenous tradition. This may be discerned through the connections readers are asked to make, the bridges we must build. For instance, in the title piece of the novel, when Lipsha decides to create a "love medicine" that will tie the aged Nector to Marie forever, that will supply the "staying power" (234) required for a strong relationship, he later admits that he dealt with powers he did not fully comprehend. This comprehension, evidently, is no longer widespread (if it ever was) but resides "in the bush" with people like Nector's brother, Eli, or, more specifically, Old Man Pillager, whom all fear. Although Lipsha's revelations about his power to heal may be construed as equally suspect, as an aspect of his own, revised self-image, we cannot so easily dismiss the possibility when we learn, later from Lulu, that he is the direct descendant of Old Man Pillager, who, like Lipsha's father, Gerry, is a "Nanapush man" with inexplicable powers (335). (Nanapush, as critics have amply noted, is a name strongly reminiscent of the trickster Nanabozho, as are Gerry's powers.) When Lipsha's instincts for such healings take him to a probable ingredient for a love medicine (the hearts of a pair of Canada geese, who mate for life), his intellect gets in his way; he incorrectly surmises that there is no inherent power in the hearts themselves but merely in people's hope for miracles: "I finally convinced myself that the real actual power to the love medicine was not in the goose heart itself but the faith in the cure" (246). This is a fundamental issue of all belief systems: are there external forces in the cosmos that operate through material elements to intervene in human lives, or is a cure other than through Western medicine simply an act of the human psyche? Erdrich places him in the moment of dilemma, and his solution is both tragic and comic. Believing cures are created solely through an act of will, he substitutes a long-dead, frozen turkey heart, and Nector chokes to death on it.

Erdrich speaks to a fundamental point of differentiation between modern, "scientific" explanations and others based in a Native worldview, a tribal realism. The results of Lipsha's rationalization are revealing when we make connections between it and other points of reference in the novel. On a fishing trip to Matchimanito with Nector, Lipsha learns that he is special because he has his brain in his heart (251). Rather than a European American dichotomy between head and heart, reason and emotion, we find the preferential merging of the two: equally a reliance upon the fundamental logic of the nonrational and a regard for old ways of expressing and enacting its dictates. Also, Nector's first encounter with Marie in 1934, as she comes down the hill from the convent and he is focused on his love for Lulu, comes about as he trudges up the hill with two Canada geese strapped to his wrists; within the world of the novel, we cannot help but wonder about the "staying power" of geese. The man and woman come together, despite the revulsion each feels at the idea, and in the scene in which they "mate" the geese become participants as they encumber both Marie's and Nector's movements. They prescribe (pun intended) a love medicine that results in the couple's marriage and the events of fifty years.

The love triangle between Marie, Nector, and Lulu clearly demonstrates the intricate entanglements to be found in life, the forces that create them, and the inadequate nature of personal knowledge in either preparing for events or understanding their significance in the moment. To expose and explore these ideas Erdrich adopts a spiral structure that circles through time to reveal with each swing more information about past events that tie the narratives together. It is Nector Kashpaw who voices this structure: "And here is where events loop around and tangle again" (128). "Thematic" concerns (more accurately, the issues and views revealed through our involvement with Erdrich's fictionalizing) and "structural" devices are intertwined to purpose in *Love Medicine*. The story is in the telling, and, as in any storytelling event, the audience has a role to play. As Ortiz says, we must participate. We must untangle events; we must straighten out the fishing line of lives, for only the reader can recognize all the ties, define the relationships, and discern the patterns. In a way, we are like "the elders," Lulu and Marie at book's end, who, after lifetimes of strife and conflict and confusion, have reached an objective distance that affords a better, more expansive perspective of the relationships, politics, and petty goings-on in the community. *Love Medicine* is built from this understanding and exemplifies how passion and compassion, pride and pity can tie people together in productive, supportive ways and thus lead to strength: the power of survivance. This is a continuation with a soul and the community.

However, survivance is always under challenge when colonialism is alive, as it is today in Indian Country. As new issues arise, Native novelists respond. For instance, by the time of republication of the novel in 1993, the economic landscape in Indian Country was changing. In the terms of the times, "Indian gaming" was coming into its own. As Erdrich's canon grew, so did the number of Native casinos. This new phenomenon, emerging as it does from the long-standing tradition of Native gambling, worked its way into the fiction of several writers, including Vizenor and Erdrich. It is interesting to see how it plays out in what was originally conceived of as a tetralogy: *Love Medicine, The Beet Queen, Tracks,* and *The Bingo Palace.* As we move into the 1990s, the four-part framework I have provided may still be useful, for gaming is more than an economic issue. It is an issue that investigates some fundamental differences in philosophy.

The publication of *The Bingo Palace* in 1994 revealed how pervasive Erdrich's concern for empowerment has been in her earlier works. Consider the title itself in light of the heated debate about Indian gaming immediately surrounding its publication. Articles in all the country's major newspapers, debates in Congress and its various committees and subcommittees, television news broadcasts, and radio talk shows featuring the United States' quintessential opportunist, Donald Trump, focused upon this contentious issue.[6] The furor that it generates is at once understandable and ominous.

For Native nations, the potential for the generation of large sums of capital carries with it the potential for self-sufficiency and therefore self-determination (affirmation and continuation), but with this potential also comes the threat of reprisal and loss. To put it succinctly, social gambling in its current usage does not simply mean gambling in a social setting but in actuality the engagement of two societies and the juxtaposing of two conflicting views of the future. Which society (European American or Native American) should have and control the funds that will determine the future for Native people? Like gamblers poised over the poker table, Native nations face off against the federal government and individual states, and at stake are the next generations.[7] This confrontation is a recurring motif in Erdrich's novels, including *Tales of Burning Love*: another locus of colonial tension but also potential transformation.

Indigenous cultures, like all others, have always had an inherent interest, a tradition, in gambling. Long before the first European tried his luck on this continent, Native players participated in the stick game, the bone game, or any number of analogous games everywhere in the land. Today, at powwows, at gatherings of numerous varieties, and—more to our purpose here—in every Native literary canon gambling can be found.

Fundamentally, all "games of chance" are games of change and power over it, and Indian gaming recognizes and celebrates that basic reality. But, as the scene with Lyman in Reno in *The Bingo Palace* reveals, Erdrich recognizes there are many ways to engage in the game. In fact, one way of reading her novels is to consider them as an exploration of the nature of chance as it engages the history of colonialism in this hemisphere and, more specifically, as a thesis on the efficacy of understanding the nature of possibility, of cusp, and employing it to one's advantage. Using this reading, we may discern a moral embedded in her stories, structured by events hinged on apparent chance. Clearly, Erdrich's fiction is, as Anishinaabe author Gerald Vizenor so aptly encapsulates in his title for a book of literary criticism, a "narrative chance" in which events reveal that probability is, like beauty, in the eye of the beholder and power is in the future of the gambler with a good heart, a love medicine.

To apprehend this thesis at work, we must examine Erdrich's overt use of gambling scenes, which are crucial, pivotal events in the long story of the central families of the Turtle Mountain Chippewa as depicted in the novels. These punctuate the history of colonialism, the chances and changes, within which the families are situated. By considering these scenes in conjunction as they evolve through the novels, we better comprehend the intricate nature of the narrative cosmology Erdrich constructs while recognizing those elements of it that seem stable, unchanging from generation to generation. One of these elements is "luck." With this in mind, let us reconsider *Love Medicine*.

From the very outset the concept of luck is prominent in the story, both its originally published version and the expanded edition. In the very first pages June Kashpaw walks down a street in Williston, killing time before her bus leaves for home. Her walk is cut short when she suddenly decides to turn from the sidewalk and go into a bar to join a man who has caught her attention; when she enters, she finds him eating Easter eggs, and when he pays for their drinks, she notes his "good-sized wad of money."[8] Why does she decide to stay with him, miss her bus, and therefore precipitate the events that are to follow in her story? "That roll helped [her make the decision]. But what was more important, she had a feeling. The eggs were lucky" (3).

Like our own lives, June's life is presented as a series of seemingly "chance" encounters or, more accurately put from the point of view of a storyteller, a series of episodes in which characters make choices that—from an audience's point of view—may or may not seem "logical" or rational at the moment. As events unfold, we need points of reference to enlighten what is actually happening and what it signifies. For June, as she gambles for the possibility of love, intuition and her belief in luck are referential; they determine her play.[9] She takes a chance, and Erdrich's canon pivots on this type of action. It is hardly coincidental that June's play is tied as well to economics and exploitation: the flute end of colonialism suggested by the oil worker's (Jack Mauser's) "roll."

There are other events in the novel equally suggestive, for instance, the scene in which Marie and Nector meet in 1934. Here, as noted above, the unlikely love triangle that motivates and informs many of the subsequent events in the novel takes shape, but by viewing it through the lens of differentiated senses of "chance," it grows philosophically deeper.

In the preceding chapter we witnessed the creation of "Saint Marie." The young Marie Lazarre, by her own admission as she tells her story in retrospect, is both ignorant and ambitious, and she perceives the Catholic Church as her sole means of salvation/success: a salvation that is described and defined in terms of social class and monetary reward. She wishes to be worshiped by those who ignore her, those who do not value her and therefore undermine any of her attempts to construct a sense of personal power and a fulfilling identity. In short, as her self-definition attests, she wants to be "above" the European Americans who hold the positions of power and therefore over the community, and part of her claim is based upon her small amount of "Indian blood" (43). She wants to "rise above" that blood, and, with sainthood, she would be adorned in gold and precious colors, and the nuns "would have to stoop down off their high horse to kiss" her toes (43).

As she comes down the hill at chapter's end her hopes, paradoxically, have been dashed and realized: the nuns have indeed knelt and worshiped her, but she will never possess the keys to the riches or power held by Sister Leopolda. In her gamble for empowerment Marie has lost one "hand" and won another. At this moment of transformation, as discussed above, she meets Nector, who trudges up the hill to sell the geese to the nuns. He tells us his story in retrospect, and he emphasizes the wonder and immediacy of this chance encounter on the hill that alters the future dramatically for the three but also for the subsequent generations of several families. In a scene in which logic and reason, "the odds," do not prevail, we have the quintessential ambiguity of an Erdrich confrontation. Neither of the two players wants to be involved with the other; however, they marry, have children, and spend the rest of their lives joined.

But why does this event evolve as it does, against all the odds? Read from the perspective of the history revealed in the other novels, in particular *Tracks*, it is even more unlikely.[10] The two young people represent warring factions within the community; Marie is thought to be a Lazarre, "the youngest daughter of a family of horse-thieving drunks" (62). The Lazarres and the Kashpaws have a long-standing enmity stemming from financial conflict: the struggle to delineate and maintain "family" lands during the catastrophic era of the General Allotment Act. However, there is more involved. For the Kashpaws, the Lazarres seem to be the "wave of the future" and thus represent the potential loss of family lands as well as the family itself: clan, culture, and community. This conflict, then, is also about survivance.

There is yet another element of the event that is enlightened by a reading of *Tracks*: Marie is fresh from a game of chance with her own mother, Sister Leopolda (née Pauline Puyat). Either wittingly or unwittingly, Marie has severed herself from both her adoptive and her biological families *and* the change they represent; in the text of *Love Medicine* that renunciation is reiterated when she turns her dogs loose on the Lazarre woman (her "mother"), who brings June to her to raise. In any event, as Marie meets Nector on the hill above town, she has lost the bright future offered by sainthood in the church, an orphan once more at the mercy of chance. Her crafting of a future using Nector is certainly understandable in this context, but it also represents the "recapturing" of a generation from families pulled into the disarray of a new, alien sense of good fortune.

Readers have the objective distance and information necessary to contextualize the event and construct meaning from it. The fictional agents of that meaning—Marie and Nector—are not afforded that power, and neither are we in "real life." In the midst of any situation we may feel empowered only to find that it was not actually so; conversely, we may feel we have lost control only to find that our best interests prevail, that we "win." The concept of chance is based upon such experiential evidence, yet each culture's conceptualization may be based upon very different experiences, histories, and cosmologies. Erdrich investigates the implications of the difference, so in Marie and Nector's case, their meeting at first reads purely coincidental, yet there remains a persistent, nagging suspicion that other forces impinge upon it. Only by reading it referentially, by investigating its inherent dynamic as enlightened by the history and the beliefs it engenders, can we comprehend the event's significance in a (re) definition of "chance."

But what of an event in which characters actively, deliberately engage the element of chance and thereby precipitate change? There are many such events in Erdrich's works, yet their outcomes are never determined by completely random forces. For the sake of brevity I will address only those most prominent and, therefore, perhaps most significant.

In the final pages of *Love Medicine*, in Lipsha's section entitled "Crossing the Water" (which is preceded in the new edition with a chapter entitled "Lyman's Luck," a chapter title clearly tied to the titles in *The Bingo Palace*), we find the crucial scene in which Lipsha and his father, Gerry Nanapush, play poker with June's other son, King. Here, their familial tie is revealed by Lipsha's marking of the cards in the deck; Gerry recognizes his mother's "signature" on the cards, since he has acquired it himself. King does not. Lulu, of course, learned it from her family, the Pillagers, and old Nanapush, the elder trickster. This ability to manipulate moments of chance, then, is tied directly to family and all that comes with it: clan definitions, character connections, and knowledge of power. This power of lineage is exerted to control events and, therefore, the future, and it is as ethereal, mysterious, and significant as the slight tick of the heart that Gerry seemingly imparts to Lipsha through a touch at book's end.

In this gambling scene, as elsewhere, luck is manipulated by those with insider knowledge who wish to reverse the ill effects of life in a disempowering colonial society. As a result of the game, father and son meet (both figuratively and literally), win, and escape. Using June's car, won by the manipulation of apparently random draws of the cards (in other words, playing with King's perception of chance), Gerry escapes the police. Using the slight tick of the heart won from his "chance" meeting with his father, Lipsha escapes the army. The seemingly disempowered victims have "turned the tables" and rewritten the "inescapable" outcome of events. In this one encounter long-standing foes—King, army, and police—lose.

The novel ends in circular fashion; for the moment, however, there is a sense of closure in a game won. Lipsha, driving "June's car," stops on a bridge that marks the edge of the reservation and, looking down into the water below, provides Erdrich's final observations about Anishinaabe life in contemporary times and a culturally defined perception of life's structure. Throughout his life he had considered himself a loser, the discarded son of a woman who did not love him. Here, he realizes that he "was lucky she turned [him] over to Grandma Kashpaw," for King has suffered far more loss and disempowerment (367). This personal revelation with its self-affirmation is framed by an even more poignant one that is tied directly to the land and the water with which it has contended for all time.[11] "It's a dark, thick, twisting river. The bed is deep and narrow. I thought of June. The water played in whorls beneath me or flexed over sunken cars" (366).

This image—the water metaphor so prominent in Erdrich's works—is fully descriptive of how life and fortune are constructed in her narratives. First, it has Lipsha on a bridge, a place of transition, and here it shifts our perspective and hierarchy, moving from the preposition "beneath" to "over." Second, it metaphorically describes the nature of life and, therefore, reorients our perception of linear chronology and, more importantly in the context of this discussion, chance. The current at first view seems chaotic and ever-changing, but it is not: good fortune comes in whorls, graces, it goes and returns, moved by numerous forces in a perceptible but also a nonlinear fashion. The general flow remains in the same direction, of course, but with myriad variations of directions and obstacles along its course. Of these "obstacles," rocks factor prominently, since this is yet one more recurrent motif in Erdrich's fiction, where stones are often metaphors for people whose lives are rounded and smoothed through adversity. Third, it connects with death and thus the potential for ultimate loss through its allusion to the red convertible. Earlier, Henry Jr. lost his possibility for an afterlife of any comfort when he drowned himself, a tragic thing for an Anishinaabe, as Lulu and Lyman tell us; immediately, Lyman sent Henry's car into the same swollen river, perhaps to make the death seem "accidental." Also, but probably not finally, it calls to mind the Anishinaabe Road of the Dead, described elsewhere in Erdrich's novels, where the dead encounter yet another test of their lives. If they have not lived a good one, they will fall from the log bridge they must cross into the afterlife and into a river where they will be lost forever. This is not a cheerful future. Lipsha, however, like June in the book's opening, crosses and returns home. Both have controlled chance and therefore mitigated loss. It is no small matter that June returns in *The Bingo Palace* to bring Lipsha some winning bingo tickets and to reclaim her car. The game does not always end with death in the fictional world Erdrich constructs.

In *The Beet Queen*, published next in the series, Erdrich carries the "chance encounter," or, more accurately, the encounter with chance, even further. In fact, taken as a whole, the novel could be said to hang solely on chance or to be structured by some very questionable coincidences. (This stylistic device continues in a later novel, *Tales of Burning Love*, where it becomes almost unacceptably overbearing.)

Left destitute after the untimely death of her married lover, Adelaide Adare is faced with a bleak and foreboding future, and when the opportunity to exert power over that future arises in the guise of a young barnstormer with an available plane, she takes it spontaneously. Unfortunately, her act leaves her three young children to sort out their own ways of survival. After their mother flies away, Karl and Mary turn to their aunt, but as they walk down yet another North Dakota small-town street on their way "home" to her, Karl chances to walk under a tree whose white, fragrant blossoms turn him aside from this one, set goal. Like June and Adelaide, he makes a seemingly impulsive decision that shapes much of what follows for decades, a decision based upon a seemingly coincidental run-in with a blossoming tree. Of course, this *is* a literary illusion, but it is one that provides an access point for Erdrich's Indigenous subtexts that tie to the ideas and concepts found in *Love Medicine*.

The novel is full of odd coincidences that, when taken together, imply a pattern of interconnectedness: Mary's best friend conceives a baby when Karl suddenly rematerializes to visit Wallace Pfeff, an acquaintance of Mary who happens to meet Karl at a convention in Minneapolis. With Karl he has had his first homosexual experience. Karl and Celestine's daughter, Dot, conceives her own child with Gerry Nanapush in *Love Medicine*, and Karl is saved by Fleur

Pillager when he jumps from a moving train and is injured. The coincidences compound, on and on, until the grand finale, when Dot impulsively jumps into a plane and disappears, echoing her grandmother's desertion, all while Mary's cousin is discovered dead in her truck by Dot's recently returned father and Adelaide's missing third child arrives, after all these years, to try to find his siblings. What are the odds?

Obviously, they are not good. The complete reliance on seemingly contrived coincidence may seem a bit much, but if one looks at it in the context of the other works, then it makes a certain sense. Considered as imaginative chronicles of the history of Turtle Mountain and its surroundings in this century, they chart an obvious alteration in the landscape and investigate the fundamental essence of that change. They dramatize "the reservation" as it evolved over time and what it signifies for the individual identity of those who live on it as well as the "newcomers" with whom they interact: the locus for Erdrich's *investigation* of what it means to be Anishinaabe, then and now. Just as Lipsha has explained in *Love Medicine*, the land now holds two cultures' gods and, therefore, two perceptions of what the future holds and how it will unfold.

There is a distinct difference between the encounters with chance found in *Love Medicine* and *Tracks* and those in *The Beet Queen*. The first two present characters who identify—to varying degrees—as Anishinaabe; the latter is comprised of characters who primarily identify as European American. Taken together, we have the various ancestries of the author. The distinction in their worldviews lies in the culturally defined ways they deal with "chance." For instance, when Pheff returns from a conference in Minneapolis, he stops along the road at a popular "lovers' lane" to think. He is alone, trying to sort out his recent experiences with Karl; immediately, he is startled by the arrival of a police officer, and, embarrassed and feeling guilty, he tries to explain his presence and thereby fumbles upon a lie that becomes the future of Argus, North Dakota: he tells the officer that he has been considering the sugar beet (a subject raised at the conference) and all its potential for their community. In other words, the characters here are moved about by chance like puppets, and, once moved, they, in common phraseology, play the hand that is dealt them. The responses to adversity are clearly delineated. One can become aggressive (as we see in the poker scene in *Tracks*) or attempt to bluff one's way through (as with Wallace); one reaction to loss is simply to work harder to overcome it and to insure success (as with Mary), or else one may lapse into an internal, a created and isolated, reality (like Karl or Sita). In *Love Medicine* and elsewhere other alternatives are posited through the interactions of the Anishinaabe characters; Lipsha determines what hands are dealt in the crucial card game with King.

Another way of conceiving of the difference is to consider the apparent lack of a crucial attachment to place for most of the characters in *The Beet Queen*, all of whom are immigrants. Even Celestine and her relatives come from the reservation to the north. Like the sugar beet itself, they are imported alterations to the landscape; like Argus, they are revisions of place who attempt to play out their tentative fortunes in a land of extremes. Perhaps the greatest irony of the characters here portrayed is that they seem to be completely self-motivated, motivated by a concern for self, yet they are wholly lacking in the power of self-determination: they do not determine their own futures, which are their "fates" in this imported worldview. Instead, they accommodate what chance throws their way, and in this way they are completely powerless, despite their apparent self-control. Once deserted by Karl, Mary eases into the secure monotony of a lifelong place in Kozka's Meats. Karl wanders the country, drifting from job to job with little or no concern for the future, and ends his life with nothing one could consider a satisfying legacy. Although Mary plays at predicting what will be, using her deck of fortune-telling cards, she is, like her fellow immigrants, moved about by forces beyond her comprehension. It seems that without this generations-long attachment to place, one's good fortune is ephemeral, one's ill fortune unbearable. In brief, the non-Indigenous character does not fare well here.

However, Sister Leopolda (née Pauline Puyat) is in Argus as well, and if there is a quality that defines her character, it is her unflappable certainty in her ability to direct the future. She emerges from the Anishinaabe community, but she also champions the immigrant ideology in that community for her own empowerment. In fact, when she describes one of the formative events in her life, she lapses not into a Native telling but into one that reflects the idea of fate derived in Europe over long centuries. As she attends the death of Mary Pepewas, she behaves like one of the Fates of old: "Perhaps, hand over hand, I could have drawn her back to shore [to life], but I saw very clearly that she wanted to be gone. . . . That is why I put my fingers in the air between us, and I cut where the rope was frayed down to string" (*Tracks* 68). In this construction only the gods have control over the future, and humans are relegated to the role of supplicants moved by the whims of those gods. This is where two cultural orientations touch but ultimately hinge in different ways when we consider the degree of characters' control over that future. Pauline was raised in the same culture as her daughter, Marie, who also wished to become a saint. Their lives, however, take very different trails and provide the basis for Erdrich's ultimate valuation of the two ways. Which one is the winner?

Of the three first novels, *Tracks* makes the most prominent use of gambling scenes. Interestingly, this was the first novel composed in the original tetralogy. There are numerous card games, games of guile between Nanapush and the Morrisseys, Pauline's manipulation of Sophie and Eli, and so on, but three events of confrontation and cusp seem to be prominent for our understanding of chance as defined in Erdrich's works: the series of poker games at Kozka's Meats, its sequel in the next world, and the "stick game" at book's end. All have Fleur Pillager as the main player.

Fleur's time in Argus is alluded to in *The Beet Queen*, where the life of Dutch James intersects both Fleur's and Celestine's (Dot's mother) lives. Pauline, who is to become Leopolda, is here as well (later she becomes the nun teaching school when Mary, on an icy slide, smashes her face into the ice to produce what people perceive as the face of Christ). Earlier, however, in *Tracks*, Pauline visits Argus as a young person who, with Russell, acts as our witness to the poker game between Fleur, Dutch, Lily, and Tor.

The game lasts for days, and as Pauline tells the story of it we find—at least in her mind and telling—there is little element of chance in it. From the outset Fleur is in complete control of the other players' perception of chance. Ironically, she seems the least likely person to be graced with "luck": she is a woman, a "squaw," and poor. There is no power in that combination for the colonized, at least from the point of view of those who conceive of themselves as possessors of all power: male, white, "pioneers" with expertise at "making their own luck." However, as the game progresses and they fail to win Fleur's money immediately, the other players look for an advantage, a way of insuring success, which they seem to gain when Tor sees Fleur's hand shake at a crucial moment. His conclusion is logical—and wrong: "Well, we know one thing . . . the squaw can't bluff" (20). Despite their supposed advantage, Fleur wins exactly a dollar every night, "no more and no less, too consistent for luck" (21). The event comes to a cusp when the men violate the rules of fair play and pool their resources to join in league against her for one last game of poker, winner take all, and the stratagem seems to work, for Fleur "played unevenly, as if chance were all she had" (23). But it is not, of course, and when all their money is in the pot and the game rides upon the turning of one card, she wins.

When luck does not smile on them, aggression is an acceptable alternative for these players. They beat and rape Fleur, at least Pauline believes they do, and the moment of empowerment is lost. But it is lost only for a moment. The next day a tornado—the Western epitome of whimsical, inexplicable chance—sweeps into Argus, sending the men into the freezer of the meat plant. As the storm screams around Pauline and Russell, whom the men have left to its mercy (i.e., certain death), the wind "at last spoke plain" (27). Pauline and Russell drop the large, locking bar down on the outside of the door, sealing the men's fate. Russell runs away with "a peaceful look of complicit satisfaction" (28). Against all odds, tossed about like Dorothy in *The Wizard of Oz*, neither is injured. "Whimsical, random chance" is a construction of one's perception; this storm is moved by a will. Fleur wins again.

Fleur ultimately returns to her home and pays the annual fee for the Pillager lands. She also gives birth to Lulu, whose parentage the community debates. Is she the offspring of a rape or of Missepeshu? In any event, she is the child of a new generation, one that brings families like the Pillagers, Nanapushes, and Kashpaws together, so the card game and Fleur's return have had a profound effect in the community, and out of it comes an equally profound revelation for Pauline, who has become a nun and thus an agent of colonization and Christian predestination: "Power travels in the bloodlines, handed out before birth. It comes down through the hands, which in the Pillagers are strong and knotted, big, spidery and rough, with sensitive fingertips good at dealing cards. It comes through the eyes, too, belligerent, darkest brown, the eyes of those in the bear clan, impolite as they gaze directly at a person" (31). Although Pauline's reliability as a narrator has been contested, her insight here is reiterated by other characters, including Nanapush and the community at large, in which the fear of and respect for Fleur are ubiquitous. Her power over chance and her bear clan affiliation are demonstrated time and time again, and these are passed down to Lulu, Gerry, Lipsha. Thus, we have both affirmation—in their ability to control chance and therefore events—and continuation, through the culturally defined DNA.

The card game in Argus has a close counterpart later in the novel, once again with Pauline as the narrator-participant.[12] Here, Pauline and Fleur travel to the land of the dead, where they encounter once more the players from Argus. Now, however, rather than play for dollars and cents, they play for life itself: the lives of Fleur's children, Lulu and a premature baby. In other words, they play for the next generation of Fleur's people, the future. The older generation has already been lost as a result of the incursion of Europeans; disease has decimated the powerful families, and those who survive question what the future will hold. Fleur loses the first hand and therefore the baby. The next hand, for Lulu, she wins, tellingly, with five queens (against the representative male kings and jacks of the others). Even in the land of the dead she is not powerless, it seems, to circumvent the plans of the pioneers.[13]

However, her inability to save her newly born child shakes Fleur's confidence. In the ensuing power plays within the community she "loses" her lands as well; the lumberjacks continue to encircle and encroach upon the lake that is her center. All seems lost; the odds are not good; yet, when the moment comes and the "inescapable" destiny, "the fate" of "inevitable" colonial domination, seems assured, Erdrich once again withholds the easy dismissal of power, the simplistic anticipation of loss and victimry. As the loggers drive their wagons in to cut the last trees, Nanapush describes the scene, and in that description there appears a veiled reference to gambling. As in Argus, the winds rise. "I heard the waves begin to slap with light insistence against the shore. I knew the shifting of breeze, the turn of the weather, was at hand. I heard the low murmur of the voices of the gamblers in the woods" (222).

Anyone who has watched the stick game or any of its analogs recognizes that gambling in some traditions is not simply a game of one completely isolated player against another. Instead, it is one group of players against another group, with one individual focusing the play while others sing, chant, drum, or verbally spar in the background. This final scene is interestingly similar to that model, with Fleur the focal point of resistance to the encroachment of foreign ideas of "resources" and extractive economies while her ancestors murmur in the background. She does not lose as much as she folds her hand without showing her cards, willing to wait for the next hand that always comes if one is attuned to the ways of chance. She deflates her adversaries' victory by sawing through the trees herself, and with the help of the wind the trees fall like sticks in a game, and Fleur walks away in control, undefeated. At the very least, the other team has developed a great deal of respect for her power, and so has the reader. With the publication of *The Bingo Palace*, the nature of that power is given further elaboration, its conclusion resonating with the motif first found in the conclusion of *Tracks*. What's seemingly lost in one story, at one moment in life, is regained through another.

The title, *The Bingo Palace*, speaks for itself. Once more, gambling becomes a central aspect of events in the text. Here, however, the element of "chance" is most clearly defined: it is indeed "in the eye (and the actions) of the beholder." Erdrich delineates two distinct modes or types of gambling, much as the previous novels delineated two distinct conceptualizations of "randomness," "chance," "fate," or "chaos," for that matter. Understandably, the ways these types of gaming work are found in the behavior of characters; Lipsha and Lyman, together, dramatize the attractions, and the ill effects, of engaging in games of chance with the wrong attitude or without the proper "luck," and the nature of empowerment in gambling is defined in their two central chapters, "Lipsha's Luck" and "Lyman's Luck."[14] The resulting concept of gambling is a telling blend of culturally determined means and motivations.

Lipsha's luck is tied directly to the past: to the power in his hands, passed down to him through the bloodlines, as Pauline has noted. It is connected in his chapter to an ancient, invaluable ceremonial pipe that is also passed to him, the chapter beginning with Marie giving it to him. Nector had been its holder, and now Lipsha has been chosen to assume that duty. Interestingly, it becomes a point of contention between Lipsha and Lyman, who considers Lipsha a lost cause and therefore believes that only he should be the holder of such an important tribal pipe and hence the controller of the people's future. Thus begins a game of power, much like the one they play for the affection of Shawnee Ray Toose.

"Lipsha's Luck" ends with Shawnee and Lipsha on a date, driving across the medicine line, the border, into Canada, and "here's where it started, that little wrinkle in destiny which [Lipsha] somehow came to believe that Zelda might have arranged" (32). The border guard—quintessential agent of colonial power—searches their car, June's car, and finds one seed, ostensibly a marijuana seed. The search continues, and he finds the pipe. He confronts Lipsha with it and Zelda's annual gift to him, a pemmican fruitcake wrapped in foil. Of course, the guards draw the wrong conclusions: that the two items are hashish and a pipe for smoking it. Lipsha and Shawnee are detained, and as the scene concludes, in slow motion, the guard connects the pipe bowl and stem, something that should only be done at certain times and places and then only ceremonially by the pipe's holder. He carries it off, also in the wrong way, slowly lowering it until its eagle feather touches the ground. The effect on the future is catastrophic.

The next chapter is entitled "Transportation." In the context of this discussion it records the transporting away of Lipsha's luck, but it also marks the initiating point of its return through the lessons he learns from its loss. It opens with a direct transition to the eagle feather touching the floor:

> WHEN I THINK OF ALL THE UNCERTAINTIES TO FOLLOW, the collisions with truth and disaster, I want to dive, to touch and lift that broad feather. . . . And yet, as there is no retreating from the moment, the only art left to me is understanding how I can accept the consequence. For the backwardness, the wrongness, the brush of heaven to the ground in dust, is part of our human nature. Especially mine, it appears. (37)

Although each chapter in the novel begins with the first line all in capital letters, here they have an added emphasis. Uncertainty, chance, is tied directly to the event of the feather touching the ground and therefore to Lipsha's luck, which has suddenly turned bad. The implication is that luck can render uncertainty controllable, and luck is tied to heritage, to the power inherent in the pipe, but, more significantly, to the obligations one has to perform duties to them both, to do them responsibly. There are many external forces that work upon luck, evidently. Moreover, the passage undermines that certainty with a telling comment about human nature: we are prone to shirk, neglect, be turned aside. How we deal with that realization and the adversity such actions bring creates character, and it is one location for the differentiation Erdrich investigates.

Later in the chapter the external forces that affect individual lives appear, as June. Alone in the bingo palace long after everyone has left, Lipsha sees her. "Now I always told myself before that there was a good side to ghosts. My reasoning goes along on the base of the following *uncertainties*: Beyond this world, is there another? . . . A ghost could answer the basic question, at least, as to whether there is anything besides the world I know, the things I touch. If I see a ghost, possibilities will open" (53, emphasis mine). Of course, he *is* seeing one; the question and answer appear simultaneously for readers, and possibilities are opened as the primal uncertainty of life is investigated and the direction of thinking scripted. June brings him a book of bingo tickets; when she leaves, she takes "her" car.[15] The epistemological significance of this event for Erdrich's character and reader is revealing: in the tribal realism constructed in the novel there is a future beyond this life, and it can have a direct effect upon the present, if one knows how to engage it.

Lipsha's education continues as he uses the tickets to win the bingo van, the top prize in Lyman's bingo palace for which people have played for five months. The process Lipsha goes through—the choices he makes and the "lucky" occurrences he has—is likewise revealing. In abbreviated form it runs like this. He observes the ways that his grandmother Lulu plays bingo: "All business, that's Lulu. And business pays" (62). He follows her model and becomes single-minded in his pursuit of the van, but with a slight and significant variation upon Lulu's: "To get the van, I have to shake hands with greed. I get unprincipled" (64). In other words, he employs the "touch," the healing power he has been graced with and which, when wrongly used in *Love Medicine*, kills Nector. He begins to charge money for his healing services, the laying on of Pillager hands: "But I do not realize I will have to give up my healing source once I start charging for my service" (64). The philosophical dilemma he faced in the attempt to make Nector love Marie, a crisis over whether or not the cure operates by sheer belief or by other external forces, is once more resolved. Finally, using only one of June's cards, which he lost but then miraculously finds again, he wins the van, then loses it immediately.

In a scene strongly reminiscent of Fleur's poker playing in Argus in *Tracks*, several Anglos, led by a man Lipsha argued with earlier, kidnap him, humiliate him, then dump him at Russell Kashpaw's to get an equally humiliating tattoo to commemorate their revenge and their power over him. They destroy the van, and the lesson is obvious. Although he has been granted the ability to manipulate events by some force external to his character, Lipsha has not won the van in the right way: he plays for self, "for the backwardness, the wrongness, the brush of heaven to the ground in dust, is part of our human nature." As a result, his apparent winnings are ephemeral, the lesson momentous. This is, of course, the lesson one finds in *Fools Crow* as well: one's abilities are of use for the community at large and not oneself.

Russell releases him, and Lipsha tells the story of how he came to be there, tied and awaiting his unwanted tattoo. He tells of the van, and Russell understands: "That's an unusual piece of good fortune." Lipsha is curious: "Have you ever had any? Any good fortune?" The answer is equally curious, given Russell's history as depicted in *The Beet Queen*: he is a veteran of several wars who has been wounded so often that he is left horribly scarred. From his wheelchair he answers, "All the time" (82). Luck, it seems, has many sides and is not always physically apparent in those who possess it, as the "loser" Lipsha signifies, nor is it apparent in the lived moment. As Russell shows him his book of tattoos, Lipsha finds the falling-star design that he saw the night of his mother's visit and later as a sign that the time was right for him to win the van. The van was not the be-all and end-all of the game, only a means, a vehicle (pun intended) to get him to where he needs to go. He has Russell tattoo it in the only appropriate place for a descendant of the Pillagers: on his hand. Lipsha has gained something unexpected and much more valuable: an understanding of his own nature and the ways it is shaped by both his own volition and forces external to his character.

"Lyman's Luck" immediately follows this lesson in appropriate ways to engage "chance." It extends the "greed" and "unprincipled" concepts Lipsha first exposes, and it is significant that Lyman's confrontation with Western concepts of gambling takes place in Reno, Nevada, "the biggest little city in the world," built on its gambling mystique and the myth of sudden gains. It is also revealing that he travels to Reno to participate in an Indian gaming conference. What we see emerge is hardly Indian gambling in the sense Erdrich has constructed it elsewhere. Gain and loss are tentative measures of any game of chance, but Lyman's losses in Reno are molded by a Western model; he plays for self, and in this framework only "the house" can win.[16] Here, we are privy to the workings of an addiction based in an overpowering desire for monetary reward and personal power through employing one's "luck": the westerning, pioneering, colonizing urge.

Throughout Lyman's ordeal in Reno we find an understated implication that he has been through all this before; what is an entrepreneur, after all, but someone who risks funds and energy in a "business venture" in the hopes of wealth and ease? However, he appears also to have felt the attraction to gambling and is cognizant of its power, and he attempts to overcome his desire to succumb. He is, of course, unsuccessful, in part because he is not at home, where, as the manager of "the house," he has the power. Instead, the whole environment of Reno is dedicated to undermining one's attempts to rationalize and therefore resist: the casino's trappings induce a "dreamlike" effect; the immediate reality—time, connections to others, physical movement—is subdued. Lyman sits down at a blackjack table and wins. As he takes his chips to the cashier to collect his winnings and leave the casino, he is drawn aside by his sense of luck again. In a description strongly imaged by automaton qualities, Erdrich makes her point: "His features were a mask. His outside expression was fixed, serene, but beneath that, on the real face that was hidden, he could feel his look of bewildered dread" (92). This is a moment of powerlessness, one that evokes an image of Greek drama and the sense of fate it enfolds, but before he can sit at another table, a man "accidentally" bumps into him, scattering his chips and gathering his willpower. For the moment he is saved. Here, in a town carved from the desert by the desire for gain, he moves like a puppet.

Later, in his room, Lyman awakes. "It was two A.M. when he woke, starting into clarity, his brain on and humming like a machine connected to that money" (92). He returns to the game and wins nearly three thousand dollars. Then he "started losing his way in a muddy sluice of sloppy plays, and he got desperate. His luck turned unpredictable and he played on, but the momentum had died" (93), and so has his "luck." He loses not only his winnings but all he has brought with him as well as the tribe's Bureau of Indian Affairs loan, and, in a last degradation, he pawns Nector's pipe for a few hundred dollars more, only to lose. In a scene interestingly reminiscent of

Lipsha on the bridge after he has won June's car in *Love Medicine*, Lyman walks to a bridge and briefly contemplates drowning himself, but the Truckee River is too shallow. He is far removed from his world, and he has no control.

There are several revealing elements to this event. First, Lyman *is* lucky, but I suggest that luck here has nothing to do with random chance. Second, when he succumbs to the attraction of the place and the chance for easy winnings, easy money, he loses his power because, like Lipsha, he has made his talent a commodity and his winnings his own, the capitalist ideal. Unlike Fleur, who wins a dollar a night to get the funds to save her family lands, Lyman plays for himself. His adversary, the player-dealer on the other side of the table, is empowered. Lyman can no longer direct probability. Third, the sense of power Erdrich exposes here is based upon the idea of predictability. In fact, his loss of power is described in those terms: "His luck turned unpredictable." Predictability is based upon knowledge. Most assuredly, one must know the odds, but there is more to it than that alone. If randomness is taken out of the game, perhaps through power and knowledge, predictability is assured. This is what Lipsha does in his poker game with Gerry and King in *Love Medicine*. In *Tracks* Fleur's coworkers feel that they remove randomness when they believe that "the squaw can't bluff." They are, of course, sadly mistaken. Power resides in vision, in an awareness that events are not based upon random chance but upon recurrent movements and motifs that swirl in recognizable patterns. In this model this recognition allows one to predict, to improve the odds, and sometimes to win. Moreover, the ability to predict is tied equally to an understanding of oneself—one's nature but also one's family and history—and human nature as revealed in the stories, as Fools Crow and Tayo learn, of the long history of life on this continent. In recent times those stories include Europeans and colonialism, courts and casinos.

The lessons in these two chapters are echoed throughout the life stories of others; the chapters of the book are named after the major characters, each with a "luck" attached. Moreover, once again Fleur plays cards for her land, lost for a time in the concluding events of

Tracks, and wins it back. But in Lipsha's odd vision quest one finds an even more emphatic statement of value, situated within the complex matrix of the Anishinaabe present of Indian gaming and land-claim issues. Here, the future of the entire community is central.

Once again, Lyman and Lipsha are united; they both go on vision quests at the same place and time. Lyman, of course, successfully completes his on schedule and in ways following the tradition. Lipsha, of course, emerges from his still wondering what he has experienced, and, of course, he appears a complete failure to the community. His "helper," it appears, is a skunk. Humiliated, smelling so bad that no one will approach him, he returns home in apparent defeat. This is Erdrich: just when one appears to have lost everything, the last card is turned. Vision comes in unlikely packages for character and reader alike. Later, the skunk offers a common refrain: "*This ain't real estate*" (218). The enigmatic statement is punctuated with Lipsha's vision of the future. (The title of the chapter is "A Little Vision," an equally enigmatic statement and perhaps a plea for people to employ a little vision for the future.)[17]

In the first segment of his vision Lipsha sees the casino that Lyman is to build. Lipsha sees its construction, which requires bulldozers, and the hauling of lake stones into the woods; each detail is significant and reflects the potentially destructive nature of change, of "development" that alters the landscape dramatically. But he also sees "revenue falling out of the sky. . . . Easy money, easy flow. No sweat. No bother" (219). The casino provides the means to insure the future because it will be built on Pillager land. Just as in *Love Medicine*, where Nector's factory requires the land upon which Lulu's house rests, this casino will require Fleur's. The casino will be situated on the spot where she played her game at the end of *Tracks* and where she lives once again, the place where the influence of Missepeshu is the strongest. In the next segment of his vision Lipsha feels the money in his *hands*; in such a place, blending Western gaming techniques (the "games") as seen in Reno and Indigenous values and perspectives, a Pillager could not lose. And then the skunk delivers his final message, the moral we must consider: "*Luck don't stick when you sell it.*" And there we have it yet once more.

The next day Lipsha's "little vision" carries us farther. Since, like Fools Crow, he knows the future of this land and the integral place gambling will hold, he shows us that such complex issues are never clear-cut: "It's more or less a gray area of tense negotiations. It's not completely one way or another, traditional against bingo. You have to stay alive to keep your tradition alive and working. Everybody knows bingo money is not based on solid ground" (221). This ain't *real estate*, indeed. He also realizes that Lyman's plan has Fleur's blessing, perhaps her influence. She is, after all, a Pillager gambler who recognizes that Lyman may be the one "who can use the luck that temporary loopholes in the law bring to Indians for higher causes, steady advances" (221). After all, she has engaged in immigrant games of chance to maintain her lands and assure the life of the next generation. Now, Lyman's plan offers a chance for the whole community.

The concluding pages of the novel are beautifully poetic. Fleur walks off into legend, but, like June, who appears at times to influence the lives of other characters, she is never very distant: "We believe she follows our hands with her underwater eyes as we deal the cards on green baize, as we drown our past in love of chance, as our money collects, as we set fires and make personal wars over what to do with its weight, as we go forward into our unsteady hopes" (274).

The investigation of contemporary Anishinaabe life through the narrative device of chance in all its permutations was carried into the next decade and the "postindian" discourse with her next novel. *Tales of Burning Love* connects, in this way, with the others. In it Jack Mauser is no longer the unnamed pickup of *Love Medicine*, the man June spent her last few hours with in Williston. Like her, he is part Anishinaabe; unlike her, he has spent very little time on the reservation, growing up in another cultural milieu. He has also had to live with her death, since he failed to follow her into the stormy night that claimed her. As a result, he has been married four times, the last time to Dot, the daughter of Karl and Celestine. In other words, this novel brings the various cultural orientations introduced in the earlier novels into a direct kinship. They become relative. Significantly, Sister Leopolda dies in the first pages.

The overt references to chance and luck abound. The night of Leopolda's death, Jack and his first wife hide in her room in the convent after witnessing the nun's departure and while he tells Eleanore of his recent marriage to Dot: "Turned out she's part Chippewa too. Coincidence or sign? . . . Do you think it's a sign, that maybe I'm supposed to do something. Identify?" (59). Much like Lipsha's interrogation of an afterlife when he is visited by June, Jack searches for a meaning that transcends the individual human life. Later, the evening of Jack's funeral, the three wives who attended go to the casino where his other ex-wife works. In a paragraph describing the game of blackjack Erdrich encapsulates a description of human society and its interaction with the luck life brings. It is, in a way, similar to Lipsha's revelation at the end of *Love Medicine*, a description of life itself:

> Blackjack is an unenlightened game that fools and drunks play well but never win, not in the long run, through mesmerized evenings. In the course of a night, a table of strangers betting idly together can turn passionate about one another's welfare, or resentful because of some irrational habit of mind. People's faults glare. Players sitting elbow to elbow close ranks against newcomers, sometimes, if their entry breaks a streak of hopeful wins. They mentally kick out a player whose dour caution brings bad luck, and draw close to someone else who wins with no letup on the averages. (169)

Such is life in the "mainstream." One hundred pages later, Marlis, the blackjack-dealing ex, extends the commentary: "You like percentages? . . . Try these. You're born. *Hey sucker, welcome to the casino!* Just remember, the house *always* wins in the end" (269).

And there is the other end of life. As Jack searches through the whiteout of a horrible plains blizzard for his son, unwittingly kidnapped by Gerry and Lipsha (as described in *The Bingo Palace*), he calls forth the image of the Anishinaabe Road of the Dead, as always a significant allusive element in Erdrich's novels. He leaves the warm cab of his snowplow and walks into a sugar beet field to investigate a mound he takes for the car containing his son, realizing that if he misses it he will "go straight west, on into the other world of the Ojibwa dead where skeletons gambled, throwing and concealing human wristbones. He saw their arms rise and toss, but he lunged ahead anyway" (384). He is lost in the storm but continues: "He walked in a big circle and then a small one and smaller, concentric, following June. It took him all night to get back where he started" (385). He returns changed, though, and he also finds his son and Lipsha, against all odds. The story has come full circle as well. Jack's walk ties directly to June's in *Love Medicine*, but here he walks into the possibility of a fulfilling, a meaningful future, one that is tied to Lyman's (Fleur's) casino. Jack will build it, and his return to the reservation to do so is conveyed in terms of survival: "Jack rocked the baby, half dreamily, his heart both lifting and sinking. . . . Now he would be part of the biggest temporary concept yet—the thrill of instant money. The power of house odds. The security of eventual small-time petty loss. Nothing new. . . . He had the sense of a swift undertow, pulling from beneath the glazed Formica table, tugging. Home" (408). The connection of games of chance to home, and the water metaphor that describes one's attraction to it, is a consistent motif in Erdrich's fiction. In each of her early novels in the 1980s the line between "suckers" and those who understand the true nature of chance is clearly drawn. However, as we find in the stories of so many of her characters, including the central one of Lipsha, knowledge does not always insure power over one's future. It only helps.

As a narrative device, however, this interrogation of the concepts of chance, coincidence, fortune, fate, and luck is central. The questions her characters ask as they fumble through their lives, attempting to understand the "true" meaning of events and plot out a future, are the questions all humankind has asked and will continue to ask. It is, therefore, a point of convergence for all cultures: a recognizable common ground as readers search for meaning. In the characters of Nanapush and Fleur as well as some of their descendants, however, we find an intriguing negotiation of culturally defined ways of answering those questions. Erdrich's Anishinaabe characters are the ones whose revelations denote the reaffirmation of Native values and ideas in contemporary times and provide the bridges between generations and, thus, the sense of continuation of those values into the future in her fiction.

The 1980s, as noted in the opening of this chapter, also saw the flowering of another Anishinaabe writer, Gerald Vizenor. Unlike his contemporaries, Vizenor has always operated on the edge of language and literary form. Unlike Erdrich, whose works are conventional in style and form and therefore easily accessible to a non-Native reader, Vizenor is an innovator, one whose work evokes and provokes sometimes heated responses, as we can see from the antithetical reactions of Sherman Alexie (chapter 3) and Louis Owens (chapter 4). In this way he is a fit voice for what followed in the 1990s and after the turn of the millennium.

Blake Hausman and I had the opportunity to speak with Vizenor about the past and future of Native literatures. Naturally, any such discussion implies imaginative fusion of sight, sound, and text, so it seemed altogether appropriate that our conversation occurred on the birthday of Miles Davis, one of American culture's most innovative and imaginative geniuses. Prior to the start of this conversation, which was recorded on two microcassette machines and then transcribed, our thoughts converged on the paradox of musical "literacy" in the creation of jazz.

John Purdy (JP): Here we go, in stereo [with two tape recorders].

Blake Hausman (BH): In stereo on Miles Davis's birthday.

JP: This is the genesis of this idea: when you were up last time, you and I walked around, and we went to Elliott Bay Bookstore.

Gerald Vizenor (GV): Yes.

JP: And when we were looking around for works by Native American authors, you were questioning what the future was going to be like in publishing.

GV: Oh.

JP: At the time it didn't seem like you were very hopeful that a lot of works, by American Indian authors particularly or publishing in general, had a very bright future. And oddly enough, when

I saw LaVonne Ruoff Brown just the other day, she told a story about, she's on the MLA Executive Board, and at one point a person of prominence in the publication industry said, quite frankly, "The book is dead."

GV: The book of any kind?

JP: Yeah. So those two things together kind of make me wonder. I thought about the past in "American Indian studies" and the publications, the numbers of books that have come out. You're the editor of two series—who better to know and talk about it? But I'm wondering, given what we know of the past, what the future holds. What it looks like, if that makes any sense.

GV: I didn't expect to be called upon for prophetic views, first question [laughter].

JP: Okay, well, let's go to the past.

GV: No, I like the future. It's safer [laughter]. I just hope to be published in the future.

JP: Yeah.

GV: That's a part of an answer, isn't it? Well, we're still riding a great time in publications, and the most impressive thing to me is that we can now clearly make distinctions—for any reason, cultural or commercial—clear distinctions between commercial writers who are Native and literary artists who are Native. And I'm not trying to draw a hierarchy but to just be comparative, that people write, for good reason, for commercial publication and find a good audience. We know who those authors are. And a lot of Native writers write for the art as they want to experiment and explore it, and they can get published, too. And that's the purpose of that second series that I edit with Diane Glancy: to find original, experimental literary artists who tell a story in a different way and also who try to make use of Native oral experience, or any other Native experience, in an original literary way.

JP: Interestingly enough, I've just finished *Field of Honor*, Don Birchfield's novel, and that's something unlike anything I have come across before . . . [confusion over the book's publication date]. I also told you that Birgit Hans has done that manuscript of McNickle's *The Surrounded*—"The Hungry Generations"—so here's a manuscript from the late '20s and early '30s that was kind of groundbreaking as well.

GV: Well, three things were going on all at once in the last generation. That was the republication of Native texts and then the publication of texts that were either unpublished or so little known or distributed that they were virtually unpublished. *Wynema*, for instance, which LaVonne Ruoff Brown brought to attention. And, at the same time, original manuscripts by Native writers. So all this material going on at the same time leads people to think there's some kind of Renaissance. But Renaissance is a European category. I'd rather think of a splurge [laughter].

BH: The splurge.

GV: A Native splurge.

JP: I like that.

BH: A resplurge?

GV: A Native circle dance.

JP: There it is.

BH: Just to play on the idea of the Renaissance—the "rebirth"—maybe as opposed to a splurge, but you mentioned Diane Glancy earlier. It's very interesting how she reconstructs. At the end of her book *Pushing the Bear* she talks about going down to New Echota, Georgia, and tracing different parts of the Removal, saying that if we can't construct culture from the fragments of the past, then what can we do? Or something along those lines—that we need to be able to reconstruct culture from what we have.

It seems that the republication of some of those texts, like the McNickle manuscript, happening at the same time as the emergence of new approaches, creates that splurge. The splurge is caused by the simultaneous reconstruction and creation—the simultaneous reconstruction and imagining where it can go at the same time. So in that way the future and the past are always going to be inseparable.

GV: I think they always have been.

BH: Sure.

GV: Well, not always. Before social science "discovery" they were. That categorized it, gave it "cultural objectivity" and reduced the generosity of spirit and sense of chance that was in all stories. But I think every Native generation deserves literary artists who reimagine their time. You can do that in a grammatical context, and you can do that in the past—you can write into the past. And I'm much more inspired by the works that reimagine the past with all its contradictions than I am with those literary artists who reimagine the past as a fundamental idea of tradition and value. Though that's useful to a lot of readers, it's less interesting to me than a liberation of the past from the dominant liturgy and cultural determinism. And also the future. I mean, you can run to the future as a responsible literary artist with Native experience, and that can be quite a negative critique on what's happening right now as a way to explain a possible outcome of things.

JP: Like *Bearheart*.

GV: Yeah. Or a utopia. And Native visionary experience has not been without utopian possibilities. I don't mean that there was a nationalism or anything like that but an idea that by living right—suggesting that if you don't, there are consequences—that by living right you bring about good spiritual energy. And that's not romantic as much as it's utopian, as a parallel literary device.

JP: Right.

GV: So is anybody doing that? Yes. Lots of poetry. And in the novel, of course again it's much easier to make distinguishing critical comments about commercial literature and literary art. That's not a value statement, but it's just an observation. And I say that because editors have an interest and try to anticipate a market, and that does influence both how people write and then how they're asked to revise, to satisfy public interest.

One of the problems I see is not in the literary art as a point of comparison but in the commercial. So far the commercial interests have not varied so widely from early romantic notions about Natives. I mean, of course we've come a long way from the notions of Karl May or James Fenimore Cooper, but the tragic romance, lowercase r romance, that satisfies popular readers— in fact, they expect it, they expect those metaphors of tragic romantic outcome to be delivered, and if it's not, they're not so sure it's Native . . . because that idea of the tragic victim is so established in American consciousness that any other outcome is not believable.

JP: It doesn't fit into the schema.

GV: It certainly is not commercially believable. Especially in this past generation, where victimry has become a primary source of consciousness, worldview, descriptions of reality in every popular medium. And it has affected alternative explanations, inspired resolutions to Native experiences as being those of tragic victimry. Or the contradictions of it, or even counters of it, but that's still a structural relationship—to counter it in a binary way leaves you with the same consciousness, or the same sources of consciousness, about tragic victimry.

That, I think, is vulnerable. People don't quite believe it like they used to, and part of it are casinos, and celebration in popular culture of Native things, fusionism in Native music. Romantic readers and viewers of Native experience have a little trouble with what it is that's traditional.

I think in art, painting, the public has come the farthest in appreciating a Native creative genius. They understand and really pay a lot of money for abstract associations, and combinations of time and place, and contradictions and irony, all these things, rather than past representations.

JP: That's a good point.

GV: I long for the time, I hope I live long enough, that people will look to literature.

JP: To the same thing.

GV: But they're not yet, not in a very large audience.

JP: Do you think your writing moves in that direction?

GV: I think it always has.

JP: Good.

GV: Not the journalism. But—

JP: No. But your novels, and haikus.

BH: I think what you were saying about liberating the past, and that phrase that comes up throughout *Harold of Orange*—"social acupuncture" [socioacupuncture]—echoes some of the ideas you're talking about now. Just thinking about that character—or a character in a story, like your character in *Hiroshima Bugi*—the character in a story that affects things, changes things, mixes things up, and throws a loop in the schema. I just have to ask you, and this is in relation to what you wrote in *Narrative Chance* about the trickster as a "comic holotrope."

GV: Yes.

BH: And I've been trying to wrap my head around that concept for a while. Thinking about what that means, and its implications—maybe there's a connection to thinking about this potential future. The idea of the holotrope, of "seeing" something, suggests a potential for literary arts to have a similar effect on audiences in the future as visual artists do now. How might that be possible, thinking along the lines of that trickster discourse, that narrative and character that will shake things up?

GV: Compassionately [laughter]. *Fiercely* but compassionately. And without direction or profit, unless it's an irony. What if I add to comic holotrope something that would make it a complete sentence, like "comic holotropes of survivance"?

BH: Right, okay.

GV: We can make a distinction now that we're not talking about comic holotropes of victimry, or gloom and doom, but a play figuratively in language. Let's take the word "comic" first, not to define but to play a little bit with where the word comes from. Comic—happy, laughter, play. Go back to Greek, to Aristotle, making a distinction in literature between comic and tragic. Both are figurative. So I'm going to say that Native storiers had the knowledge of Aristotle about this being figurative, the story. It's not a story of direct representation or mimicry.

Let's take the tragic first, Aristotle's idea that tragedy is the imitation of action that arouses strong feelings in the reader or the audience. In the case of his description that's theater. But it's a narrative nevertheless, it arouses strongly. Emphasizing imitation, not representation. Imitation. Now that's a really good idea and insight into narrative. Unfortunately, social scientists have taken Native stories as representation, not as figuration, because they're not literary artists. They're methodologists looking for objects to represent, a faux reality.

The comic, he points out, is communal. And in theater it's variations of characters, of audiences or witnesses or readers, knowing things the characters don't know, or the other way around. Or combinations of that. But it's always communal because you can't have a play of the comic, or humor, or even tragic humor without people being in on it to know where the metaphors play. You don't have to be in on tragedy because it's an imitation.

JP: You observe it.

GV: It's provided for you. So if I were a Native oral literary artist, a narrative artist, and I was hearing stories about Aristotle, I'd think, Smart guy, we've been doing that for a while. And clearly, he understands, in his discussion of the comic, that our play is communal. Now when you get to the written page, though, you don't have community, you have an individual reader. So comic holotrope is the question—it's communal, and it's "all" figuration, the entire figuration—you have to re-create it, which is the entire figuration—of the community. You have to create a play of readers and listeners in the story itself. That's the comic holotrope.

My most successful comic holotrope was *Griever: An American Monkey King in China*, and that's where I sort of put the word together because my character is holosexual. He's all. Everything is erotic, on all sides, including all the pronouns are of erotic play for him. And he's the comic holotrope, because the story is told as an imitation of things, of communal context on multiple levels, of community reimagined, of Native interests being played out in the context of another great historical community, Chinese opera, the Monkey King opera, in the modern context of a Communist state.

JP: Right. Of repression and compression.

GV: Lots of contradictions about what our community really is. The whole thing is a comic holotrope.

BH: Like the Shakespearean play within a play within a play—the idea of the reflection of the audience and community, and within that another reflection of audience and community, and within that another reflection. Going back to the idea of communal experience, or communal knowledge such as Aristotle's theater, and thinking about literary arts in the future, to what degree is the progression of literary arts in publication somewhat dependent on the visual? There's the technology of filmmaking and of course the history of film and representation and the problems we might face with that.

GV: Film has to represent, or not. *Harold of Orange* had to represent. Shorthand structural binaries are comic in that community of players, Harold and his warriors. The Warriors of Orange, they're in their own context. But you have to represent. You can't represent the subtleties of metaphor on film. You have to show it, and usually the metaphor is one of action. Sometimes sight gags, although there are no sight gags in *Harold of Orange*, and that is funny. It's not suspense in any way, but you're in on it. Probably the most dramatic example was getting off the bus.

JP: The T-shirts.

GV: And then Harold changes twice. It cancels out even the binary irony of the play. And then his advice to one team and then the other, and then he changes T-shirts.

JP: "Remember what the missionary said, our ancestors said . . ."

GV: On both sides of the binary it doubles the play of the contradiction. What Shakespeare depends on is general understanding in his time, a general understanding of the crown and the hierarchy of privilege. That's pretty well understood, and everything plays on that understanding. Other factors that are so well known, too—greed, sexual intrigue, dishonesty—but that's a great framework. To do that about Native experience for another audience, which is what social scientists have done, but they have to reduce it by methodology to be recognizable, literary artists have to find a way to deliver that, and I think literary artists have unlimited metaphors to do this, because they're not obligated to linear or reductive ideas of culture or anything familiar.

The truth is, don't give a shit about the reader. The reader has to come to them. And that's not antireader or hostile, but I don't know who the hell the readers are either. I don't think anybody knows who the readers are, except those people who write genre literature. They know who the commercial readers are. But James Joyce didn't have a reader. Melville didn't even have any readers, much less anticipating them, for his lifetime. Look at that fantastic book, *Moby Dick*, and—I choose examples in the English language—and look at James Joyce. Apart from *Dubliners*, which is family and communal, the other work is extraordinary. I mean, readers aren't there yet. Now, most readers will say, Well, I don't give a shit, he owes it to me. And my response to the readers is, Fuck you, don't read it. I don't give a shit if you read it or not. I don't.

Now I say that because I make my living with state money [laughter] and have the liberty to write the way I want to write. And with rare exception I've been able to do that and get published. Which is extraordinary, because it's not easy. And if I were writing commercially I couldn't do that. I'd have to find a reader, and I'd have to talk to an editor to find out where that market is and to play on certain metaphors as they would understand Natives. I challenge that. I think that only perpetuates the rubbish, not that the work is rubbish, but it perpetuates that rubbish expectation, and it allows all kinds of other writers to play on that too, because they know where that audience is, too. There's one place where "other" writers can't get, and that's in the literary art of Native experience. They can't get there. I don't think they can get there. Maybe some extraordinary people can, and if they do, they deserve a lot of recognition. Hal Borland did.

JP: *When the Legends Die.*

GV: That book was so powerful, I was convinced he was Native. He's not.

JP: That's the first one I read that got me going.

GV: I used it in class all the time, thinking he was Native. And he is, I mean, by imagination. His identification with the character in the closet was so profound and powerful, he had to imagine that life experience, and he did it brilliantly. Compared to Native literature now, it's not that great a book.

JP: No.

GV: But at the time it was an extraordinary voice.

JP: Well, it was assigned in my class that Montana Walking Bull taught.

GV: Really?

JP: Oh yeah.

GV: I did, too, all the time. I was surprised he wasn't Native, but I have to say it didn't bother me. I said, Well, let's adopt him, he ought to be [laughter].

JP: Get him up to Point Roberts here, we can change his DNA [laughter].

GV: He doesn't know [laughter].

JP: He's descended from Columbus.

GV: Yes he is. He's one of those Columbus boys.

JP: Well, I'm wondering though, too. You edit two series at university presses, and I know university presses are feeling the pinch. Not necessarily for the fiction or literary art that they're publishing but for the scholarship in the humanities, which I learned just recently . . . sometimes the average is they lose $10,000 a book. There's an issue in MLA discussion now, and the profession in general, wondering about whether or not monographs are a thing of the past, that tenure and promotion will be decided by articles rather than books. So I'm wondering what effect that will have. Will university presses start to publish more fiction? More marketable maybe?

GV: They are.

JP: Make more money.

GV: Lots of presses are.

JP: That would seem to open the door even a little bit wider. Instead of having to have a list that would cover 75 percent scholarship and 25 percent fiction to fund the scholarship, maybe a revision to that equation.

GV: I think that people will be able to publish monographs, but not in print form. It'll be electronic.

JP: Well, that's part of the argument, or part of some of the proposals.

GV: Several things are going on. It's the edge of some very radical changes. In journal writing, peer review—very difficult to get published. And the cost of publication is so expensive. The subscription rates are prohibitive now, libraries can't afford them. And several scholars have found a way around this in the sciences, just recently, to publish electronically. And it's free. In other words, they're dedicated to scientific publication and peer review, and as quickly as possible.

JP: Which was the original idea behind the print form as well, that got commercialized and co-opted.

GV: And presses of course started out mostly to publish things like that, monographs. When you look at some of the early publications of university presses, they're dreadful. I can't imagine anyone feeling a responsibility to publish some of that, but it was very important at the time to make it available for other scholars.

I don't know if that will happen in fiction, but I think there's still a pretty strong market for critical studies and Native literature. Maybe not so strong in the social sciences, although political science and law and things like that have a pretty strong audience because of growth and interest in that field. And it's very practical—government interest in that area. But if literature went electronic, I don't know.

JP: There are some journals that are publishing both ways, like *Weber Studies*. There's a print version, but also you can access it online.

GV: You can also download the electronic version of many books online for a little less than half the cost of the print version.

BH: Thinking about the future and technology and current developments in computer technology, it was about eighty-five years ago that Mary Austin's *Indians Book* was writing down Indigenous songs by formatting them into the five-line notation of written Western music. Now we can record sound directly into digital format and see it represented as a visual graph. It's entirely possible to imagine, within another generation maybe, having access to multiple forms of text simultaneously—entirely audio and audiovisual at the same time. People theorize about secondary orality.

GV: Walter Ong.

BH: Right. But there still is a sense of imagined presence, I suppose. And thinking about the business of publishing, thinking about literary art, I wonder. What will the technology open up for us? Will we lose something that is inherent in the play on metaphor that you get on the page? I think we would gain something, too. Seems like quite a paradox. Thinking about sound—the sound as the primary thing—if you can get the sound coming through the technology, and there is a way to communicate that dramatic irony if the narrative is oral and literary at the same time.

GV: The written text, though, doesn't have an electronic sound. It has an imagined sound in the reader, and it has to be that because it's written for that. An example would be asking readers to read your own work. You would think, Well, a writer knows what the play of emphasis of metaphors are. But some writers are dreadful readers, and if you had to listen to them, you'd never read them again. I mean, T. S. Eliot sounded like he was whining.

JP: Faulkner even.

GV: Right. You could hardly stand it.

BH: I sometimes like hearing other people read Allen Ginsberg's poetry more than hearing Ginsberg read it himself.

JP: The variation of that is we don't read on screen the same way we read on paper, for those of us who are born and raised reading on paper. And the way the language changes on screen, the way e-mail words are truncated, that new kind of variant of English that's being used, one wonders what the future will bring with that.

GV: In *Hiroshima Bugi* there are two narrators, two voices—one, the character who does these marvelous things, and then a friend of the character's father who knows about him and how things have gone and provides some thoughts for the reader, and he does this because in fact the character asked him to do this, sent him his stories and said, "Add some background here," so he adds a chapter following. It's a way to avoid third-person omniscience, which is a giant false voice.

But the style I wrote it in is the first narrator. My character Ronin Browne is not speaking to a reader. He's speaking a kind of poem, and the dialogue is without direction or notation. You just have to hear it as it goes. That is, it is between someone. There's no "he said she said" and nothing about the quality of voice. It has to be imagined in the imagistic reduction of the quote. And it's very short sentences. That's also the style of ka-buki, so I've borrowed this literary sentiment and practice in kabuki, which is also a fantastic play embellished with costume and gesture, and then these short dialogue sentences that you really have to pay attention. And I expect readers to pay atten-tion. If they don't, well, go read the newspaper, then, where it's "he said she said" because they talk bullshit.

JP: Yeah. Were you working on that long poem at the same time you were working on the novel?

GV: I was working on that long poem for about five years.

JP: Oh.

GV: I couldn't find the narrative.

JP: What's the title of that?

GV: *Bear Island, the Battle [War] at Sugar Point.*

JP: That's right.

GV: But I did the research about five years ago, and then I hired someone to do some additional research to exhaust every library source. And then read it several times, took out interesting ideas from the material. I thought at first I would write an historical es-say, but it bored me. Most of the material is newspaper story, some government documents but not much—it wasn't quite enough for an interesting historical thing because you'd have to fill it out a bit, and then you get into a creative historical narrative. I just didn't think that was satisfactory, that people would be critical and dissatisfied for different reasons about the same text.

So I thought, Well, I'll do a long poem. And then I started a kind of descriptive narrative, poetic style. I didn't like that either. I wound up with too many connections, causative statements, prepositional phrases. It just ended up junky and kind of ponderous and phony. So I ended up imagistic. It's one fifty-page haiku imagistic poem about this battle. So I finished that and I was really pleased, but I realized that I'm not going to get many readers because they don't know what the hell this is about. I can't depend on any common knowledge. If I were writing about the civil war, maybe, or something like that. So I then wrote about a ten-page prose introduction, laying out and touching on, historically, everything in the poem. A sort of short prose narrative, historically based, as an introduction. So I figure readers can fake it [laughter].

JP: A holographic fake, huh? Oh, interesting. So what's next?

GV: A novel on Jesuit sexual abuse.

JP: Really?

GV: Indian boarding school. So far I've got the action figured out. A group of boys refuse to be victims—my theme of course—and they just outwit and outmaneuver and overwhelm this corrupt, perverted agent of God, or the pope. And they're good hunters, so they start out as snipers. And they stir up the snow around him, they shatter bark near his ear. They never shoot him, but they let him know at any moment, at any time he's visible, he's a target. And they drive him pretty close to insanity. They do sacrifice him, though. And they do it with lilac coup sticks. They whip him to death.

JP: Wow [laughter]. Lilac coup sticks. I love that.

GV: Lilac's got a nice strength. I used to make slingshots out of lilac. It's got a good spring to it. And they whip him to death. I have the action part of the story, but I don't have the sentiments of community and what happens, except I'm inclined to say that several priests disappeared somehow in this community. No one knows what ever happened to them.

JP: Interesting.

GV: They're never charged, you know. No one would bring a charge against them.

JP: I see a trend developing here—disappearing administrators . . .

GV: Right. That's right [laughter]! *Chancers.* I suppose what I'm trying to do is disappear before I disappear. I have to disappear all those bastards I've known.

JP: I'm also stuck on the idea of a fifty-page haiku poem. We were talking a little while ago about the way that the haiku informs your prose. So do you figure your novels are 150-page haiku prose?

GV: I think Kim Blaeser picked up on that really well. Really well. Good insight. I was really complimented by her thoughtful reading of that, and she did a lot of background reading, too, things that I had read, so she was trying to understand how I had come to this, and that was really nice.

JP: It makes a lot of sense. I've always wondered how you construct your manuscripts. At times, it's almost like you're working a word at a time.

GV: Some are.

JP: We all are, obviously, when we write, but I mean somehow there are those places where your prose gets very deep, and they turn on the associations or connotations of one word or the denotative definitions of one word and the way that the sentences are structured.

GV: Well, I don't take words as representation, but they do have history. And they deserve a greater meaning, many words. So I bump into one of them. Well, "survivance" is one, that's not a neologism but a borrowed French word that I give a different meaning. And it's a condition of survival in the French, but I give it another meaning, I think a greater meaning, and that's what language has always been. I've also created a lot of words, neologisms. People don't like those. Most people don't like that, they really get pissed off at that.

JP: Really?

GV: It's really interesting.

JP: My students eat it up. They have fun with it.

GV: I got an e-mail from somebody named Nova, and this person said about this: "There are women warriors, too." So I replied, and said, "Naturally, what's the context?" Nova replied by quoting Vizenor quoting Ishmael Reed about women warriors just playing the scenarios of gender division or something. Sounds like something I'd say. And I thought, You know, this is really sad. Someone is probably obligated to read this for some course or something and is resisting the play of language, mask, and identity. Ishmael Reed in that scene, and I'm sure what Nova was referring to was *Hotline Healers*, a scene about triple identities with masks, and that context of contradiction and mask says something, and she represents it as my view. It's such a limited, impoverished interest in the written word, much less imagination. Someone like that ought to go into banking. You can keep accounts, but not an imagination.

JP: Yeah, there it is.

GV: So I responded, saying now that is a simpleminded twist of a fictional scheme. And she didn't reply but sent the message back.

JP: Which was a reply in itself.

GV: So I sent a message back without a reply. I think she finally killed it. I was prepared to do this for the next ten years [laughter]. Every time I open up my e-mail, just hit "reply" to that one.

JP: There ought to be a way to program the computer to do that [laughter]. There are those simplistic knee-jerk reactions.

GV: I get a lot of correspondence like that. I don't answer much of it. One recently was from St. Cloud—I could tell by the "edu"—so I gathered up whether it was assigned or not. I doubt if it was assigned. It was about *Bearheart*, I think it was probably on a supplemental reading list or something. And the first message was, I thought, entrapment: "How do you view bestiality?"

BH: Uh-oh [laughter].

JP: Through my window [more laughter].

GV: Safely. Double-paned.

JP: Tempered.

GV: But not reflective! And I said, What's the context? She said, Well,

I'm reading *Bearheart*, and you seem to really like bestiality. I wrote back and said, It's a work of fiction. It's an imaginative story, and is there something wrong with relationships between humans and animals? Is that a Western hang-up? It was quite a long time before he or she answered that, and the response was evangelical.

JP: Oh, okay.

GV: That I'm sick. "How could you possibly think of anything like that? You need help," or something.

JP: You know what happened in Sodom and Gomorra.

GV: Right. I didn't answer that because it was an entrapment. But I did get a lot of that when the book first came out, about "How can you possibly write about that, what the hell's the matter with you?" And I say, Well, it's literature. It's like a good Native story. It's a good myth, humans and animals have relationships, have children who are mixed bears and mixed wolves and beavers and all kinds of things. You see, that's myth, that is not worth considering. So then I challenge it by saying, Well, what exactly is the problem between humans and animals? And it ends up being only sexual, because the obscene indulgence in domestic pets is something to worry about rather than the sexuality of it.

JP: Incredible. You must have gotten a lot of reactions for that. Good.

GV: It's still kind of amazing. Maybe it'll be resurrected in the oil bust again, because it was written during Carter.

JP: Oh sure, during the oil crisis.

GV: That makes it about thirty years old.

JP: Yeah, I was thinking about this same thing. Wow.

BH: Before we end this conversation, I want to ask you about the idea of imposing a narrative. You spoke about this kind of imposition earlier today, imposing a narrative consciousness on the details of the story. Thinking about this book that you're working on now, it seems tricky because people are going to pass judgment. And maybe you're coming from the perspective to begin with that the reader's going to do what the reader's going to do, if they're even there.

GV: Well, I'm doing something similar to everything else I do. I'm doing survivance, not victimry. The secure narrative right now is victimry. I'm just amazed that nobody's told a survivance story. Kids saying, "Fuck him, that crazy old bastard." It's all like it's determined. Damnedest thing. I knew sick priests. I think they ought to go talk to Italians. Italian families have known for years, for generations, that priests are weird. They wouldn't have trusted their kids on some camping trip with a priest. What is this mentality? It's the American repression of sexuality as a real experience. It's just crazy.

JP: Denial, awareness.

GV: So they think that a priest is one of these perfect people that has no sexuality.

BH: And that's where the social acupuncture comes in.

GV: Exactly.

To highlight a couple of ideas for future discussion, Vizenor says in one place that narrative

arouses strongly. Emphasizing imitation, not representation. Imitation. Now that's a really good idea and insight into narrative. Unfortunately, social scientists have taken Native stories as representation, not as figuration, because they're not literary artists. They're methodologists looking for objects to represent, a faux reality.

The comic, [Aristotle] points out, is communal.

This idea of the interplay of reader and narrative is worthy of further exploration, for it enlightens as well the four-part structure of DIAC. I would argue that the novels already discussed are, indeed, imaginative imitations, but I would also say that they investigate fundamental ideals and/or attitudes and thus become their own distinct articulations of them. As he says, "You have to create a play of readers and listeners in the story itself. That's the comic holotrope."

3 | THE 1990s

In the last decade of the twentieth century the canon and numbers of authors continued to grow. Yet another generation emerged to extend what had been accomplished and to increase Native artists' presence in other genres and media. Filmmakers such as Victor Masayesva in the late 1980s proffered a new aesthetic for movie viewers, just as Sherman Alexie's *Smoke Signals* took the issues central to Native written literatures into the popular medium and neighborhood theaters. As the authors previously discussed continued to build their individual canons, new fiction writers such as Eric Gansworth, Gordon Henry Jr., Susan Power, Thomas King, and, although she had published quite a bit already, Elizabeth Cook-Lynn found a growing market for their narratives. Once again, these are only a very few of the decade's voices emerging to share their own ideas about the canon: what it is and where it is going.

The "Returning the Gift" gathering in Norman, Oklahoma, in 1992 helped generate an energy similar to that of Flagstaff in 1977; here, however, hundreds participated rather than dozens, with an equally expanded geographical distribution. This included an expansion of genre as well. In 1995 A. A. Carr published his first novel, *Eye Killers*, a vampire story set in Albuquerque and Laguna Pueblo, and this movement into popular genres once again opened inroads for those who would come in the new millennium, such as D. L. Birchfield.

And as the canon changed the discourse about it changed as well. As critical theory became even more energetically deployed, the issue of a truly Native critical theory took new force. Although scholars such as Michael Dorris had argued in the 1970s—at the same time Leslie Silko published her "Old-Time Indian Attack"—that Native stories should be "read" from the cultural context that produced them, others began to question such an "anthropological" approach. As mentioned in the introduction, scholars such as Robert Warrior and Craig Womack explored the possibility of a Native-centered reading of texts. Louis Owens developed the idea of "cross-reading." No matter how useful these discussions may or may not have been, they are still an attempt to examine a wide array of texts through a lens. While the lenses may have changed, the "object" under study, the fiction, still operated with the elements discussed earlier: DIAC. Even the writings of Gerald Vizenor, so markedly different from those of his colleagues, exhibits this shared quality, and it is his work that moved most deliberately into the realm of critical theory, to co-opt and subvert, often with humor.

Sherman Alexie is another author who deploys humor in productive ways, and his career—there's no other way to say it—skyrocketed in the 1990s. His short fiction collections, *The Business of Fancydancing* and *The Lone Ranger and Tonto Fistfight in Heaven*, were published in 1992 and 1993, respectively, with his first novel, *Reservation Blues*, coming two years later. Much like Erdrich in the 1980s, Alexie's popularity rejuvenated the discourse about Native arts, and his commercial viability helped broaden the market for other writers and filmmakers.

I had occasion to ask him about the canon and its future, the same issues I had discussed with Paula Gunn Allen earlier. The conversation took place on a rainy autumn morning in an east Seattle café near Alexie's home. My colleague and former student Frederick Pope went with me to talk with Alexie, who was/is much in demand; in fact, that evening he was scheduled to read at Left Bank Books for a benefit to provide books for Native American inmates of this country's prisons. As always, it was an interesting and dynamic discussion, and on our trip home Fred and I agreed—it was candid, wide-ranging, profoundly playful.

John Purdy (JP): I understand the filming of the movie [*Smoke Signals*] went well?

Sherman Alexie (SA): We're premiering, screening at Sundance October

15. We'll know shortly after that if we're in [the final competition] or not.

JP: Fantastic. . . .

SA: We developed it there, so . . . we're in, but we need to get in the competition, and that's only sixteen films. We need to be up for the awards. [The film made the final sixteen and won.]

JP: Lots of good films have come out of Sundance.

SA: Yeah, but ours is better [laughter].

JP: Tell us a bit about the movie.

SA: It's a story; it's from *The Lone Ranger and Tonto*, "This Is What It Means to Say Phoenix, Arizona," that story. Victor and Thomas go to Phoenix to pick up Victor's dad's remains, so it's a buddy movie. It's pretty funny. Thomas is Thomas. The actor who plays him is amazing—Evan Adams. He's had small roles in Canadian productions; he's a First Nations guy from up there. He's just amazing. He's sort of taken Thomas. I can't write about . . . I tried to write a short story with Thomas in it, but I couldn't. I kept seeing him. . . .

JP: Seeing Adams?

SA: He's taken him away from me. He's so convincing, so real, so Thomasy. He's an adjective now.

JP: So he's typecast . . . as Thomas?

SA: He's so right for the role, it's scary to think that he's always going to be playing some weird Indian.

JP: I don't recognize the name.

SA: No. The movie has Gary Farmer in it, from *Pow-Wow Highway*, Tantoo Cardinal. . . .

JP: *North of Sixty* [a Canadian television series] . . .

SA: Yeah. Adam Beach, who was Squanto. Harvey Bernard. Michele St. John, Ella Miles from *Northern Exposure* . . . am I missing anybody? Buddy Lightning, who was in *Grand Avenue* on HBO. Baker, who's on *North of Sixty*. Tom Skerritt has a role, Cynthia Geary, who was on *Northern Exposure*. . . .

JP: That's a good cast. And what kind of role did you have in it? Did you have much control over it?

SA: Oh yeah. I wrote the screenplay; I was the coproducer. Five songs of Jim Boyd's and mine are in there. Two 49s [a song genre] in there I wrote. So . . .

JP: You can do it all. . . . You're doing 49s now?

SA: For good or bad, whatever, is in there.

[Interruption]

JP: So, did you have fun making the movie?

SA: No [laughs]. Yeah, yeah I did. The scary thing is that it was so fun, and so intense, so immediate, that if I start doing really well at this, I might wind up being a good screenwriter. I'm going to direct *Indian Killer.* I'm scared that if I make it I'll give up writing books.

JP: Whoa. And move to Hollywood. . . .

SA: No [emphatically]. The thing I think about is that probably 5 percent of Indians in this country have read my books. *Maybe* that much. Probably more like 2 percent, or 1. You take a thing like *Pow-Wow Highway*, and 99 percent of Indians have seen it.

JP: Well. It's a powerful medium. So you didn't make Gary Farmer wear a wig, did you?

SA: For the first scene. Then he doesn't have it. Then we let him be Gary. But he gets to be young in the movie. Twenty years difference.

JP: It's just that the one he wore in *Highway* was so much a wig. So you're directing *Indian Killer*? Are you dealing with the same [film] people? I hadn't heard about that.

SA: It's not official yet, we haven't signed the contracts, but it's happening.

JP: Where will you shoot it?

SA: Seattle. Right here.

JP: This all sounds time-consuming. Do you get to write, other than what you're working on [for the movies], or is the schedule so intense that it takes you away from writing?

SA: I'm working on a new novel.

JP: Want to talk about it?

SA: Yeah, but I don't know if it's going to be the next one published.

I've sold it, but I don't know if it's going to be the next one. Essentially what it's about is . . . it's set in the future, although it's set in the 1950s, an alternate 1950s, and I don't want to give too much of it away. Basically, scientists have discovered the cure for cancer involves the bone marrow of Indians.

JP: Carrying the cure for the world, huh?

SA: Yeah. Essentially, we start getting harvested.

JP: You and the yew tree.

SA: It's called *The Sin Eaters*. Pretty intense. And I'm working on one about the Mafia in the '20s and '30s and Indians, but I don't want to give away more than that, though.

JP: I think that's what they call the tease. . . .

SA: And it's based on a true story about the Mafia and the Spokane Indians in the 1920s.

JP: Oh no. Well, we have our research cut out for us now. Interesting.

SA: Well, actually, it's based on a true *sentence*. There's only one sentence that mentions this Mafia connection in one book. I came across it and I can't find anything else about it. I'm taking that one sentence to create a whole story.

JP: So it's the greatest cover-up in the world. One sentence and all the other information's yours.

SA: Exactly.

JP: I love the life of a novelist, right?

SA: I'm going to use that one sentence as the first sentence in the book.

JP: The one set in the alternate '50s—you say you've already contracted that. When do you think that will come out?

SA: Next year. Same press: Atlantic.

JP: And now into movies and writing 49 songs.

SA: I've been doing that forever, did that long before I ever wrote a book.

JP: Did you play around with songs, then, when you were young?

SA: Yeah. I quit for a long time, sort of getting back into it again and realizing I forgot how to sing. Maybe it's a mental or emotional block.

JP: You were playing with the language, then? Is that attractive to you? My son and I do that all the time. We take a song and rewrite it, play with the language, it's fun.

SA: Exactly. 49s are just fun that way.

JP: Well, I didn't know you were doing a movie of *Indian Killer*. You did the script *and* you'll direct?

SA: I'm doing the screenplay right now. Just about done.

JP: One of the questions I wanted to ask you is what you have envisioned for your future. It sounds like you don't have time to envision a future.

SA: Yeah, well, movies, definitely. I mean, I feel the only concept for me is poetry. I kind of get bored with other things. Novels take so much energy; it's so *hard*. Hundreds and hundreds and hundreds of pages of writing. They're *hard*. I think I'm just a decent fiction writer. I tell good stories, but sentence to sentence, verb to verb, noun to noun, I don't think I'm all that, you know. . . . Everybody else seems to think more highly of my work than I do. Suppose that's a good thing, eh? But I like the poetry; I think I'm good at that.

JP: So you still work at it?

SA: Oh yeah.

JP: What have you done with it?

SA: Publish it. I just had a new book out last year, which makes seven books of poems now.

JP: True. I remember when *Fancydancing* came out, I was on a flight, one of those small commuter flights, practically falling out of my chair. I had a colleague sitting in front of me who said, "What are you laughing at?" and I said, "Here, read this." Spoon-feeding bits and pieces of the book to him, and not just the humorous ones. Comes pretty quickly though, doesn't it? A lot's happened to you since then.

SA: That was published in January of '92. Yeah, I mean five and a half years later I'm an eight-hundred-pound gorilla [laughter, of course].

JP: One of the things that came to mind as we e-mailed back and forth about this interview is the memory of hearing you read at places like Village Books. It's fun. But when you read at Bellingham High a few years ago, with Dian Million, Tiffany Midge, Ed Edmo, it was a different thing. Do you see your audiences as different in some sense?

SA: Oh yeah. When you're inside a bookstore it's much more static; there's many more expectations of what's going to happen. I like to play with them. I've come out and done my characters, or come out and been Angry Indian Guy, or Funny Indian Guy, took on a persona and messed with the crowd.

JP: And you do it well, by the way. I want you to know. When you read with Linda Hogan that one time, you could hear the hackles on the back of their necks going up. And you, just looking back at them, with a smile on your face.

SA: Oh yeah, I had a good time with that reading. Part of that was good time, part of it was just a *bad* mood. It depends on the environment. At Village Books everybody's crowded into such a little space, you have so little room to work with up in front, it's really much more of a reading reading, but if I'm on a stage, I'll get nuts.

JP: It was fun that night at the high school. Jim Boyd was there, too. You were working on *Reservation Blues* then. You were running some things by us, and there were a couple of times when you'd stop and say, "Yeah, that works. The audience bought that. Let's try something else over here."

SA: That's a way of doing it. I mean, you always get tired of the question, y'know, of "How does your work apply to the oral tradition?" It doesn't. I *type* it [laughter]! And I'm really, really quiet when I'm doing it. The only time when I'm essentially really a storyteller is when I'm up in front of a crowd. Growing up with traditional and nontraditional storytellers, and they're always riffin' and improvvin'. . . .

JP: That's the fun of it.

SA: Sure. You can just imagine! The reason, I tell people, that Indians . . . that whites beat Indians in wars was not because they were tougher; I mean, we'd beat them on any given day. But then the whites would want to fight the next day again, and we just didn't want to do that. We'd want to go talk about it. You can hear the stories, the next day the warriors going "Man, remember when you dodged that bullet?" and the day after that it was "Hey, remember when that guy shot you nine times and you survived?" After the next day "Remember when you jumped over that cactus, got shot nine times, grabbed that horse, crawled inside of it, hid for nine hours while they stampeded around you, jumped back out, grabbed the general by the throat, slapped him twice, and ran away?" *Yeah. . . .*

JP: Yeah, tell it again.

SA: I come from a long line of exaggerators.

JP: One of the problems with editing a journal is we have people who get interested, get caught by those stories and then read a lot, but all of a sudden someone comes through with a new novel that does something else, something that comes around for the first time, and we're right back to where we were in the '60s and there's a raging debate about "Is this Indian?"

SA: Actually, SAIL [*Studies in American Indian Literatures*] is just fine. I've been subscribing for the past four years. Some essays are great; I've never seen a wider difference between good or bad in any academic journal. The bad ones are even more interesting, because they embrace, hang on to old ideas. I mean they're not bad scholarship, they're not badly written. What I mean is that no one has figured out a new way to look at Indian literatures. Above all else, *Indians* aren't looking at Indian literature. There are very few Indian scholars, very few Indian literature critics examining it. Those who do, like Gloria Bird or Robert Warrior or Liz Cook-Lynn, are still using the same old lit-crit tools. I think we have been far too nice to each other for too long now. I think Indian writers have grown enough, that we're not going to get any better unless we really start hammering on each other.

JP: I think that's true in the scholarship, too. One of the things we try to do in the journal is that, rather than get everyone to follow in lockstep, to take articles with widely varying points of view, so sometimes we have two essays in one issue that give opposing arguments. It is tough, too, not only for the people who submit but for the people who read the submissions, because those people cover the spectrum, too. We often have two readers, one who will say, Publish, this is great stuff, the other saying, Throw it out. Okay. What do you do now?

SA: The thing that gets me with that is the Vizenor thing. I mean, he's the god of the Indian lit-crit people.

JP: Why do you think so?

SA: It's obtuse prose, a lot of wordplay and word masturbation, essentially, that results in nothing.

JP: Did you ever read his *Narrative Chance*?

SA: Yeah. I mean, I can get into it, it's fine, but I've sort of been struggling with this idea, what does Indian literature mean? If Indian literature can't be read by the average twelve-year-old kid living on the reservation, what the hell good is it? You couldn't take any of his books and take them to a rez and teach them without extreme protestation. What is an Indian kid going to do with the first paragraph of any of those books? You know, I've been struggling with this myself, with finding a way to be much more accessible to Indian people.

JP: I was at a workshop once in Santa Fe, and Vizenor was there, [Louis] Owens, Anna Lee Walters was there, and some other people from the Navajo Reservation. Someone asked her, "So who are you writing for, Anna?" She said, "Young Indian kids on the rez."

One thing I like about my classes is that sooner or later students are going to be asking that same question: "What is this Indian literature?" And then they wrestle through all those questions of audience and definitions, by biology or whatever, and just when they start to feel comfortable, then we complicate it. Take the book for the book.

SA: But see, that doesn't work.

JP: What?

SA: Taking the book for a book.

JP: In what way?

SA: In an Indian definition you can't separate the message from the messenger.

JP: That's not the same. I think "the book" can carry that. Your work carries it.

SA: Yeah. But I think you're referring to identity questions and such.

JP: Oh. That's how the issue shakes out because that's what the students are interested in, but the question is how to take them back to the book, to the story itself.

SA: Most of our Indian literature is written by people whose lives are nothing like the Indians they're writing about. There's a lot of people pretending to be "traditional," all these academic professors living in university towns, who rarely spend any time on a reservation, writing all these "traditional" books. Momaday— he's not a traditional man. And there's nothing wrong with that, I'm not either, but this adherence to the expected idea, the bear and all this imagery. I think it is dangerous and detrimental.

JP: It's the '90s, and now it's time to move on. So, we get back to the discussion of what "it" is.

SA: Well, I want to take "it" away. I want to take Indian lit *away* from that and away from the people who own it now.

JP: I think you do in your writing.

SA: That's what I mean. I'm starting to see it. A lot of younger writers are starting to write like me writing like I do, in a way, not copying me but writing about what happens to them, not about what they wish was happening. They aren't writing wish fulfillment books, they're writing books about reality. How they live, and who they are, and what they think about. Not about who they wish they were, the kind of Indian they wish they were. They are writing about the kind of Indian they are.

JP: Sure, and it makes sense. Whenever you have any group of individuals in any literature who start to define the center, then everybody has to ask whether or not that's sufficient over time.

SA: We've been stuck in place since *House Made of Dawn*.

JP: But there's some interesting work coming out. Have you read Carr's *Eye Killers*?

SA: I hate it.

JP: You did? Well, that's right, it does have that traditional thing going on, but to move into the genre of the vampire novel I thought was interesting.

SA: That's fun, but I thought that book was blasphemous as hell to Navajo culture, the way he used ceremonies and such. I have a real problem with that. I don't use any at all. And a white woman saved everybody.

JP: But she *was* a teacher [laughter].

SA: But it read like a movie turned into a novel. I was supposed to review it, and I didn't.

JP: Tell me this. What do you see coming out right now that is doing what needs to be done?

SA: Irvin Morris. I like his book [*From the Glittering World: A Navajo Story*]. I think Tiffany Midge has a good future, once she stops copying me.

JP: She did a great reading that night in Bellingham High.

SA: The thing is, she was so into my work then; she's not so much now. That night—ask the people who saw me read before that night—she read exactly like me. So even that night I had to change the way I read. I'd never heard her read in public before, and she got up and read and I thought, O my god, that's me, that's my shtick. So I literally had to figure out a different way to read.

JP: Do you see anybody coming up through Wordcraft Circle [an offshoot of the "Returning the Gift" gathering]?

SA: I'm in Wordcraft Circle; I'm a board member and all that. But I get worried. I think it's focusing too much on the idea of publication, the idea of writing as a career. It's becoming very careerist.

JP: So you either make it . . . if you don't publish and not doing it for your whole life, then you shouldn't be doing it? Is that the danger you see?

SA: Well, it's becoming less and less about art. The whole thing is full of publication opportunities, money to win, scholarships, news about Indian writers publishing. . . .

JP: "Done good."

SA: Done good, yeah. Which is all fine. We're having a meeting soon, and I just want to share my concerns with them that I'm worried that the focus has gone wrong.

JP: That the joy of it is not there?

SA: Exactly. One percent of one percent of the people in Wordcraft are going to have a book published. I think it's setting up unrealistic expectations.

JP: There's a group that Liz Cook-Lynn is involved with, a storytellers' circle, and they publish what they come up with themselves. The focus isn't on selling it but on doing it.

SA: Yeah. The act is the thing. I know people who would rather be where I'm at now, but I'm jaded as hell. About publication, about the "art" of it. I sound like I'm complaining. I'm glad to be where I'm at; I worked hard to get where I am. But there's also a lot that's shady about it. Being a successful Indian writer and being an Indian, a "good Indian" (in quotes), are often mutually exclusive things, and there's a lot of pressure. I spend a lot of time alone, working. Selfish. My friendships suffer, my relationships with my family suffer, my health suffers. To be where I'm at, to do what I do, you'd have to be an obsessive compulsive nut [much laughter], and I don't think we should be encouraging our children in that direction [more laughter]. Or at least letting them know. I mean, Wordcraft should be talking about the ugliness, too. This is what happens. Hard truths about publishing.

JP: The reality rather than the ideal image of the author dashing about the world, vacationing on sunny beaches.

SA: Exactly.

JP: But there are other rewards, right? The joy?

SA: Money and attention.

JP: Besides that.

SA: Don't let any writer fool you.

JP: Now, a little bit ago you said the poetry was still there, that that's . . .

SA: Yeah, but nobody buys that.

JP: Yeah, true. I almost said that. But they buy movies and they buy novels.

SA: First and foremost, writers like to get attention. Don't let any writer tell you different.

JP: Yeah, well, in my world it's tenure and promotion, so . . .

SA: Which is attention. We want to be heard. We're standing on street corners shouting. If that's not a cry for attention, I don't know what is. And Indian writers, all writers in general, but Indian writers, too, were the weird kids, the bizarre kids. The ones who question institutions, the ones who were not all that popular. The ones who people looked at weird. There are big burdens involved in all of this, you know.

[Interruption]

JP: You were on the state governor's book award board, and one winner was Carolyn Kizer. She has a great poem, "Afternoon Happiness." It says the poet's job is to write about pain and suffering, all that is "grist for me," but all she wants to do is write a poem about being content, and this poem does it.

SA: Actually, I'm doing it, too. My next book is all happy rez poems.

JP: That ought to start a buzz.

SA: Yeah. All the joy I remember from growing up.

JP: Good. Think it will sell well in Europe?

SA: It's not corn pollen, eagle feathers, Mother Earth, Father Sky. It's everyday life. Remembering taking our bikes and setting up ramps to jump over the sewer pit. That kind of stuff.

JP: And making it!

SA: Yeah, yeah. Or *not* [laughter]. And some of it a little sad. I'm working on this poem; it's not very good right now, I just wrote it last night, but I remember, I remember, I dreamed it a couple of nights ago, but during the winter we would . . . In winter, we'd take our gloves and put them on the radiator in the old school whenever they'd get wet. But I remembered some kids didn't have gloves because they couldn't afford it, they were too poor. And I didn't have gloves this one winter, and I remembered that. And so I had this dream where I was sitting in the classroom and there were twelve pairs of gloves on the radiator and thirteen kids in the classroom, and so everybody's looking around trying to figure out who's the one who doesn't have gloves, so everybody's hiding their hands. So I'm working on that poem and that image of everyone hiding their hands so nobody will know who didn't have gloves. Kind of sad, kind of nostalgic . . .

JP: But positive in ways . . .

SA: And that is also funny, I mean. Another one's about . . . There's this series of lullaby poems, actually, that I've written, they're really rhymey lullaby poems. Powwow lullaby poems, I call 'em, 'cause where we live on the Spokane rez the powwow ground is a couple of miles away, and at night you can hear the drums and the stick game players playing all night long, and that would put me to sleep at night during powwows. I'm writing poems about that feeling, or walking in the dark back from the powwow grounds, hearing the drums, or walking to the grounds at night, or falling asleep in teepees, or in Winnebagos, or when we were real little, at a powwow in Arlee or wherever, and you'd end up sleeping in cousins' teepees in just a big pile of Indian kids. Those are the kinds of poems I've been writing.

Like the last book, *The Summer of Black Widows*, I thought was technically good. My last book of poems, technically good. I thought it was probably my best book. But very few of the poems Indian people would relate to. Whereas a book like *Fancydancing* I think is incredibly Indian. I want to go back to writing the kind of poems I wrote in *Fancydancing*. I'm more happy now. I'm a happier person. When I wrote these books . . . I'm getting happier and getting healthier. Some people say I always write about drunks. Well, no I don't, but if you look at the books you can see a progression, actually. The alcohol is dropping out of the books because the alcohol is dropping farther and farther out of my life, as I've been sober for more and more years.

JP: And I can see a bunch of kid poems coming out in the near future, then?

SA: No. No, I won't write about him [his son], I mean I write about him but I won't publish them unless he's old enough to let me know it's okay.

[Interruption]

JP: What's needed, then, is a new press.

SA: I'm going to do it. Actually, next year I'm going to start up a literary journal that's called *Skins: The Poetry Journal for Indians and People We Wish Were Indians.* I figure to start publishing books out of that.

JP: Fantastic. Great. It's been done. Lots of people have started presses that way.

SA: I've the money and the influence. I can print a thousand copies of a poetry book. I'll be able to do that kind of thing, and I can get distribution. Poetry books will still only sell three hundred copies, but I can get them out there.

JP: Well, even one, two, or three.

SA: One a year, two a year maybe.

JP: How long have you been thinking about this?

SA: Since the beginning. I just had to get to a place where I had the finances to do it. I didn't want a little mimeograph, I wanted a very, very professional journal, ah, very beautiful. The very best paper and the very best design. I wanted to wait until I had the finances there to have the best-looking journal possible. I just said *Skins*, and I can see it. *The Poetry Journal for Indians and People We Wish Were Indians.*

JP: People have talked about it over the years, and presses have come and gone, presses have had interest in it and other times none, and I bring that up because we get back to that model "if it's not like this . . ." we don't buy it. The reason some young writers get caught in trying to write like that, the convention, is that they might get published.

SA: That's all they know. That's all they've read or been shown. I don't know about you, but growing up all I got exposed to was Mother Earth, Father Sky stuff or direction stuff. That's how I thought Indians wrote. I didn't know I could write actually about my *life* [laughter].

JP: The first revelation, right?

SA: Yeah, I could write about fry bread and fried bologna. And the great thing is, I didn't know you could combine the traditional imagery and fried bread and fried bologna, the way I lived my life, and the way inside me, and the way I thought, which is a mix of traditionalism and contemporary culture.

JP: Right, which is reality.

SA: Which is reality. I didn't realize I could do that, something you can. I can write about, you know, Ray-Bans and powwows.

JP: How soon do you think you will do that, *Skins*?

SA: Next year sometime. We haven't figured out submission policies yet. For a while I think we'll just recruit, get it established, and then open it up to submissions. But with editorial guidelines—"no lyric poetry" [laughter]. "We want narrative."

JP: No lines that end with the word "blue."

SA: Right.

JP: Well, the *Bellingham Review* has been around for seventeen years or so, started by a colleague of mine who has retired.

SA: Yeah—a guy named Knute.

JP: Yeah, Knute.

SA: He rejected me like ten times while I was in college. I bet eventually he probably rejected half the *Fancydancing* manuscript.

JP: Oh, wow. "Click!" That's interesting. He wasn't the colleague on the plane with me who I showed the book to, but he did, though, what you're talking about. He set up a press with just that idea, that out of the journal submissions he took some poets and made them books. And it worked.

SA: Do you know Jim Hepworth? Confluence Press? He rejected *Fancydancing*, the book.

JP: Good. I mean, oh, that's too bad.

SA: No. I harass him constantly. He goes, "Oh, I didn't read it, I couldn't have read it, one of my readers must have. I would have remembered it." And I started laughing. I said, "Jim, you sent me the letter. I still have the letter. You said, 'This is encouraging, this shows lots of potential. But not ready for publication yet.'"

JP: Yeah. I know. So do you send him reviews of the book on the back of royalty reports?

SA: Well, he knows what happened.

JP: Wish you the best of luck on that project. It's good.

SA: It's going to . . . The reception we get at literary journals is terrible. The standard literary journal rarely publishes us. And when we do it's always part of a "special issue" or a special section. "The Literary Reservation." I'm looking for new young writers, the undiscovered voices who are telling us things. I want to read poems where I recognize the characters and I recognize the words. Where, ah, I'd also like to publish poems that people will not get, at all.

JP: Insider jokes.

SA: Yeah, I load my books with stuff, just load 'em up. I call them "Indian trapdoors." You know, Indians fall in, white people just walk right over them.

JP: I thought it was supposed to be the other way around. Hmm.

SA: Ah. So that's the kind of thing I'm imagining. Poems that work in all sorts of ways, but I really want the subtext for Indians.

JP: This is exactly how, as we were talking earlier, it will be done, how it will move on. Others have been at work doing it, like *Greenfield Review*. Now that things are established, it's time for the next phase. *Skins*.

SA: And just stay with poetry, because fiction costs too much.

JP: Yeah, yeah. Takes up a lot of space: more short stories, you have fewer poems.

SA: And I'm sorry, but I think generally speaking, Indians just don't write good fiction: it's not in us.

JP: I take it, then, that you're not going to do a serial of *Almanac of the Dead* [Silko's second novel]?

SA: No. I just don't think . . . It's just not natural for us. I think we're meant to write poems. All of our traditional communication, it's about poetry. So I think in some sense, genetically, we're poets. Culturally speaking, we can become fiction writers. We can sort of . . . But it's one of the problems with some of the criticism, some of the criticisms directed by Liz Cook-Lynn and Gloria Bird and Robert Warrior talking about how there needs to be more tradition in Indian writing. I thought . . .

JP: What's more tradition?

SA: But also, I mean, we're writing in English, 99 percent of our audience is going to be non-Indian, so how the hell do we do that?

JP: And, if you take that a step further, then should you?

SA: Exactly. We shouldn't be writing about our traditions, we shouldn't be writing about our spiritual practices. Not in the ways in which some people are doing it. Certainly, if you're writing a poem or story about a spiritual experience you had, you can do it. But you also have to be aware that it's going to be taken and used in ways that you never intended for it to be. I think it's dangerous, and that's really why I write about day-to-day life.

The responsibilities of being an Indian writer are enormous. Even more so than any other group of people because we have so much more to protect.

JP: [an aside to Fred]: You ever heard this before?

SA: I mean and it's so funny, people, like some of these writers, will think of me as being this very contemporary, very nontraditional guy, and I am, but I'm a lot more conservative in my take on Indian literature than any of those people are. I think . . . like some of the Navajo stuff and some of the traditional chants, or like some of Momaday's stuff, when rendered into English, means nothing. Means *nothing*. Our traditions are all about being, about taking place in a specific time and a specific geography. But when in a book that goes everywhere to anybody, it's like a traveling road show of Indian spirituality.

JP: Think of it this way, too, one of the elements behind that is the impetus for putting it in English and putting it in a book.

SA: To sell it. There's no Indian who would stand—well, very few—on a roadside singing traditional songs to make money. Yet they will put it in a book and sell the book. To make money. I think the passage of money invalidates any sort of sacredness of any of the ceremonies that are placed within a book.

JP: Someone asked, I think it was Vine Deloria Jr., how to tell a plastic shaman, and he said to just ask how much they charge. Pretty well says it.

Well, I'm glad you're going to do that; it's a really good idea, the journal and the press, and to put out the poets who come through who have promise. That's good.

SA: Yeah, I'd like to nurture careers. And to have a space for Indian writers to develop. I mean like this idea of featuring a poet per issue, a young, unknown person, featuring them, and also charting the growth of these young poets over a few years, and then into a book. I've seen a number of first books by Indian poets recently that really needed editing help.

JP: I've noticed that, too, lately. Even fairly well established presses are putting out things maybe too quickly, not carefully enough.

SA: And then the books, because they're bought, disappear, and it does a disservice to the writers. That's one of my problems with Wordcraft, it's rushing people into print before they're ready. And when you get a bad poem published, or a flat poem published, you don't learn anything. They've published bad poems of mine, and I've suffered for it. There are bad poems of mine in books.

JP: It becomes embarrassing later as well [laughter].

SA: "Oh my god, I wrote that? No, somebody slipped that in there when I wasn't looking."

JP: It's a strange business, isn't it? I'm glad that you're keeping at the poetry, some balance. So when's the movie coming out?

SA: We're doing distributor screenings over the next couple of weeks for Miramax, Sony, and all of that. All the big ones. If there's been an independent movie over the last five years, whoever's released it, they're coming. It's a good movie, comparable in level and quality to *The Full Monty*, the performances are amazing. These actors finally got a chance to play human beings rather than wind-o-bots. I think it's really going to go. I think we'll get an awakening here, and we'll get about a three-year window to make Indian films.

JP: The doors will open quickly. . . .

SA: And close quickly. What's going to happen is there will be a flood of Indian movies, most of them will be bad, they won't make money, and then the door will close again. We'll have the chance for a couple years here, I think.

JP: Just like we were talking about awhile ago, things get rushed into production instead of . . .

SA: What I'm hoping to get from this movie is so . . . We told the story but at the same time it is also very subversive, to take on "Indian cinema" and the images in the movies, about the Warrior, about storytelling, there's all sorts of little jokes along the way about the ways Indians get viewed in the movies, and in culture, as we're telling the road movie stories. I'm hoping it will kill, make it impossible for anybody to make this type of movie again. Like the way *Blazing Saddles* killed the western for twenty years.

JP: If it accomplishes just ten years, it'd be wonderful.

SA: Six months, three days, two hours. For dinner after they see the movie, if they can see Indians as nothing else but human beings, it'll be a success.

JP: We could boycott the whole thing, Hollywood. One day.

SA: One day. One day of no anti-Indian thoughts. Not going to happen. I can dream.

JP: So you have a something going on tonight?

SA: It's called Books for Prisoners. It's affiliated with Left Bank Books.

JP: Well, I hope you have fun.

So, for Alexie in the 1990s Native fiction writers all faced similar issues for publication: either to conform to those elements of literary "tradition" that had become conventional for the canon or to write another view of contemporary life that resists often romanticized and essentialist images. And thus a canon refines and redefines itself. In this sense there may not be as great an ideological distance between what he argues and what Vizenor argues.[1] Their narrative styles and subjects are remarkably dissimilar, but does this also mean that they do not want their works to mark them as "Native" (however they define the term), then reveal what that means, and reaffirm that sense in contemporary times and into the future? Should *all* texts in a canon be directed to a specific audience, the average twelve year old on the rez, and should all the criticism about the texts be driven by one imperative? One wonders.

GERALD VIZENOR: Revisiting *Darkness in Saint Louis Bearheart*

Given the attitudes about the state of Native literatures in contemporary times, the concerns about the future of this canon, and the ideas about criticism directed at the canon expressed in the previous interviews, I would like to revisit a novel from the 1970s using these ideas as well as those raised in the examinations of the early novels of the first two chapters.

I do so for a simple reason. As Alexie notes, a canon evolves when its practitioners "hammer" on one another. This hammering is called criticism, but, as I note in the introduction and elsewhere, as with any audience, critical reactions to texts are shaped by lenses. We all know this (although it was not commonly held to be true fifty years ago), but in the common discussion of this phenomenon, and in particular as it is directed into studies of Native literatures, the lens in question is defined in a Native/non-Native binary. In other words, the critical discourse, as it shaped itself in the 1990s, began to draw artificial battle lines between critical approaches to texts that had more to say about whose lens should be authoritative than about the real issue: how Native literary texts resist, deconstruct, and reconstruct authority.

As Alexie also notes, Native writers have a clearly layered sense of audience that also operates from the binary of Native/non-Native, but the critical discourse as it evolved over the years called for a revision of the critical sense of only one side of that binary. In other words, the criticism focused primarily on the way that non-Natives have read, read, or will read works by Indian writers and only peri-odically acknowledged that the reading repertoires of this audience evolved as society changed over these crucial decades. Rarely is it acknowledged that the Native readership and its reactions to texts have changed as well. In 1936 the readers of D'Arcy McNickle's first novel, *The Surrounded*, did not respond as the readers in 2006. In 2006 readers of Native descent responded to it very differently from those of 1936. The reasons are the result of all the historical events that intervened as well as the advent of all the writers who have ex-panded the canon. Times change. I would argue that the two previ-ously perceived audiences' readings will, at some point, converge in direct proportion to the canon's evolution, and that leaves us with the ultimate question. *Is* the canon evolving, or, as some critics/ writers discussed thus far contend, is it "on the brink of extinction," threatened either by a growing lack of interest in "Indian things" or by a gradual homogenizing process?

Critical reactions must accommodate this change in audiences over time and allow for an inclusive rather than exclusive discourse. As Paula Gunn Allen says earlier, it is not about a priestly class telling an audience how to interpret; critical discourse must allow the texts to provoke the right questions, and the more the better. Previously, in other times and circumstances, the critical canon required exclusivity for the simple reason of self-survival and self-determination; presently, exclusivity narrows the discourse as well as publication possibilities and audiences for Native writers. For over three decades Gerald Vizenor has been at work to bring more and more readers and critics into the discourse, teasing them, challenging them to question, and encouraging them to clean their lenses for a better view. This is my reason to revisit his first novel at this point.

In the spring of 2005 Gerald Vizenor graciously agreed to answer some questions posed by the students in one of my courses. They had read *Bearheart: The Heirship Chronicles* (the 1990 edition of *Darkness in Saint Louis Bearheart*) and were working their way through their own (oftentimes) confused and convoluted reactions to its story. It was an interesting exchange, and, as one would expect, it had its humorous, trickster moments, including the "answers" he gave them. Much like the title character in his movie *Harold of Orange*, who challenges another character to consider the sources of his own question by telling him "Your questions are my very answers" (79), Vizenor's responses challenged the students to translate, reflect, and (re)interpret.

One of the questions was this: "What elements of the novel do you feel have not received adequate critical attention?" His answer was brief and direct: "Pure Gumption and the other mongrels, and the brilliant, wounded women in the scapehouse at Cache Center."[2] I would like to return to this novel from the 1970s/1990s now to examine those characters through a lens that blends critical approaches, then and now: a melding of a New Critical eye for detail with Reader Response, with an ecocritical spin. Using Vizenor's personal responses to the students' questions as an opening to do so, I will provide some of my own reactions to them, with the hope that this will speak to a point of commonality in a text so different from its contemporaries in the 1970s, if not as much in the 1990s.

First, however, I would like to comment upon one of the valuations in that set of questions: "We [my students] perceive the novel to be prophetic." I agree with them, and I will come back to the nature of its prophetic qualities. For the moment, though, I would like to note that, unlike so many if not all of the novels produced in the 1970s by people deploying Indigenous content, Vizenor's/Bearheart's story of Fourth Proude is forward-looking: it imagines a postapocalyptic future and as such carries with it an inherent and profound cautionary message about the ultimate payoff of the values by which many people in the United States and elsewhere operate. In the old phraseology, what goes around comes around, politically, spiritually, and ecologically. I might add that this may be true for criticism as well. Despite the horrific setting, the novel valorizes Indigenous values and thus reaffirms them, even as they accommodate a "post-Indian" (Vizenor's term) reality. In what ways can this novel speak to us in this, a new millennium, and, given its postapocalyptic setting, can it still provide a sense of continuation thirty years after its original publication?

My students asked, "Was the idea for the novel derived from the events of the times during its conception and this sense of impending collapse, and/or does it reflect Native peoples' desire and ability to return to old ways of life?" Vizenor's response: "The energy crises of the '70s (and again this past year [and I will add currently]), the inevitable end of petroleum, and the story of a government that forever turns to native resources, were the obvious background metaphors and narrative sources of cultural tension in the novel. I considered empty interstate highways, and how gangs would declare sovereignty at every rest stop across the country." Given recent history in the Middle East, the congressional push to open Gwitch'in lands in the Arctic Wildlife Reserve for oil extraction, and myriad other events driven by short-sighted thinking (what Vizenor calls "terminal creeds," or values and ideas that are inherently self-limiting, restrictive, and destructive), the narrative becomes even more layered and richly prophetic and therefore even more frightening.

There are two other events from the decade of the original publication that I would like to recall. First is the NEH-funded institute in Flagstaff. One further effect of that event was a renewed push for the inclusion of Native American literatures in college and university curricula, hence the resistance of the National Association of Scholars. This event and the reinvigorated critical discourse, out of which came the issues that shaped the next three decades of criticism, also helped shape Vizenor's canon and the literary production of many writers. So in a way it makes sense that the novel was rereleased by the University of Minnesota Press in 1990; in other words, I believe it is also prophetic in the ways that it anticipates that discourse—the critical word wars and the culture wars, if you will—but also the issues of identity politics, new historicism, and of course postmodernism, to name just a few. I will add to that list "ecocriticism." After all, one other historical event of note in the 1970s that informs my reading of the book is the Boldt Decision, which acknowledged the treaty right of the Northwest tribes to one half of the salmon harvest, and in the first chapters federal agents claim one half of the timber on the reservation for the federal government. In Vizenor's canon the intersection of political and environmental issues informs historical events, and his first novel is no exception.

Furthermore, and this is not an event but a phenomenon: there was a television commercial in the 1970s that was so popular it became a case study in textbooks about advertising and pop culture: a lone Indian (Iron Eyes Cody), dressed as if he came from an age long distant, paddles his canoe ashore through the litter and flotsam of a material culture gone mad only to step on equally polluted land to secrete one lone tear. As a window into the culture of the time it provides a vision against which Vizenor's novel rebels in imagistic if not ideological terms. The imagined Indian materializes from the past to cry for modern consumer culture and thus acts as Nature's conscience (only to slip back into History, no doubt). Rather than perpetuate this recognizable image, Vizenor complicates it, and he does so in the novel with other types of consumers: crows and dogs, a differentiation of note. "How do you view bestiality?" Indeed.

Both crows and dogs are prominent in the book and, as others have noted, are primary actors in its drama. The dogs first appear in the chapter entitled "Migis Sandridge." This is the first chapter devoted to the narrative-within-a-narrative's "future-present," the story of Fourth Proude Cedarfair. The occasion is significant enough to mention. This chapter provides the transition between a history of the Cedarfair Circus and the pilgrimage Proude, Rosina, the crows, and the mongrels undertake. That pilgrimage is precipitated by the incursion of federal agents sent to evaluate the cedar trees as a source for firewood, and, as Vizenor's response to the students' question attests, it is "the story of a government that forever turns to native resources." However, Proude learns of this imminent intrusion from the seven "warning crows," who stir up the other birds in the circus and the dogs as well to convey the message to Proude, who, we are told, comes to understanding through their intervention: "Silence and languages of animals gave him power" (17).

Now, I do not want to run the risk of romanticizing this idea or essentializing the character (as Alexie and others have noted as a flaw in critical approaches) and therefore end up like Belladonna later in the novel, done in by her own terminal creeds and just desserts. This is, after all, a work of fiction, but it is one that at first seems to differentiate in ways that some non-Native authors, as Alexie also notes, often deploy. However, the eagle, bear, and so on as narrative devices in those works function in different ways and to different ends.

First, I want to call attention to the behavior of crows, fictional or otherwise. If one walks through a forest and comes upon crows, one notices very quickly that they call attention to themselves and that they do so through utterance and silence, through sound and gesture. Many animals do, dogs included. However, there *are* in fact differences in their languages, their sounds and gestures: a raven does not talk like a crow, nor does a crow talk like a dog, but we all share the same generalized ideas of communication, of utterance and gesture affecting others. This is the way it is, so that takes me to a question: What is the metaphoric potential of these fictional crows, and a sacred number of them at that?

As Proude tells Rosina in this chapter, the crows agitate the other animals, including humans (he and Rosina), and this is also part of their repertoire, so the lesson here is that we can either turn away from their agitation discourse, as Proude does at first, or do as he comes to do: listen, shift focus, look for sources, and thereby discover significance. This leads me to a hypothesis: one of the functions of the character crows is to interrogate the interrelationships between character species but also, in the terms of literature, the ways readers listen, or do not listen, to the language of others, and this is, fundamentally, an issue of values, of what or who the reader privileges. As scholars and students have noted time and time again, *Bearheart* is not a comfortable read; if it were, it would lack significance and fall squarely into the literary genre of the "traditions" Alexie finds so problematical. If one "hears" its sources, though, one is agitated to self-reflection and action; if one does not, one continues to walk through the forest and thereby miss an opportunity, perhaps to one's detriment. In this way the novel creates (and operates upon) a linguistic discomfort that leads to an aesthetic of agitation.

Moreover, oftentimes the agitated "utterances" of animals in the book carry ecological signification: a few pages later, the evil tribal chairman, Jordan Coward, who wishes to cut down the sacred cedars and destroy the Cedarfair Circus, comes to confront Proude, and all the crows defecate on him. This is a crow idiom full of signification.

However, in this scene the five dogs also participate in the drama: they "jumped against him [Coward] knocking him down," another significant gesture, indeed (24). The pack takes down its prey. As we learn much later, in the story of Lilith Mae and in it the story of the woman who loved a mongrel and gave birth to puppies, crows, mongrels, and humans have a long-standing relationship; it is the crows who turn pups into human form and teach them to dance and laugh. Such mythic transformations abound in the novel.

Mongrels, dogs, abound as well, so let's consider some linguistic basics. Consider the three-letter word itself: dog. The denotative meaning is pretty clear and widely accepted: a domesticated species that is often thought to derive from "wild" kin. And there it is; *Dances with Wolves* becomes "Dances with Dogs" (or, given the chronological order of production, vice versa). Dogs come in a variety of "breeds" and are thus of "pure lineage," as determined and documented by the American Kennel Club, the AKC, or of mixed lines and thus a "mongrel." Connotatively, the two words carry semantic differences: dog is generic, and when it is used in conversation, it is usually followed by the name of the breed. Mongrel, however, often carries a derogatory edge that also has a level of significance. Mongrel suggests a wanton disregard for the supposed sanctity of bloodlines and thus a sense of chance derived from sexual action that results in a contamination; in the case of the use of these terms in the novel, the word brings into sharp relief underlying value systems that privilege one animal over another, and, like race, this is a social construct.

Mongrel and breeding also question the idea that humankind has some innate right to alter its world and other species to fit its own agenda. Call it eugenics, genetic engineering, blood quantum, whatever. In this adheres a wide array of Western ideologies located under other terms like Judeo-Christian, capitalism, Puritanism, utilitarianism, and choose-your-ism. The word "bloodlines" itself opens up the convention of primogeniture. In many ways, then, the words "dog" and "mongrel" in the novel suggest that the AKC and the BIA are not that different. There is another element to this sense of purity and hybridity, and to illustrate it I want to tell a story.

Her name was Missy. When I was ten or eleven, my father got her from a Basque man who was on a crew that traveled about shearing sheep for those who raised them. She was a small puppy, a multicolored ball of fur. Brown, white, gray, with black spots, and by now many readers have probably narrowed down the possibilities of her lineage to two or three breeds. In this case, given the story of her coming to us, it may be surmised that she was, in fact, an Australian shepherd. However, the Basque man swore that she was half coyote, the result, it seems, of a lonely night and chance meeting on the prairies of eastern Oregon, where he herded sheep for the larger portion of the year. To put it bluntly, we did not believe him; there is a lot of folklore about this type of liaison out West, and besides, her appearance clearly spoke her breed.

Missy had all the features, including the looks and—in the terminology of the time—the instinct to herd. She herded sheep, she herded kids, she herded chickens, although she was a bust when it came to cats. She was a wonderful, kind, sensitive pet and a good friend. However, as she aged the obvious changes came, and at one point she was pregnant through the guile of a neighbor's mongrel. Things changed. She turned aggressive and late in her pregnancy burrowed under the roots of a pear tree, creating a den, a trait not noted in purebred dogs but certainly in coyotes. No one went near her, for she let us know she would attack. This changed character was not the result of "conflicting instincts," as in the discourse of the time; it was the result of her ability to draw upon behavioral resources to fulfill her needs of the moment. She had more than one language from which she drew, and both worked. She was a mongrel and adapted to changing circumstances quite effectively.

Once again, in the critical discourse about dogs we find a resonance with that attached to the sign "Indian," historically and in literary production. Domesticated is equated with serving the goals of the master, and in this camp we have Chingackook, Quequeg, Tonto. Wild (savage, etc.) means that one is an obstacle to those goals, and thus we have Magua, Crazy Horse, Gerald Vizenor.

In *Bearheart* Vizenor oscillates between the words "dog" and "mongrel," sometimes using both of them within the same paragraph. While this certainly avoids monotonous repetition, the continuous shifting also foregrounds the ways words shape our perception of "the other" and the fact that we often find meaning not in the sign itself but in the silence/space between it and its socially constructed binary. For readers, this is where real negotiations take place. It is, I believe, an element of the "rhetoric of gaps" Kim Blaeser uses in her book, *Gerald Vizenor: Writing in the Oral Tradition*, and it is a co-opting of word wars and word wards that blurs lines, including those constructed between animal and human. The concepts of dog and mongrel apply to the human pilgrims in the novel as much as the four-legged ones.

As Vizenor phrased it in one response to my students' question:

Mixed-bloods, cross-bloods, are the real natives, as the fuller poses are versions of irony. These racial contradictions, degrees of blood by an arithmetic measure of identity, are brutally stupid, and yet these racial notions prevail in many references to natives.

The characters in my stories forever contravene racial categories. Only the separatists play to racial purity and privilege, and that has been the dreadful human condition in the modern world, any world, anytime! There is no other source of native consciousness than cross-bloods, and that naturally is the heart of this bear story. Everyone, everywhere is a cross-blood.

And there one finds a central message to the stories in the novel.

There is one further consideration for this discussion. Inbred "instinct" limits agency in the dog: a terminal creed of the breed. From a limited, external point of view, the breed does something ingrained that seemingly brings it pleasure: herding sheep, fetching a ball, killing a neighbor's child. However, consider the implications. The animal moves and responds in ways determined by its "blood," its engineered nature. Ironically, in this way it resembles many of the monsters that inhabit the stories of Indigenous cultures that also act in predictable ways; oftentimes, these automatic responses to certain stimuli actually doom the monster, if the hero of the story is clever enough to understand these limits of thinking and power and thereby anticipate the monster's reactions, turning them against it.

The mongrel, however, is liberated in that the strength of "the instinct" is diminished and others have appeared in the mix, and this is a *positive* element of its character, as is the number of instincts (i.e., "breeds") it may draw from: it can retrieve a skill/behavior when necessary but set it aside as well. As with Missy, it allowed for alternatives and options to fit the situation. In her case her changed behavior and therefore her language saved her puppies from the fate of most unwanted litters on the farm; instead, they were sought after by neighbors who recognized the benefits of hiring an adaptive survivor who could protect their flocks. In the terms of the novel not only do the mongrels have agency, they *are* agents. The word accrues the status of an objective correlative, but, given its implications, I would suggest it is more a "subjective correlative" that opens up the social constructions of blood for readers.

And this makes a certain autobiographical sense as well. Before I read it in print, I had the pleasure of hearing Vizenor's story about

Lucky, the mongrel he befriended in Japan who agitated him to action and thus saved him from being killed by a tree falling on his tent (see Vizenor's autobiography, *Interior Landscapes*). There are other dogs as well—Chico and Bull—whose characters no doubt helped shape the mongrel characters who have a special place in his canon because they are smart and resourceful; they encounter each situation as an opportunity, as a chance, much like tricksters but without the guile and certainly without the usual Coyote consequences.

The mongrel pack in the novel adds a member with the first stop on their pilgrimage at the scapehouse on Callus Road, where Pure Gumption joins their ranks. (Although it is unnecessary for this discussion, it is interesting to note the potential of seeing this place as a reference to the pub the Scapehouse Inn on Scapegoat Hill in Huddersfield, England.) For the moment, I will simply note the obvious language play on both "scape," as in "scapegoat," and the sound's evocation of "escape" as well as "scape" with its visionary implications. The language play continues throughout this section with the description of the people who inhabit this precursor of Biosphere II, for the scapehouse presents an ecosystem wherein, as Proude notes, "the outside is inside" (36). Here, the plants and animals are born and die under the care of the women poets, the "weirds and sensitives," as they are called, and, as with "dog" and "mongrel," these are loaded terms.

Sensitives are perceptive individuals with heightened awareness, often—as the term suggests—through heightened senses, and the description of the scapehouse and the actions within it are highly embedded with sensual detail. From the smells of soil, baking bread, and perfumes, to a catalog of the various calls of the animals, to the scene where Rosina touches the welts on Sister Willabelle's scarred body, the senses guide the telling of these women's stories. In brief, this sensuality complements their wounds, and together they generate the women's "brilliance," their uniqueness, such as Willabelle, whose body fed the insects, worms, and fish of the jungle as she struggled to survive. Each woman's unique skill/character is not the result of breeding but of experiential knowledge. And, as a result of their various wounds and skills, they have banded together to provide and perpetuate a secure location within which they share all things (no pun intended) in a sustainable environment. This communalism is the centerpiece of the concept of "tribal" and acts as a measure by which the other neotribes along the pilgrim's route are judged. For example, consider the enclave of the "Gay Minikins," so narrow and terminal in its creed compared to the scapehouse. Thus, the scapehouse as literary device provides the obvious: that such interdependency, tempered with a willing acceptance of new members (pun intended) and thus an "intermixing," is at the very core of an ecosystem and its survival, a fundamental truth of ecological discourse. This interdependency is the foundation of these women's society, and it is the antithesis of personal obsession, which drives the vast majority of the characters in the novel, often to their doom.

However, the women are also termed "weirds," thus evoking the Fates of classical mythology as well as, through Old and Middle English *wyrd* and *werde*, the possibility of controlling the outcome of events. The Fates, alluded to in the discussion of Erdrich's *Tracks*, were the daughters of Themis and thus necessity, much like the scapehouse women, who form a society out of necessity. The connection to Greek mythology is strengthened by characters such as Sister Dimetria, who was the goddess of the harvest, but then extended by Sister Caprice, the butcher, who fulfills a function similar to Atropos by ending lives at the proper time but whose name suggests a whimsical decision-making process rather than the fulfillment of a predetermined destiny (Pauline Puyat's antecedent). In brief, these characters represent a system constructed out of "Western Civilization" and its historical trajectory, but one that seeks to reclaim the fundamental interconnectedness of life forms, the basis of Indigenous myth, including those of the West prior to the intervention of Christianity. Bestiality, indeed.

The one point of complication and contention, the cultural tension Vizenor notes in his response to the students' question, comes during the evening meal, when Proude refuses to eat the "stuffed kitten" because it has not been "praised." The dialog, then, unpacks the shades of meaning in the terms "to celebrate," "to exalt," and so on.

In essence, the dialog suggests that if we acknowledge our colleagues in the ecosphere for our fundamental interconnectedness and the function we each fulfill within it, we have shifted from the terminal traditions of Western history and into a fundamental discourse with our environment. However, as with any human discourse, this risks a movement to overgeneralize, and this is the tendency Proude resists. Meat is not always meat, and his resistance takes us toward a behavior that is no longer terminal in the universal and abstract but one that is localized and personal in its acknowledgment of "the other."

This proffered discourse is tied throughout the novel to the mongrels, who interact with their environment without the baggage carried by other pilgrims. This is to suggest that they operate as agents of meaning in the novel and in most cases of ethics. Of them all, there is one dog who exemplifies this trait. To help the pilgrims on their way, Sister Eternal Flame hands them Pure Gumption, the glowing dog with a blue aura, a sensitive healer. As her name signifies, she is courage incarnate. When she is agitated to action, she exemplifies the "gumption," the boldness, that comes from pure interests, and the results are curative in effect.

Briefly, I will note that it is she who is excluded from the final gambling game with Sir Cecil Staples, the Evil Gambler; it is she and Private Jones who reunite the spirits of the murdered children with their bones and with their parents and then rebury the bones and defend them from desecration by Bigfoot; it is she who completes the pilgrimage; and, most significantly, it is she who draws the deformed, wounded hordes to her healing power.

These hordes are significant for the purposes of this discussion because these are the characters who provide the prophetic ecological character to the horrific landscape Vizenor describes. These characters are much like Sister Jacinth in the scapehouse, who is dying of cancer caused by the preservatives in the cold meats she ate as a student. They are all deformed and dying from a culture based upon a capitalist model that extracts resources, engineers them for profit, and thus generates its own demise. This is the "flute end of consequences," the completely logical, predictable end that we all wish to ignore.³ Avoidance is "scapism," but the narrative in *Bear-heart* will not allow us to do so because it agitates us into awareness. Futuristic novels are often just that, an escape from reality, but Vizenor's is the antithesis of this convention: marked from the open pages as fiction, stylistically calling attention to the fact as surely as any crow in any forest, it resonates with the concept uttered by Chief Broom in Kesey's *One Flew over the Cuckoo's Nest*: "It's true, even if it never happened." But the ecological apocalypse the novel presents *is* happening.

Ironically (perhaps), as I was completing the first draft of this section of the book, I stopped and took a break for lunch. My mail arrived, so I opened it while I ate. In the mail was a flier from a local bookstore with notice of a reading by James Howard Kunstler. The subject of his talk is his book *The Long Emergency* from Atlantic Monthly Press, Alexie's publisher. The subject of the book, the blurb tells us, is the demise of the fossil-fuel age, and, it seems, with this impending crash "our models of global industry, trade, food produc-tion and transportation are unlikely to survive. . . . Globalism will wither and life will become profoundly and intensely local." Given the subject of this chapter, one may say that Kunstler's "revelation" is old news, thirty years old, to be exact. For those who listen to the crows and mongrels in Vizenor's novel, Kunstler's observations are redundant. These readers are already watching for weird sensi-tive women and mongrels of many colors. For those who have not listened—for whatever reason—and whose actions are thus directed by generations of Western breeding and thought, one must suggest that they should now turn to the road maps of the nations to select the rest stop of their future before they are all taken.

Although the novel, as a novel, makes use of animal and Native characters that might be seen as conventions of popular literature about Native cultures, the mongrels and bears operate more as they do in spoken literatures of those cultures: they are imaginative imi-tations. Vizenor further undermines the convention in two ways: through the use of "mongrel" instead of its wild kin and in the frame for the novel itself—the novel-within-a novel as told by Bearheart. These subversions of the conventions further strengthen its conformity to DIAC. Apocalyptic as it may be, there is no doubt that its moral center is of value—for Native and non-Native alike—and that it will endure despite the threats of modern technologies and ideologies.

Bearheart is hardly an overtly humorous novel by any stretch of the imagination, dealing as it does with postapocalyptic horrors, and in this it is very different from Vizenor's later works, which deploy humor and irony throughout. As Vizenor tells us, the genre of comedy resists the attempts to make tragic victims the central trope of the canon, so it is small wonder that humor became by the 1990s an enhanced element of the written canon. So let's consider the ways that circumstances provided a new spur to the directions of that canon in the 1990s: the increased use of humor as a narrative device, the increased use of film as a medium of choice, and the ongoing discourse about what Native literature is and does. To do this let's begin with another novel, from 1993, modifying the personalized reader response above by looking at the origins of those responses for the reading audience from the 1970s into the 1990s.

THOMAS KING: *Green Grass, Running Water*

It is a sad statement of marketing fact, but for every individual who sits down to read a work of written literature by a Native American, many, many more sit down to watch movies or television programs in which Native characters, issues, and/or beliefs—real or, more often than not, imagined—play a role. So where and how do people form impressions about cultural issues and each other? As critics have pointed out for decades, the visual media often fail to provide accurate images of Native peoples, the history of North America, current resistance movements . . . fill in the blank.

In a recent article I argue that the 1950s were the crucial years in the development of contemporary Native American literatures not because of significant Indian texts that were produced in that decade but because the contemporary audience for them was shaped at that curiously complex moment of time (see my "The Babyboom Generation"). In brief, I discuss the baby boom generation and Walt Disney's rise to power through his manipulation of my generation's imagination. In fact, in this context I believe his continual use of the word "make-believe" ironically conveys the agenda he had—to make believers by manufacturing make-believers—and his ideological descendants in the entertainment industry have not lost his touch. The question that concerns me, though, is, how does one fruitfully engage a deeply inscribed, invisible, make-believe interpretative mechanism that does not provide a productive understanding of current or historical events and people? Particularly one that may have springs of self-interest and gears of gratification as its clockwork and has as its focus Native peoples?

Humor is one strategy employed by some Native fiction writers to counter nonproductive understandings, and, like any other methodology, it has many degrees, shades, and effects that, I believe, demonstrate one further element of differentiation as well as a methodology of resistance. Thomas King (Cherokee) is one such practitioner, and he, too, is a boomer. As he says in an interview with Jeffrey Canton:

> If you write humorous material, or if you write comedy, the great danger is that they [the audience] will not take you seriously. I think of myself as a dead serious writer. Comedy is simply my strategy. I don't want to whack somebody over the head, because I don't think that accomplishes much.
>
> There's a fine line to comedy. You have to be funny enough to get them laughing so they really don't feel how hard you hit them. And the best kind of comedy is where you start off by laughing and end up crying, because you realize just what is happening halfway through the emotion. If I can accomplish that, then I succeed as a storyteller. (6)

It is an intriguing insight into the psychology of revelation, a strategy of surprise; in other words, King suggests an active audience participation in its own deconstruction that, as I argue in that article, is absolutely necessary to make visible, destabilize, and possibly reprogram that interpretative clockwork.

One of the prominent targets of his humor in *Green Grass, Run-*

ning Water is, in fact, the medium of choice by so many baby boomers and thus subsequent generations of audiences: the visual media of television and movies. Of course, Hollywood—both the ideological and the mythological entity—is an easy target. It has been critiqued, condemned, and lampooned ad nauseum since its first rise to power in the popular culture of America in the twentieth century, but nonetheless it continues to operate as customary, providing audiences with assuring, comforting tradition, the presold value of its resurrected movies and plots documented with dollars. In fact, practically concurrent with the publication of King's novel, Disney Enterprises released an animated remake of the Pocahontas and John Smith myth, thus extending that tradition into the next generation. King's approach is therefore timely; however, as his ideas about humor as pedagogy suggest, his critique is much more complex than a simple lampooning of the medium and its penchant for misrepresentations.

Instead, King exposes the fundamental nature of its power on the human psyche, operating from the ur-assumption that the world is determined by story, including the narratives we construct about ourselves or others construct about us.[4] But whose stories tell us who we are today? In the novel the origin stories of Christianity are interwoven with those of Indigenous North American traditions, the latter forming the overt differentiation of the novel, made initially prominent by chapter openings in Cherokee. Moreover, the stories Hollywood has, over the decades, turned into a visual literary tradition are embedded in the fictional life stories of characters that frame the narrative. King thus "grafts" literary traditions, including filmic traditions, at several levels, all of which are connected through humor.[5] As we laugh at his revised reenactments of popular narratives, though, we come to recognize the apparatus through which some institutions, such as Hollywood, have insinuated themselves into all our lives. We have met the apparatus, and it is us. Like Changing Woman, Old Woman, Thought Woman, and others, we fall through King's trapdoors (in Alexie's term) into a new world where our internalized—often comforting in their self-serving nature—mythologies are revealed and, hopefully, left behind. Surprise.

But first, let's consider food. One of the humorous stories woven into the novel that is never foregrounded to any degree is the story of Lionel's parents, Harley and, interestingly, Camelot. The name Camelot, of course, opens up a number of potentially interesting mythical stories, ones that particularly resonate for a boomer reader: the Arthurian legends of England and the dynasty of President John Kennedy. Both were eras of illusory comfort, security, and potential, and both of these power narratives are hero centered and driven.[6] However, this happily married couple is on stage very little, and their one identifying characteristic, apart from their family affiliations, is that Harley seems to be trying to get Camelot to expand her cooking horizons. In our first encounter he has given her a book of Italian dishes, later it is Hawaiian; more than an attempt at sophisticated cuisine, it is gastronomic globalization. The couple inhabits a space somewhere between Jack and Jackie, Desi and Lucy (from the popular television show *I Love Lucy*), but the activity that is continuously connected to Camelot is, I believe, the central defining metaphor for King's novelistic humor and perhaps his idea of contemporary times for Native nations. Although Camelot follows the recipes, she always substitutes local ingredients for "the other," the foreign, the exotic. Moose meat replaces octopus and so on. In other words, this is what King does as well: he adopts the recipes—and here I would like to substitute a term more specifically aligned with my discussion, scripts—but puts a decidedly personalized, humored flavor into them. What emerges is a hybrid narrative that encompasses all others in its stew, grafting new ingredients to old processes.

King's scripts for the novel come from several sources: as mentioned earlier, there are the mythologies of Christian and Native peoples and of Hollywood, but he also co-opts the personal stories of historical characters that have been rendered in written texts—for instance, captivity narratives as diverse as Mary Rowlandson and the Native prisoners of war captured and taken to Fort Marion. Moreover, he weaves the concept of grafting scripts into all levels of the novel; an obvious example is the idea of "Christian rules" that continuously creeps into the narratives in which a female creator of Native tradition meets a male character from the Bible. Here, "rules" are the fundamental plot elements and embedded values of Christian narrative and thus King's audience's orientation. They are scripted to reflect the patriarchal and self-serving ends for the biblical character (Noah wants a submissive woman with large breasts), but the rules are easily deflected by the female's lack of concern for someone else's story—the script that tells actors how to behave and speak—of how the world should work. At one point, in fact, the female character is captured by soldiers and taken to Fort Marion due to this lack of concern for the rules of her assigned role. Her deviation from the egocentric script, in other words, calls attention to her, marking her "otherness." To escape she simply dons the mask of the Lone Ranger, thus momentarily appropriating a popular story from her captors' canon. Once she conforms to the outer forms of the script, she has easily and successfully manipulated their orientation, and she walks away their hero.[7]

King's tease is effective: the scripts we have learned from narrative sources—popular literature, film, television, history, mythology— have shaped our interpretative mechanisms, the images and their evocative emotions and attitudes that are brought to bear as we interact with stories and through which we make meaning. And he makes little distinction between "sacred" scripts and "profane" ones in the ways that human perception is referential to learned narrative potentialities and the repeated reinforcement of our ability to make those potentialities "work out" through aligning ourselves with the plots and resolutions that are rigidly "ruled."

This is, of course, nothing new. Oftentimes, though, in critical studies, novels, movies, and so on that call attention to it, it is engaged in an oppositional binary as limiting and terminal in potential as the original: you either maintain your original misconceptions or throw them all out. Either-or. I believe that this is in part what "whack somebody over the head" means. In other words, King's critique does not condemn film per se, nor does it approach filmic misrepresentations as a documentary would, and it is thus more evocative, provocative, proactive. Much like the conference in Salt Lake City where Lionel is to read a prepared speech only to have this easy script derailed by an American Indian Movement (AIM) demonstration, the direct confrontation can carry its own set of uncontrollable and counterproductive plots. King is, indeed, a successful storyteller, hitting the audience with issues wrapped in humor.

One aspect of King's investigation of contemporary life and culture reveals this idea. The Hollywood images and mythological narratives are as compelling for Blackfoot characters as for non-Natives. As the character Babo comments several times: "Now, isn't that the trick." Yes, it is. To confront a popular tradition so insinuated into society's value systems as to be invisible, and to do so with your own, one that cuts across class, culture, gender, and then to rewrite the fundamental fantasy of social identity by which all others are assessed, now that is quite a trick.

Lionel's character is determined by his early inspiration, the one hero he would like to replicate: Marion Michael Morrison, aka John Wayne. Even his childhood friend turned nemesis, Charlie, uses this hero as a measure of Lionel's failure, continually asking their mutual love interest, Alberta, "nothing personal, but you're not sleeping with John Wayne, are you?" (44). By the end of the novel-movie, when Lionel returns John Wayne's bullet-riddled jacket to the four old Indians, he enacts the revision of his identity that he has effected through his experiences, through which he recognizes the fantasies Hollywood has created for/in him, and thereby those he has created himself. It is, indeed, his birthday.

But I'm getting ahead of the story. I must emphasize that it seems that King is operating on more than a level of critique, that he is in fact attempting something in this multilayered narrative that is a blend, a grafting of film and written fiction that has serious implications. Let me illustrate this with a discussion of a simple technique and then one that is even more complex and intriguing.

One of the difficulties with such a sprawling and disjointed, such a postmodern, story is that audiences are easily lost trying to fit the pieces of the plots together in some controllable pattern. This is particularly true early in the script, as the audience learns the cast of characters and their relationships with one another. This same difficulty is inherent to the visual medium of film, particularly those that interweave several plotlines or employ flashbacks, and so on, where crucial editing decisions are often determined by the need to provide visual cues. For instance, in the case of quick cuts that can take our attention across geography and time literally in the blinking of an eye, how do we reorient? Through it all there is a need for continuity, for some sense of interrelatedness between scenes. In the novel this is accomplished quite subtly. Consider King's section shifts—much like cuts—where we reorient to the story being told through the usual, obvious visual cues, such as characters' names or the storyteller or the dialog of events that are referential to previous events in the story. This works well enough as long as the shift is to another point in the story being "left," but this is rarely the case. More often than not there is a dramatic displacement from one story to another as we cross the white space—perhaps an ironic phrase—in between. However, King provides some interesting continuity in less than obvious ways that carry subtexts with them. In this way King's narrative operates much like "intercutting": the joining of two (or more) film sequences or plot strands through parallel editing.[8]

For example, at one point the quintessential baby boomer, Bill Bursum, is in his appliance store watching The Map, a huge display of televisions organized to resemble a map of North America. Tellingly, the store is in Alberta, Canada, and therefore the display is a fit symbol of the pervasive, orienting, global influence of Hollywood, and what he watches is a central symbol for the novel: his favorite movie, *The Mysterious Warrior*.[9]

> The best Western of them all. John Wayne, Richard Widmark, Maureen O'Hara. All the biggies. He had seen the movie twenty times, knew the plot by heart. Even knew some of the lines.
>
> "Yes!" Bursum whispered as the movie opened with a shot across Monument Valley, and he clutched his hands in his lap as if he was praying. (211)

This is followed by a section break, and we are to the Blackfoot characters' story, with Latisha, Lionel's sister, returning from work to find her young son Christian fixing dinner as his siblings anxiously wait. "'Ssh!' Benjamin whispered, his hands clutched in his lap. 'If you talk too loud the food will burn'" (211).

The scene shift works on several levels, including the "visual" as we move our eyes down the page and make the leap to construct and then make referential the actors' body movements—the hands clutched in their laps—that link the two dramas they watch unfold, one a movie, one a cooking session, each of which requires quiet concentration and participation.[10] The overt connection between Bursum's devotional act and Benjamin's speaks to the fact that in one scene the script is known, the outcome certain, and in the other it isn't. Concurrent with this is Benjamin's sense of agency, that what one does can affect the working out of the script: indeterminacy with a gastric immediacy. For Bursum, of course, the script is locked and will, viewing after viewing, continue to chronicle the colonial sense of agency, of history fantasized.

This may seem a tentative reading of the scene. However, let's consider the movie Bursum watches, the epitome in the novel of Hollywood's fantasies that are so compelling for all people. Obviously, *The Mysterious Warrior* is a John Ford production; Monument Valley was his location of choice, particularly for the movies of his protégé, John Wayne. This is where Ford shot the western "classics": *Stagecoach* and *The Searchers*, to name only two. In all, of course, Ford invented Indians for the scripts: Navajos playing Comanches, tribal affiliations of no consequence as long as the stand-ins could demonstrate the professional skills necessary to evoke the stereotype: "how to mount a horse without a saddle, how to ride bareback using just the mane and your hands, how to drop to the side of the horse so you couldn't be seen. How to fall off" (202). This is the milieu of Charlie's father, Portland, whose career is made in Hollywood playing such supporting (and here I am indeed punning) roles. However, although a Blackfoot, he does not fit the visual representation the audience has come to recognize, so he is made to wear a fake nose. Thus King lampoons the behind-the-scenes, absurd surrealism that exists within the power of the fantasy manufactured.[11] The Native acts as a stand-in for the imagined, the scripted, the Invented Indian.

In Bursum's folded hands and exultation "Yes!" however, there is a seed of the sacred; here, the Bible's stories are reverberated, prayed to, reinscribed arbitrarily onto an invented western landscape and peoples. Lands and peoples are of no consequence. They are merely resources to be moved about and reconfigured to fit the script, the rules that ensure the ascendancy of Western civilization and the inevitability of the plot called Manifest Destiny.

Each of the characters, though, at some point or points in their stories is caught by the same movie, a very similar moment of quiet regard. Alberta, Charlie, and Lionel find it on their televisions as they converge on the off-reservation town of Blossom. The movie is ubiquitous and thus provides a thread of continuity for weaving these stories together while carrying the subtexts of King's investigation of Hollywood's influence on the psyche and thus the identity of individuals. It becomes the objective correlative of Hollywood's rendition of history. Of course, this makes his revision of it even more poignant later.

There is one important character, though, who does not see the movie: Eli, Lionel's uncle. Eli has spent his whole adult life away from the reserve. He is a retired literature professor who has lived in Toronto, married to a white woman who is more interested in his ethnicity and maintaining ties with his family than he is. It is she who convinces him to visit the Sun Dance one summer, but she is unable to do so again. After years of marriage she contracts an illness somewhat like leukemia but dies, with it in remission, in a tragic car accident. Retired from his position, Eli returns home to the cabin his mother built with her own hands that sits right in the way of a hydroelectric project. He battles the project in court and wins an injunction that effectively blocks the company from opening the floodgates to generate electricity and thereby flood his home. Each morning his nemesis, Sifton, comes from the dam to read a scripted legal plea for Eli to move, and each morning the dramatic event, the plot, ends the same way, with Eli saying "No." Like Bursum's movie, the action is predictable. Each of them knows how this drama plays out, and each knows his lines by heart: one an affirmation of "progress" in the John Ford tradition, the other its negation. This Indian refuses to fall off his horse.

However, there is a grudging amiability about the daily scene as well. Sifton often brings Eli books, castoffs from his brother's bookstore. One morning as he sorts through them Eli selects a western, *The Mysterious Warrior*, which, as the cover announces, is "based upon the award-winning movie" (178). In essence, so is *Green Grass, Running Water*. Moreover, King reverses the usual process, whereby popular novels become the basis of movies; the medium, in other words, is inconsequential, for the genre of romance-fantasy works in both. Here, the western is much like the Vietnam War movie-book, *The Deer Hunter*. Like it, *The Mysterious Warrior* is a war romance story that is set in a cross-cultural, colonial paradigm; like it, the lovers can never find a satisfying relationship with one another, thanks to the war that shatters the comfort of their arbitrarily constructed identities and thus the freedom to reconstruct them. The parallels are interesting.

In the "real world" of Eli's life he has lived a cross-cultural romance as well: Indian man, white woman, just as in the novel he reads. However, it works. To extend the fantasy, though, she is even a rich, white woman whose parents accept Eli with none of the racial discrimination and tension expected in the genre. (*Guess Who's Coming to Dinner?*) His life-script, in other words, reads in stark contrast to the fantasy of the popular romance. Even his wife's death, a predictable plot device in the genre, does not fit the recipe: she passes on after a long relationship and at a time when the future looks promising. That's how life works, despite the ways it has been represented in film and fiction, particularly in the convention of racially constructed romance. Moreover, even Eli's death in the battle against the forces of colonialism, also a predictable plot device in the tradition, is rescripted; he dies after a successful career within that colonial society, but his death also marks the death of the dam. These subtle revisions of the familiar plots of filmic fantasy with the lives of his fictional characters through intercutting is also a subtle way of revising the stories that have formulated audiences' interpretative mechanism, much like a recent psychological study in which patients haunted by nightmares were relieved of them through "imagery rehearsal." In this therapy they evoke the nightmare's script and revise it when awake.

And revise them King does. The most comical instance of this (and perhaps the most provocative, since the technology exists to make this a possibility) is when the four old Indians revise Bursum's movie as several people watch. These Native characters are of indeterminate tribal affiliation, gender, and age; in other words, their ethnic identity is not made significant other than by the sign "Indian." In still other words, they are The Mysterious Healers, and in that is their identification. From Dr. Joe Hovaugh's logs we know that they have escaped his institution thirty-seven times over their long stay to fix the world, a process that is obviously a complex and difficult one. As they tell us, it requires that one "fix" small things that will then have a profound ripple effect upon larger patterns, a reverberation of chaos theory turned into socioacupuncture, in Vizenor's term. As Joe Hovaugh reminds us, though, each time they fix something a "natural" catastrophe is a side effect: erupting volcanoes, forest fires, and so on.

Their names are relevant: Hawkeye, the Lone Ranger, Ishmael, and Robinson Crusoe. The missionary tradition of renaming is humorously subverted here with the appropriation of fictional heroes who all had an Indigenous "sidekick."[12] The "small" things one fixes, in other words, can often be the internalized mythologies emerging from popular stories and the ways we orient to and thus identify with their characters. In the case of the movie, though, fixing merely requires a simple editing cut.

On Lionel's fortieth birthday most of the male cast of characters converges in front of The Map in Bill Bursum's appliance store. The movie shown on all those myriad screens is, of course, *The Mysterious Warrior*. The script has reached its climax, one of violent confrontation as a means of plot resolution, as befits the western-romance genre. The scene is set on a river, where John Wayne, Richard Widmark, and the surviving soldiers of their command are barricaded behind driftwood logs awaiting an attack by a much larger force of Indians. This is the quintessential Hollywood scene, and it deserves a moment of careful scrutiny, because for each of the characters in King's novel it has an inherent attraction, despite some of their attempts to dismiss it as fantasy. That is fantasy's power: it whispers to the psyche in very personal terms of self-empowerment.[13]

The scene is much like the one found in the Hopi filmmaker, Victor Masayesva's, wonderful film *Imagining Indians*, which, interestingly enough, was released the same year as *Green Grass, Running Water*. I will look at the movie in detail below as a point of filmic comparison with King's text, but for the moment there are a few things that are relevant to this scene in the book.

In Masayesva's film he interviews a member of the Northern Cheyenne who played in the scene of a Cecil B. DeMille movie (I believe it was *Cheyenne River*) in which Gary Cooper and his troop are barricaded on a riverbank waiting for the attack. It is identical to the one King describes, including the fringed jacket Cooper wears. In the interview it is revealed that the director asked the Natives assembled for someone to play the chief in the attack, and one venerable old man stepped forward, saying that, since he was a chief in reality, he should stand in for the role. As a result he led the charge right down the streambed.

What he didn't know at the time was that the film crew had rigged a trip wire under the water so that when Cooper and his troops "opened fire" the horses of the Cheyenne out in front would be tripped, thus simulating a "realistic" image of Indians dying in a volley of gunfire, falling off their horses. This piece of information, I believe, helps focus the scene in King's novel, for it demonstrates the wide gap between lived reality and fantasy. The disrespect shown the elder and the others speaks volumes. But the scene also enfolds the myths that have become internalized by almost all the characters who watch the movie in Bursum's store. The Invented Indians' frontal assault is illogical, so they stand in opposition to rationality. Logic and technology will win; Indians will lose. Firepower and stars will prevail. Hollywood chiefs always get soaked.

The four old Indians are the obvious flies in the ointment of such reasoning. The reader already knows that they had tried to "fix" the film before and failed: in their room at the motel they, too, see the movie as the others watch the night before but with different reactions: "'Isn't this the one we fixed?' said Hawkeye. . . . 'Oh, oh,' said the Lone Ranger. 'Looks like we got to fix this one again'" (247). When they "fix" it, they reveal the methodology, mythology, and psychology of the fantasy the audience expects. We laugh as King hits us.

Consider the dramatic moment for Wayne and company. First, the heroes of Manifest Destiny, who are here equated with the forces of modernity in opposition to those of "primitivism," are surrounded and outnumbered. The future is in question. Who will survive? Whose culture will prevail? Of course, the film was made after the future of Manifest Destiny had become history, so an audience is curiously situated at an easy distance from contemporary issues of that history. Much like the more recent romance-war fantasy, *Dances with Wolves*, the dissociation from the past, which is perceived as remote and unchangeable, allows a comfortable voyeurism. It is a "guilty pleasure," literally, much like Eli's, the literature professor who sneaks in the reading of the romance novel. (To his credit as a character and in defense of literature professors everywhere, though, he fast-forwards, that is, flips through, most of it.) The popular romantic genre in both film and fiction is easily evoked for King's reader, but King withholds the gratification that comes from watching the script work out as one has imagined and expects (its "logical" resolution), implicating the audience in the process. We like scripts like this, yet we are also attracted to surprising plot twists and turns, which are not usually the convention in the western romance.[14]

In a word, in this genre the plot is predictable, and therefore it requires no conscious effort on the part of the audience. We relax our critical processes, since the genre is devalued and thus not worthy of critical analysis, and watch the script unfold. This sense of inevitability and passivity is at the heart of the internalized mythology. Here, one does not require an interpretative, only an emotive mechanism. This is the subliminal message that has to be reinscribed if one hopes to "fix" the film. But how does one accomplish this? Can one deploy a version of Vizenor's aesthetic of agitation?

The old Indians, who sing a new script into being as Bill Bursum watches horrified, simply remove one element in it, an element that had become so ubiquitous in midcentury westerns as to become cliché: the cavalry riding to the rescue. As the old Indians sing, the soldiers simply disappear. On one level this reediting calls attention to the obvious fact, sublimated by the convention of the motif, that it is a very contrived and unrealistic ending: literally a deus ex machina. The hand of John Ford has reached down to resolve the conflict against all logic, against all odds. The sudden reversal—of victory snatched from the jaws of defeat, and one cannot help but lapse into cliché to describe it—is to be an uplifting experience, as it has been for Bursum but also is for Coyote, when both shout "Hooray" as they are swept up into the emotion of the moment with the blast of the trumpet sounding the rescue. The desire for a "happy ending" is shown to be universal but, more often than not, unidirectional and unrealistic. The reality one lives is never quite the same as the imagined narrative we help construct.

Of course, once that trumpet and the man blowing it disappear, one realizes that it was all a fantasy anyway, sleight of hand, images on celluloid, make-believe words in a script that was manipulated by the imagination of a writer and a director. "Now, isn't that the trick." Indeed. Once the illogical enforcement of power is removed, the script works out naturally: Wayne and all his men are killed. The Little Bighorn revisited. For the fictional characters, this is revelatory. Bursum, of course, once his fundamental mythology has been destabilized, is disoriented. When his assistant wonders if the "glitch" (i.e., the virus) has infected all their westerns, Bursum responds in the only way possible in the face of such a possibility: denial. He escapes to his other fantasy, also to be destroyed in his near future, his lakefront property with its imaginary house.

For the others, though, particularly the next generation embodied in Lionel and Charlie, the "new ending" is cathartic. For Lionel, the old hero dies. He has been given Wayne's hol(e)y jacket, which, he comes to find, is much too constrictive; it does not "fit" him. He has to imagine new heroes closer to home: his uncle Eli. And for Charlie, who watches the Indian leading the charge closely, it enables a reconnection with his father, whose role is reinscribed from victim to hero:

> Portland turned and looked at Wayne and Widmark [after the cavalry disappear], who had stopped shouting and waving their hats and were standing around looking confused and dumb.

Without a word, he started his horse forward through the water, and behind him his men rose out of the river, a great swirl of motion and colors—red, white, black, blue . . .

"Get 'em, Dad," [Charlie] hissed. (357)

Once the production crews roll up the trip wire, pay the extras, and return to Hollywood, once the editors have done their tricks, and once the "text" is locked and sold, King implies, it's open season. Nothing is fixed (i.e., locked and immutable) until it is "fixed" (i.e., made to be reflective of reality rather than historical fantasy).

There are no boundaries to stories or media in King's novel, where characters refuse prescriptive "rules" of scripting. Coyote jumps back and forth between plots and tellings, as do we; the "real" Blackfoot characters' life stories shadow those of popular romances, as do ours; and the fundamental scripts of biblical myths are reverberated through Hollywood fantasies: all Wayne really wanted was a submissive woman with big breasts. As Tayo's grandmother says in the conclusion of Silko's novel *Ceremony*, I think I've heard these stories before. However, like Silko, King makes the scripts visual and thus visible, along with the ideology they carry, and re-edits them accordingly. By blurring the line between movie and fiction, by deploying humor through filmic device, he also disrupts the easy hierarchy of sacred and profane, "serious" and popular texts, and spotlights the ways audiences make easy allowances and passive deferrals (or defaults) to some media over others, thus opening the way for the imaginative inscription they carry with them. His reinscription (with emphasis on "script") provides ample reaffirmation of Native story and belief as well as their continuation. This reframing took many forms and directions in the 1990s, particularly in film.

VICTOR MASAYESVA JR.: *Imagining Indians*

Masayesva's movie is a good example. It covers eighty years of Hollywood's Indians, from the silent *The Battle of Elderbush Gulch* to *The Dark Wind*. However, the core of the film is comprised of long sections focused upon the commodification and appropriation of Native materials and lifeways in general, including sacred objects as well as contemporary art. Thus, Masayesva's eye is far-reaching, and his narrative makes no distinction between these issues and those provoked by other analyses of Hollywood's canon and, by extension, the canon of fiction. Like the blurring of the two media of production for King's *The Mysterious Warrior*, *The Dark Wind* is from a Tony Hillerman novel.

Throughout the documentary portions of the film Masayesva juxtaposes Hollywood footage—its images and history—with interviews of Native people who were in some way concerned with or involved in the movies' productions. Given the fact that for many people Hollywood provides their initial, sometimes sole, image of Indians (Masayesva's thesis), this use of film footage, with a new context surrounding it, is well considered. At times he juxtaposes newspaper clippings (and thus "real-world" controversy) with the spoken words of the people he interviews and in one section presents the words of promoters of Hollywood movies with an overlay of a comic book; thus, he destabilizes "truth" and "fact." The packaged images the public has been fed clash sharply with the "truth" of events behind and beyond the camera. The image and thus its mystique are shown to be false, the elaborate construction of romantic, self-serving imaginations employing the artifice, the "tricks of the trade."

Given the bulk of his examples, then, and the numerous interviews, the pervasive nature of the appropriation and misrepresentation he sees at work in society are revealed. The evidence should be compelling, but his hope to dislodge that propensity in society may not be accomplished through this element of the film alone. Pointing a finger at the myth and calling forth reality may not effect significant change; contemporary political campaigns suggest as much, wherein the "image" is everything and reality only at times tangentially interesting. In other words, documenting the inadequacies of the apparatus through which he is working holds a convenient escape route for his audience. The documentary element of his movie, despite its innovative use of techniques of the trade, allows an objective distance between text and viewer.

To counter this, Masayesva provides a central, metaphoric drama—a fictional story—that interweaves throughout, providing a frame for the film. It dramatizes the attitudes explored "objectively" in the documentary, providing the differentiation that, ostensibly, an "objective documentary" should avoid. Interestingly, Masayesva makes use of the gendered-contest convention so prominent in Hollywood's imagination and King's novel, pairing a white male dentist with a female Indian patient. Significantly, their interaction takes place within a room that has a collection of movie posters covering its walls. One of them, in fact, is for the movie *Captain John Smith and Pocahontas*. There are two Hollywood film genres that are pervasive in this section of the film and represented in the posters on the walls also: the "captivity" and thus cross-racial romance narrative and the war narrative.[15] The dentist-authority, patient-subject motif, then, replicates the personal and painful implications of the two genres as well as the Pocahontas myth.

Despite the fact that he tries to "anesthetize" the woman, the dentist—dressed in medical garb but also a bone choker—is oblivious to her continued discomfort; tellingly, she is silent throughout as he articulates his own agenda, thus revealing his beliefs. To do so he evokes *Dances with Wolves* and his hero, Kevin Costner, with whom he identifies. (The blurring of actor-enactor is telling.) The dentist is impressed by how easily "he learned your language, and you picked up on his"; how "you took him into your hearts"; and how he could relate to "the spiritual lifestyle you people had." The lack of distance between romantic fiction and reality is apparent subtext to the monologue throughout the scene, with its emphasis on and indictment of the verbs' past tense: the implied loss of all the dentist deems valuable and therefore worthy of appropriation. The pronoun, of course, underscores this as well with its generalized antecedent.

John Smith lives again, but his is now a safe, a privileged voyeurism. The dentist has a plan to bring the historical lessons from the movie into being. He has made contacts with "some New Age people who are into real estate and travel, down in Phoenix," and together they intend to build a "Higher Consciousness Resort" where—for a price—people can come for weekend-long, "intense Indian Spiritual Seminars." As with the Disney(land) model, the seminars would be dramatic play through imaginative, revisionist enactments. Masayesva is being satirical, of course, but the satire is closely aligned with the New Age reality that Geary Hobson wrote about in the 1970s (once again, see Hobson's "The Rise of the White Shaman"). His portrayal of it is comic in context but hinges upon attitudes inherent in a long-standing colonial paradigm, the mystique of colonialism itself: the profit to be derived from promoting one's revised image of "the other" and then depriving the other of lands. The desire for a quick reversal of fortune—here both spiritual and financial fortune—in our hero's favor is a compelling tradition. John Smith was a seventeenth-century realtor, after all, as Erdrich well knows.

The fact that Masayesva's investigation takes place through a gendered contest is important, especially when one considers the conclusion. Here the patient rises up in revolt, attacks the dentist, and takes away his drill. With this she attacks the lens, the camera, slowly and deliberately etching it with the colonist's own instrument: a reinscription with a vengeance. Once the image the camera records is completely obscured she pushes the camera over. The screen goes black, and a dialog begins in an Indigenous language. This Hopi filmmaker has made his statement, using conventional tricks of the film trade to topple the apparatus and perhaps the audience's reliance upon it. The message is clear.

GERALD VIZENOR: *Harold of Orange*

There are tricks, and then there are *tricks*. In fact, the most common word used to discuss Gerald Vizenor's art is "trickster." This is understandable, given his consistent wordplay and his construction of characters very obviously patterned after trickster characters to be found in Indigenous literatures. However, it is in his own employment of dramatic, comic reversals—the elemental business of the trickster— that Vizenor reimagines popular representations of history and Native peoples. At once humorous and poignant, these scenes truly delight and instruct and thus impress new perception on old conventions.

The central character of Vizenor's movie is Harold Sinseer, de facto leader of the Warriors of Orange, "tricksters in the new school of socioacupuncture" who "talk about mythic revolutions on the reservation" (55). In other words, from the opening scene one is aware that a "new school" is derivative of the old, that it employs a pedagogy based in language ("talk"), and that it is founded upon the idea that applying pressure to sociological points can have a curative effect for the body politic. As in acupuncture, the point where one must apply pressure is not necessarily in near proximity to the pain or ill being treated, not, in other words, on the economic or political reality of Native Americans but upon the often stereotypical images of American Indians that feed if not create that reality. Subjecting the popular myths to the pressure of Vizenor's reversals thereby forces his audience to reassess them on a level beyond reason and logic, beyond op-ed ruminations: the playing ground of the trickster where drama carries the message.

This approach is indeed a "mythic revolution" through the remagining of the myths of representation so ingrained in the social psyche as to be comprehended as "fact" and therefore functionally invisible. As King says, it hits the audience with the suddenness of an epiphany and may indeed prove painful. As Harold says as he and the Warriors depart for their meeting with an Anglo board of directors of a charitable foundation, once they have had their way "that foundation pack won't remember nothin' we tell them but the truth" (58). There are numerous examples in the movie in which "truth" emerges from the sudden, abrupt, comic reversal of popular untruths. I will focus on three that are representative: one dealing with a popular myth of history and two with the dynamic of cultural interaction as espoused by Hollywood through the genres of romance and war movies.[16]

As the Warriors of Orange escort the board of directors to various points around the city there are several scenes in which Indian and Anglo are paired as they travel on the Warriors' "school" bus, a configuration reminiscent of King's four "old Indian" characters and their antecedents. This pairing generates dialog—a dialogic interaction—that has misunderstanding as its basis, healing as its goal. For instance, in one scene an older trustee raises an old and pervasive theory that purports to explain the presence of Native Americans in this hemisphere, a long-standing dilemma dating from first European colonial contact.

ANDREW: I have considered the origin theories of the American Indians . . . Some are *quite* interesting. I find the Bering Strait migration theory to be most credible . . . How about you then, what are your thoughts on the subject?

NEW CROWS: Which way, east or west?

ANDREW: Which *way*? What do you mean?

NEW CROWS: Which way across the Bering Strait, *then*?

ANDREW: Yes, I see . . . Well, I hadn't really thought about it that way. Which way do *you* think?

NEW CROWS: From here to there, we emerged from the flood here, the first people, unless you think we are related to the panda bear. (66)[17]

When Andrew counters with the observation that there is "so little evidence to support your idea," New Crows responds in a way to bring into relief, reverse, and thereby shake the fundamental beliefs of his audience: "Jesus Christ was an American Indian" (66).

In very short order Vizenor has dramatized images, popularly ingrained in his audience, that are an attempt to explain phenomena under the guise of scientific (and therefore objectively verifiable) fact, history. By reversing those images—by problematizing the directional framework inherent in the paradigm—he imaginatively demonstrates the ideological and thus ethnocentric foundations upon which they are based. Simultaneously, he valorizes Indigenous origin stories—the elemental narratives of who Native peoples are and how they came to be where they are—and challenges written "history" with myth, including that of Christ. He has forced a remagining of orientations, frames of reference, and thus representations with which we are all familiar. He has made us laugh, then reassess. Vizenor, it appears, is the Anti-Disney.

Later in the movie the Warriors take the directors to a park, where, as they step down from the bus to play a game of softball, Vizenor once again reverses our orientation. As noted in the interview, the members of the wholly Anglo board are dressed in red T-shirts that bear the word "Indians" in white letters, and the Warriors wear white T-shirts with "Anglos" in red lettering. In preparation for the play, the conflict, Harold moves between the two teams as they huddle, changing shirts accordingly to match those of his audience, first the Warriors and then the board members. He admonishes the former: "We are the 'Anglos' and we're here to win and win big . . . Play by the rules if you must, but rape and plunder to win the game" (76). Violence, sex, and colonialism again, but here the war genre—the racial conflict—is mitigated by the nature of the game itself. To the "Indians" he makes a call: for them to remember "what the missionaries said our elders said around the fires" and that they "are made in dreams and the white man is the one who must win . . . When we help him win we are free and soon the white man will want to be like us" (77). Harold utters the Disney model, the modern variant of Cooper, Longfellow, and May against which the authors I've discussed resist.

It is difficult not to equate this exchange also with the history implied in the illustration of Smith and Pocahontas; it is she who will "help them win" and he who wants to appropriate or co-opt the Native. However, here the straightforward articulation of the colonial agenda is complicated by the humorous image of Indians labeled as Anglos; the rearticulation of the Pocahontas agenda—to aid the colonist—is undermined by the cutting irony of the "translators": the missionaries who take possession of the words of the elders, the ethnographers who write down Native history and thus control attitudes and therefore the future. The inevitability of colonial domination, so prominent in the history book and illustration of Smith and Pocahontas, is called to question, and the true agents of the conquest are made apparent. Vizenor's audience laughs at the absurdity of it all.

Thus, socioacupuncture works. The movie abounds with similar examples, and at the center of them we find the dynamic, gendered contest between Fannie and Harold. Interestingly, in the screenplay's opening scenes there is a reenactment of a woman-man configuration reminiscent of the Pocahontas-Smith binary, but with an interesting twist.

As Harold walks into the coffeehouse the "screen is filled with a large photographic silhouette of Harold and Fannie posed like the statue of Hiawatha and Minnehaha" (55). The statue represents two other popular literary constructions dating from colonial literatures: the Anglo imaginative mating of two romantic figures.[18] This is, of course, analogous to the Smith-Pocahontas myth, but since Fannie is not a Native American, it aligns Fannie (Anglo student of Native lifeways) and Harold (Indian) in a comic reversal of the Smith-Pocahontas paradigm. The Indian here owes the Anglo; Harold borrowed a thousand dollars from her in college, and now she wants to be paid back. Also, Harold wants her help to secure a large grant from the foundation that will help his Warriors live well from the "tax-free bonds" in which they will invest the monies that are supposed to fund the growing of coffee "pinch beans" on the reservation. In this instance Harold has become the seeker of financial ease—the colonial agenda of John Smith—and the Anglo board the possessor; Harold's methodology humorously reverses their respective situations as he moves to dispossess funds from the other. Harold tricks Fannie, though, so that the debt is absolved without costing him anything. With her passive assistance they manage to get the grant, using one board member's stereotypical, racist ideas about Indians as the final selling point. The "grant" will thus fund the revolution.[19] The colonial agenda has been called forth, reversed, and situated in a comic rather than deadly and tragic narrative. In its entirety the movie moves systematically through DIAC and productively presents tribal self-determination.

SHERMAN ALEXIE: *Smoke Signals*

At the risk of turning this into a survey of films but in the interests of circularity and symmetry, I would like to mention briefly Alexie's first film. As noted in the interview, it won the Sundance festival's prize and was subsequently picked up by Miramax for wide distribution. It did, indeed, open a window of opportunity for Native filmmakers, including Chris Eyre, who directed *Smoke Signals*. While it certainly deploys humor as a device to investigate contemporary life and tragic events of the past, it does so in a conventional style that lacks the sudden reversals we see in King and Vizenor or in the parallel genres of Masayesva's documentary framed with fiction. In all, however, the differentiation is immediate, the investigation elaborate, and the affirmations telling. In each, the plot resolutions speak to the obvious fact: Native cultures are alive and dynamic, and the story will be continued.

In his introduction to the screenplay Alexie reiterates some of the ideas explored above in the discussions of the other texts. Films are deeply insinuated into American culture and the ways we perceive our world. The introduction, a work of art in its own right, begins simply, "I love movies" (vii). 'Nuff said. To explore that reality, Alexie blends the physical reality of family members' reactions to the filming and premiere of the movie: his mother cries as she watches young actors rehearsing, one of whom reminds her of a young Sherman, and his brother cries at the end of the first showing of the final product, catching Alexie as he walks down the aisle to field questions and hugging him "until I could hardly breathe" (x). Alexie describes what happened at one shoot:

> My dad was watching us film.
> We were filming in DeSmet, Idaho, the small town on the reserva-
> tion where my father was born.
> Yes. A few feet away from the exact spot where my father was
> born.
> I watched the crew set up the lights.
> My brothers and sisters were drinking coffee a few feet away from
> the lights.
> I watched the producers huddle together.
> My brothers and sisters huddled together in a van to take a break
> from the cold.
> I saw the breath of our young actors as they spoke into the cold
> air.
> My brothers and sisters talked about all the movies they loved.
> I knew that no matter what else happened during the making of
> *Smoke Signals*, I was going to make movies for the rest of
> my life. (ix)

The alternating, poemlike couplets underscore the conjoining of fiction and reality: life and its mirror. It is a family event that ties the lived experiences of kin to the production of a fiction, but it is a fiction that is compelling through the power of the medium itself. There is a section break, and after the white space Alexie proclaims, "I used to think that movies were real. / I mean, I thought, I truly believed, that every movie was actually a documentary" (ix). And there it is. The medium lives in a related but removed reality. Moreover, this is a fit description of the ways the film follows the conventions of the craft with staged events and dialog, much like those of fiction and novel.

I will examine two scenes that allow for the investigation of contemporary experience for Indigenous people and relate to the discussions above. Both scenes take place on the main characters' (Thomas Builds-the-Fire and Victor) journey to Arizona to repatriate Victor's father's remains. The first evokes the power of Hollywood to shape perceptions of the other, using once more the movie *Dances with Wolves*. As they converse, Victor finally confronts Thomas with his primary personality trait:

> I mean, you just go on and on talking about nothing. Why can't you have a normal conversation? You're always trying to sound like some damn medicine man or something. I mean, how many times have you see[n] *Dances with Wolves*? A hundred, two hundred times? . . . Oh, jeez, you have seen it that many times, haven't you? Man. Do you think that shit is real? God. Don't you even know how to be a real Indian? (61)

While this could suggest, as Victor surmises, that Thomas is affecting a persona, we come to understand that he is not. Thomas *is* a medicine man or something, for he certainly works a cure for Victor's alienation from his father. Also, Thomas *is* the resident storyteller, the one who builds a fire in those who listen. Taken individually and collectively, the two represent the wide spectrum of what it is to be a "real Indian" in today's society.

This is shown directly a few scenes later where the two Indians face off against the cowboys who have taken their seats, a diminished version of colonialism with one's place lost to the other. Although they protest and try to show their "warrior" faces, they do not get their seats back. As Thomas notes, "Man, the cowboys always win, enit?" (65). Although Victor disagrees, Thomas lists the honor roll of cowboys who do: "Look at Tom Mix. Look at Roy Rogers. Look at Clint Eastwood. And what about John Wayne?" (66). And there we have it: the cowboys of Hollywood fame and that King so cleverly co-opts and kills. Alexie also co-opts them, for in the next lines Victor and Thomas improvise a 49 song about John Wayne's teeth, questioning if they are real or fake. The nature of reality, lived experience, as opposed to that which is perceived and received through the popular medium of film, is pervasive in Alexie's screenplay and film. In this way it, too, is in keeping with the other works discussed above, adding yet one more voice to the investigation of that lived experience while challenging the images Hollywood has made conventional.

In brief, *Imagining Indians* ends with the violent overthrow of the apparatus through which representations and images have been created and perpetuated; of course, though, this is all accomplished by means of that apparatus: Masayesva's camera and direction, which dramatize events for us. In *Green Grass, Running Water*, *Harold of Orange*, and *Smoke Signals* the violence may be deferred, but King, Vizenor, and Alexie also manipulate the apparatus itself—the evocative power of novel and film respectively—to turn the stage upon which images of Indians have been imprinted into an imaginative quagmire, a humorous destabilizing that ultimately has as its goal a reimagining of images and the theoretical foundations upon which attitudes of "the other" rest.

Unlike the Disney pedagogy, in these works we cannot imaginatively identify with the colonial hero, for to do so would require us to conceive of ourselves as absurd, our agenda flawed, and our "sidekick" our equal if not our superior. When boomers laugh in these works, they laugh at themselves and thus the Disney tradition of resurrecting and perpetuating the myth of colonial correctness and its portrayal. This is perhaps the most powerful tool that can be employed: an imaginative and dramatic self-reenactment through self-doubt, the angst of our generation and the genesis of postmodernism. Methodologies aside, each artist has a finely tuned awareness of the pervasive nature of the myths that have driven much of this country's history and a "sinseer" desire to reinscribe them.

Thus, the means and implements of DIAC grow as the number of works by Native authors increases and new genres and media are brought into the discourse. With this in mind, I would like to turn back the chronological structure of this discussion and look at a work of fiction that predates the 1970s yet anticipates the issues raised by the works I've discussed. By revisiting a novel predating the Flagstaff conference, I will extend the discussion in both a critical and historical framework. In the next chapter I hope to bring all this together into a reconsideration of DIAC by going back to some origins. To do this I would like to consider some ideas for a prominent critic of Native literatures: Louis Owens.

4 | The New Millennium and Its Origins

Since the 1970s critical studies about Native fiction abound. Most notably to date, Louis Owens's *Other Destinies: Understanding the American Indian Novel* does a fine job of exploring and discovering the major issues in the fiction written by Natives, and its coverage extends into the 1990s. As mentioned previously, concurrent with the growth of criticism as a field of study and application, in the United States there were heated debates about "authenticity" (cultural and/or ethnic verisimilitude), "authority" (who is authorized to speak from a specific cultural or ethnic perspective), intellectual property rights, and the appropriateness of applying Western theory to non-Western texts, all of which enlivened the latter decades of the century and continue to shape the ways we think and talk about texts and the meanings they may provoke. I had the opportunity to talk about these issues with Owens in his home in the mountains near Albuquerque, with its clear view of the Sandia Mountains. It was the comfortable setting for this, the last installment of four days of wide-ranging conversations about fly-fishing and politics, espionage and University of New Mexico basketball, contemporary higher education and the environment.

John Purdy (JP): So, where to begin? Let's start by talking about your novels. How did you start writing fiction?

Louis Owens (LO): The first novel I wrote was *Wolfsong.* I began it in my attic room in the Forest Service bunkhouse in Darrington, Washington, one fall after the snows came and almost everyone else had left for the year. I wanted really to write a novel about the wilderness area itself, the Glacier Peak Wilderness, making the place the real protagonist of the novel and the characters ways of giving the trees and mountains and streams and glaciers a voice.

JP: Did I tell you the story about the first time I used that novel, at Western [Washington University near the locale it describes]? I had a student in the back who, when we first began discussing it, furrowed her brow and said: "Where is this town, Forks? These characters seem familiar." I asked her where she was from, and she replied, "Darrington" [the community that is the model for that in the novel].

LO: Well, actually, I named it Forks because I wanted to disguise the town. Also because the rivers [the Skagit, Sauk, and Stillaguamish near Darrington] come together [ultimately], and that is symbolic. But I had somebody who actually made a pilgrimage to Forks and came back to tell me how great it was to find the town where the novel is set. [Forks is on the Olympic Peninsula in Washington State.] I didn't have the heart to tell her that it wasn't Forks.

JP: Well, Forks is a lot like Darrington. They're both small logging communities.

LO: Darrington may be meaner, at least way back when I lived there in the '70s. The first words spoken to me there were by these three loggers who wanted to know if I preferred to have my hair cut off with a chainsaw or burned off with kerosene.

Anyway, that's how I started writing the book, and then I put it down and went back to school, where I picked it up again to work on while I was writing my dissertation. Bill Kittredge was a writer in residence at UC Davis at the time, and Bill read a draft of it, liked it, and did me the great favor of sending it off to his agent. It was read by Gary Fisketjohn, who I think was at either Random House or Knopf at the time, and he said he liked it and that he was sure they'd publish it. I thought, Who says being a writer is so hard? But the novel was turned down, nominated by Fisketjohn for the Pushcart Press Book Editor's Award, which it didn't receive, and then reconsidered and rejected a second time. That's when I put it on the shelf for about a decade. Basically, I was young and had my heart broken as a writer. I was pretty naive.

Wolfsong was finally published because I happened to be talking with John Crawford of West End Press one day, and he asked if I had any work he might consider. I said that, well, I did happen to have a novel somewhere, and that was that.

JP: And *The Sharpest Sight*?

LO: I started *The Sharpest Sight* in '82. Actually, I'd started it years before with a short story about a friend in high school who committed suicide. I tried to write about him in a hundred different ways and just couldn't do it. Finally, his story became embedded in an invisible way in *The Sharpest Sight*, a novel that is primarily about my brother who vanished in the U.S. after three tours in Vietnam. I worked on that novel off and on over the years as I also did other more academic things—the things you do to get a job, get tenure, and so on. During that time I also wrote *Other Destinies*, a critical book, plus a couple of books on John Steinbeck.

JP: Scholarship and fiction? Different voices . . .

LO: In a way. Anyway, it got published rather strangely, too. Oxford [University Press] was interested in it. They said they wanted to publish it, but they kept stringing it along without a contract for six months or a year. I can't really remember. By then Oklahoma was starting its new series, with Gerald Vizenor as editor, and I ran into Kimberly Wiar at a conference. She asked me if I had any work they could consider. I sent her the manuscript of *Other Destinies*, and she got back to me within a couple of weeks saying they wanted the book. So I withdrew it from Oxford, probably ruffling some feathers in the process, and officially submitted it to the University of Oklahoma Press.

While talking about *Other Destinies*, Kim—who [was] a senior editor at OU Press—asked what else I was working on. I said a novel, and she surprised me by asking if they could consider it. That's how both *Other Destinies* and *The Sharpest Sight* came to be published by Oklahoma in the American Indian series.

JP: That was announced at the MLA [Modern Language Association's annual convention] in San Francisco that year. I remember the reception and Vizenor's speech.

LO: That was a good reception. It's a good series. These books [the two novels] were really written for myself, but they were published with these presses because I happened to bump into the editors; things happened to come together at the right times.

JP: I've wondered about that—the time frame itself but also the publication, the writing of *Other Destinies*. I remember it came out so closely to *Sharpest Sight*. And that would be a question: Do you see the work on fiction and criticism as a balance to one another, or do they interact in some way?

LO: I think . . . inevitably they will interact. They have to. The mind works as a whole, so to say while writing a piece of fiction that the ideas from reading and writing criticism don't work in somehow would be dishonest. It may not be conscious, but it has to have some effect. Gerald Vizenor is perhaps the best at making it obvious, at blurring the line between the two in the minds of his readers.

JP: One of the things he does is to take that whole universe—academics, scholarship—and put it into his fiction: Arnold Krupat's there, you're there, the whole lot of us.

LO: For Jerry, the line between fiction and nonfiction does not seem to exist. For him, his fiction is certainly metafiction that generates its own story.

JP: Well, that takes us through *Sharpest Sight*.

LO: Let's see. *Bone Game*. I remember the first time I went to Santa Cruz in the '70s. The place had a feel to it, a—I don't know—a dark presence. I had forgotten about that, but when I moved back there [to teach] in 1990, I felt it. I could feel it in those mountains and canyons.

JP: You could feel it in the place you lived?

LO: No, we lived about seventeen miles north, in Boulder Creek, deep in the redwoods. I felt okay there, but Santa Cruz had a definite haunted feeling for me, and I began researching the history of the place. What really stood out for me was what seemed like a pattern of almost ritualistic violence spanning almost two centuries. I came across a reference to the killing of a Spanish priest at the Santa Cruz mission in 1812, and I found an interview conducted with the son of one of the Ohlone Indian men who killed the priest. That became the genesis of *Bone Game*.

That book was very different from anything I'd written before. I wrote it in a small room I'd built into my garage about a hundred feet away from our house, off in the trees. Instead of working in the mornings, which I prefer, I found that I had to write that at night because if I got up at four a.m. to write, my young daughters would inevitably get up with me. So I had to work after they went to sleep, usually between ten p.m. and two or three a.m.

JP: The witching hours.

LO: Yeah. It was scary, actually. There was an owl that took up residence right outside the office that would hoot all night.

JP: That's a haunting book. I remember when you came to my NEH seminar [summer of 1993] and read from the manuscript; it was eerie.

LO: In some ways it's my favorite of my novels, the one in which I took the most risks and experimented most radically. I wanted to write a nonlinear novel, one that worked rather like a mosaic. I imagined it completely before writing it—though of course many surprises happen when you write, and that is maybe the greatest pleasure in writing. But I wanted it to be a story in which all times and all actions coexisted simultaneously. I felt that I couldn't convey the fabric of violence in that place any other way. It can be confusing for a reader who may have trouble figuring out when or where or within what consciousness he or she is at any given moment.

JP: So it's a geospecific place that is deep with the history of violence.

LO: And to convey that . . . I wanted to explore that sense, the enormous sense of loss that the Indigenous people of the Santa Cruz area, the Ohlone, experienced. Within a single generation—the matter of a few years, even months—so much was lost, changed forever, as the result of the coming of Europeans. That's why the novel begins with the lines "Children. Neófitos. Bestes. And still it is the same sky, the same night arched like a reed house, the stars of their birth." I wanted to convey in those lines the extraordinary shock of recognizing that the world has not changed at the deepest, most important levels, though one's people or culture may have vanished. It's a haunting sense to me.

JP: Then the killing of the priest is the apt, the perfect act to precipitate the events in the novel, the evil that came with the change.

LO: Yeah. That's how I felt. And in a way Santa Cruz is a microcosm for the U.S. There's been so much violence perpetrated in its history.

JP: Yesterday, we were talking about the possibility of making films from your novels. You said you thought *Wolfsong* would be the easiest to film; do you see *Bone Game*, then, as the most, or one of the most, difficult?

LO: I think it would be the most difficult, given the time shifts, but *Wolfsong* and perhaps *Nightland* might be easily filmed. In fact, *Nightland* has already been optioned for a movie. *Bone Game* would probably be very scenic or filmic, but structurally it's complicated by the nonlinear plot. *Nightland*, on the other hand, was an experiment for me in writing as purely a linear plot as I could. In that novel I wanted everything to follow rapidly from the single event in the opening scene—a body falling out of the sky. I tried to create a feeling of an inevitable rush of plot beginning with the first line.

JP: Well, it's certainly dramatic enough. A body falling from the sky; it gets the reader right away.

LO: It should hook the reader. It hooked me as a writer, actually. The whole novel began with a vision that came to me one day of a body falling from the sky. I'd also been reading a newspaper account of buzzards attacking barnyard fowl in West Texas, a true and strange account, and that merged with the image of a falling body to create the opening scene. Of course, for Cherokee readers a body that looks like a buzzard and comes from the west will have some disturbing resonance.

JP: Well, producers or directors seem to be looking for that kind of hook, but one that has another level of meaning is even more interesting.

LO: I guess I didn't impress them [laughter]. Seriously, though, I don't know what they really want. Does anybody? Filmmakers or publishers? Trying to figure them out would probably drive you crazy or make you write what they want instead of what you want. That's probably one of the few benefits of having a job, to have the luxury of writing what I want to write.

Nightland was written in large part for my aunt Betty, to whom it is dedicated. I'd written about my father's people, who are Choctaw, and drawn on our family's experiences living in Mississippi and California, but I hadn't written anything about my mother's Cherokee roots. My aunt, who is the last surviving member of my mother's family, called one day to ask if I'd do some research for her on her Cherokee family. That made me realize that I should write a story about Cherokee mixed-bloods like my aunt. Perhaps my mother's death about ten years ago had made that kind of writing too difficult until now.

At any rate, the mythology that structures the foundation for *Nightland* is Cherokee, not pan-Indian or anything like that, but Cherokee. And I knew my aunt would recognize a lot that most readers of the novel will miss. I never believe in explaining my own writing, though I happily explain other people's, but I will say that the Thunder Twins, or Sons of Thunder, are very important mythic figures in *Nightland*.

JP: Those are the things that weave their ways through the narrative.

LO: Sort of. Anyway, I did some research for her, so she told me what her grandfather's name was and her grandmother's, which she thought, since she had no written record. Actually, only half the family's on the Dawes rolls, and they're all on the 1910 Oklahoma Indian census. It occurred to me that I really should have written a book about my mother's family, too. The Cherokee side. And that's how a body came to be falling from the sky.

JP: So your aunt helped put the context to your falling body.

LO: I figured that, maybe, 1 percent of the people who read the book will get that, if anyone does at all. [The tie of the present with the older stories.] But she read it and wrote back in one of her few letters, saying "You're a real writer!"

JP: Did she ask where she was in it?

LO: No, but she did mention that "there's some bad words in it."

JP: Well, it has some of the same qualities of your earlier novels, that sense of layered time and events. What happened in the past is being felt in the present.

LO: Yeah, that's true. I guess one thing I'm working on in most of my writing is the way America has tried, and continues to try, to bury the past, pretending that once it's over we no longer need to think about it. We live in a world full of buried things, many of them very painful and often horrific, like passing out smallpox-infested blankets to Indians or worse, and until we acknowledge and come to terms with the past we'll keep believing in a dangerous and deadly kind of innocence, and we'll keep thinking we can just move on and leave it all behind. That's a reason that one of *Nightland*'s protagonists, Will, ends up living on a ranch containing a world of buried things, including even a smashed Range Rover.

JP: Out of sight [buried, in fact] but still a part of the story . . .

LO: Right. But he's going to stay there. You can't run from that buried history.

JP: In a way, that rings of Santayana—those who don't know history are doomed to repeat it—and Faulkner's "dead hand of the past," and Silko's "if you don't know the stories, you don't know what's happening now."

LO: It's about processing the past, consciously and unconsciously. James Welch's work deals with it, too. *Fools Crow*, and one of his best, *Winter in the Blood*.

JP: It has one of the great lines, the revelation that comes when Old Bird farts.

LO: An epiphany carried on the wind. We just talked about that in class. That's a great novel.

JP: So now you have the new novel in production, *Dark River*.

LO: *Dark River* will be published by Oklahoma next winter, and incidentally, I'm very pleased to be back with Oklahoma after an unpleasant foray with Dutton Signet, who published *Nightland*. *Dark River* is very different again from what I've written before, and I'm sure it also is very similar. I wanted to overturn a lot of conventions in this novel, disrupt stereotypes in comic and violent ways, with the emphasis upon the comic.

JP: I see what you mean. I like how you play with them. The "weekend warrior" who is out there trying to experience the "thrill" of war . . .

LO: The militia . . .

JP: Yeah, but even more insidious than that in some ways, less blatant. The professional person who comes from the urban center to learn the ways of the "wilds" and to hunt humans. Then the convention of the Vietnam veteran, the Black Ops type of characters, and you take them all apart.

LO: Well, good. I'm glad you think that. And actually, the militia were inspired by a group of guys I ran into when I was backpacking on a reservation. They were wearing camouflage uniforms, out practicing war. Disneyland with weapons. I know there are people like that, practicing violence against others. By the way, those weekend militia guys were white and they were on the reservation illegally but in such a remote spot that nobody else probably would have come across them. There is quite a bit of violence in the novel, but I like to think it has an almost slapstick quality to it, disturbing and comic at the same time.

JP: That group is an interesting group because it has such a wide array of characters; they're all participating in the same type of activity but operating from different backgrounds and values, so there are these moments of crisis for some of them: "Are we going to kill these women or what?" It is no longer a game, and they have to decide.

LO: Ironically, in a group like that the most violent are often the individuals who never experienced war.

JP: They haven't had to live the aftereffects.

LO: Well, yeah. You were in Vietnam. You know what I'm talking about. I wasn't, but my brother was there for three years, and a lot of my friends were there, and a number of them died there. It seems to me that it is almost always the people who haven't experienced the immediacy of violence who are capable of getting involved in it as a game.

But that's just a part of the novel. I wanted to bring together a whole convergence of different characters. Stick them all in one place and see what happens.

JP: And it has such a wide array; I mean, not just the characters in the canyon but on the reservation, too. In fact, a little while ago you were talking about the genesis of that reception in the casino; it came from one you attended on a reservation once. That's marvelously funny: "stranger than fiction."

LO: Well, I hope there's a lot of humor in it.

JP: There is, all the way through. And I won't ask about the conclusion, since the book has yet to be released, but I like how you bring those various conventions from several genres together.

LO: You know, it's a strange conclusion, and some people will probably be unhappy with it, and some people may not. I like it myself. At the end of the novel I sort of wanted to deconstruct the novel, I suppose, and the whole process of storytelling. Explore what it means to say stories have no ends. And I wanted to take apart all the clichés, and that's why I have this major character in the novel, one I really like, who's running around shouting Italian phrases at women. This was a character actor in Hollywood who learned his Italian from Sal Mineo and other actors and says Sal didn't speak Italian very well. He's a very good friend of Iron Eyes Cody and has Cody's cat. And wig [laughter].

JP: And that poor cat [more laughter].

LO: A grim fate.

JP: Before I ask you about that collection of essays you have coming out, and I do want to talk a bit about it, I have to ask you. You have a lot of fly-fishing in your novels . . .

LO: I like to fish. . . . Well, you know water has always been an obsession. I guess I'm really obsessed with it. Jerry Vizenor pointed this out to me recently. You see, he's obsessed with tree lines for some reason, and for me it's water. I've always lived near water: by the Yazoo River in Mississippi, the Salinas River and Coast Range creeks in California, I've always fished. My earliest memories, really, are of fishing. I could barely walk. And my teenage years, adolescent years, I was *obsessed* with it. I spent all my time on that water. And Cherokees have a medicine called "Going to Water" which is one of the most powerful of all medicines. I think maybe that's why we've survived this long. Water's really important.

Of course, I lived in the North Cascades, where you're wet all the time, and that's another aspect to it. But I love to fish. I love to try to imagine what the fish are thinking.

JP: When you use it, it seems to be a very positive characteristic or quality for people who have other problems.

LO: I guess it is. It's clearly an escape, in a way. I like to go fly-fish a river by myself, backpack in, and I'll start fishing in the morning, and the next thing I realize, it's dark. I've lost a whole day, fishing and reading the river all day, and that's as close to any kind of a Zen experience I've ever had. I try to give that to my characters. And it's a connection, clearly, trying to connect to something.

The nicest moment in Thoreau's *Walden* is the description of fishing at night. That connection.

JP: He does it in *The Maine Woods*, too. His journals of his trips up there.

Then, of course, some of us connect and others don't, or more often [laughter].

LO: You're more obsessed than I am!

JP: Well, what about the collection of essays. You told me about it while you were working on it, but we haven't talked about it since.

LO: It's a collection of essays I've written over the past several years and new essays put together [see *Mixedblood Messages*]. A really eclectic bunch of pieces that deal with mixed-blood identity, representations of Indians in films like *Dances with Wolves*, there's an essay in there on the invention of John Wayne, which actually came out of a request from a magazine to write about Wayne from a Native American perspective, as a hero. I went back and watched a lot of his films, so I became a minor expert on John Wayne; it's fascinating, that evolution. So I have Wayne and Kevin Costner, and a fairly severe critique of *Dances with Wolves*, I guess. Invariably funny, because you can't help but be funny when you talk about that movie.

And about three environmental essays, one called "How Native Americans Can Save the World." I'm looking at Indigenous attitudes toward the environment and Native epistemologies. There is a sense of responsibility that I think is a tradition to many Native Americans, traditional Native American beliefs that stress responsibility to the world we live in, which is the only way we're going to survive as a species. Somehow, we have to learn this, and unfortunately most of us have not learned it. Still bulldozing and cutting, no real sense that if you clear-cut a rain forest in Brazil, you affect the climate of Scandinavia.

And I have several autobiographical essays in there as well, along with about fifteen or so photographs of my family that go back to about the turn of the century. Pictures of my mother's family in Indian Territory, log cabin. Mixed-blood Cherokees hanging out in the Territory. Just surviving.

What fascinates me about that, looking at these old pictures, is that you end up with this rainbow coalition. One photo is of a family, a neighboring family of my mother's great-grandmother, her neighbors, a mixed-blood Indian family, with about six or seven kids, and they form an arc, like a rainbow, parents in the middle. There's one little boy who's brown as a coffee bean, and beside him is his blonde brother, and they look *just* alike, but they're different colors, and the rest of the family is a range of complexions and hues. A wonderful, beautiful picture to me. It seems to me that what these people were doing down there in Indian Territory was creating their own borderland. They were living everything we like to write about and theorize about today, as in Gloria Anzaldúa's book, and they were doing it just out of necessity for survival. No one making a big production out of it. Just living as human beings, and I really admire that.

JP: When you were talking about *Bone Game* a few moments ago and the California experience, that dramatic, world-shifting, world-changing interaction in one generation, you wonder how humans can respond to that, react and accommodate that type of an experience. But here, you're suggesting that in other places, then, that can be handled generationally, that it is done through generations as an act of survival.

LO: It's a totally human act, you know. In the Southeast . . . well, a lot of people don't really understand; the Cherokees, for example, are the butts of many jokes: "I had a Cherokee grandmother who was a princess," right? And a lot of blonde Cherokees running around. The fact is that the Southeast tribes met, married, and intermingled with European traders very early, Irish, English, down in Mississippi and Louisiana there were the French. The Welsh came in, Scots. And that's why you find the repetition of those European surnames among the tribes, and that was a process that took place over many generations. That's why you find a Cherokee principal chief named John Ross. Ross becomes a big name among the people, or McCurtain, or Garland. That's fascinating, such a different history from those of the Plains tribes or Northwest, or inland nations.

That's what fascinates me about this whole area of study and why I keep doing it in spite of a lot of misgivings—that is, the diversity, the complexity in the contemporary Indian world is so profound. I'm trying, really, in my writing to get at that. I'm trying to point out that not every Indian in America is riding a spotted pony across the plains chasing buffalo. That there were people who didn't arrange their teepees in circles but instead lived in towns with roads and cabins—the Cherokee or Creek, for example—or they lived in long houses or reed houses like the Ohlone in California. There's a tremendous diversity; today I think more than half of Indian people live in cities. They don't live on reservations, and most are mixed-bloods, so there's this extraordinary range of experience that needs to be represented in art in all ways.

I don't have any patience at all with the essentialist attitudes that say non-Indians shouldn't read things [written] by Indians or talk about Indian literature or whatever. Certainly, you have to have respect and be careful, but it's absurd to say things like that because writing is about communication, and art is about dialog, and that's what we are trying to do. It's almost criminal when someone who doesn't know a culture will come in and exploit it, whether it's in writing or art, visual art, or anything else, just to make money. It's using Native Americans as an extractable natural resource. And you don't have to go very far to find examples, but at the same time we write books that have to be for everybody, and I think every artist should have the right to work with whatever medium he or she wants to work with, but some of the results will be bad and some of them good, some of them will be honest and some of them dishonest. You can't tell somebody that if you're a woman, you can't write about men, or if you're a male, you can't write about women; if you're black, you can't write about white people, or if you're white, you can't write about Indians, or vice versa. That would make it impossible to have a Ralph Ellison, Alice Walker, Maxine Hong Kingston, Scott Momaday, anybody.

JP: That's interesting in the context of *Dark River*, with the New York anthropologist who knows all the old ways and the language.

LO: Yeah. The anthropologist is more "Indian" than the "Indians." He's done his research, and he's hell-bent on living traditionally according to a static idea two hundred years old. The Indians, of course, just want to get by. They want to have a four-wheel-drive pickup and a microwave oven, if it's handy, and want to live like real human beings today, but he wants . . . he comes up with the idea of a theme park . . .

JP: Right. That's a marvelous exchange . . .

LO: He wants the Indians to turn their reservation into a theme park to live like they did two hundred years before, and they'd get all sorts of grants, of course, to do that. But the first idea the tribal council comes up with is to hire hippies to imitate them. The Indians decide to live in Scottsdale [Arizona].

JP: I just about fell out of my chair when I read that; that was a hilarious council meeting.

LO: Well, you know, it's satire, so that stuff is always a little extreme; it's beyond reality, but it's to make a point.

JP: When we laugh, we laugh at some of the odd ideas we have, so it's all worth it.

LO: Well, I read recently, came across a statement that Sherman Alexie made; he was talking about Adrian Louis, and he said that whenever he sees something Adrian Louis writes, he knows it's true because Adrian lives on a reservation. Adrian happens to be Paiute, I believe, but he's living on the Lakota Reservation, and if you follow that logic out, that would make anthropologists the best novelists, the most honest, "truest" writers because they live on reservations, too, and they study the cultures intensely, so maybe anthropologists should write all the novels. Make our movies [laughter]. Some are, actually. There are "Indian" novels by anthropologists.

JP: Or anthropologists' partners, like Theodore Kroeber. Well, there goes the syllabus; we'll have to redesign the whole neighborhood.

Anyway, what's in the future? Want to talk about anything you're working on or want to work on?

LO: I don't know what's in the future, although I'm interested in perhaps writing another book about John Steinbeck, believe it or not, as a very early ecologist. I think that's an aspect of Steinbeck that has never been appreciated enough.

JP: You worked on him for your dissertation.

LO: I did a couple of books on him, actually. He's one of my favorite writers, and the funny thing is that if there's one writer I can count on Indian people in Indian Country having read, it's Steinbeck. He's very popular.

JP: I wonder why.

LO: I think it's because his worldview is very close to what you might find in those communities, and what Steinbeck is arguing in his writing is that we have to be responsible for what he terms the whole thing, known and unknowable, in a very deep way: that if you step into a tide pool, you have to realize that that step has changed the entire universe, and that will fit neatly into what

Silko's arguing in *Ceremony*, the whole sense of having to be careful, to walk in balance, to be responsible for knowing that every single act of humanity changes the world. Steinbeck was arguing that sixty years ago, before anybody in white America really was, so I'm thinking about going back and doing some more work on Steinbeck, as in critical, and then as far as fiction is concerned, I may not write any more. Or I may write about international espionage.

I don't know. It is a very frustrating thing, I think; trying to be a writer is extremely frustrating. I always tell my students that they should do it only if they can't help it . . . because I think writing is rewarded for all the wrong reasons. In order to be a successful Indian writer, and I talk about this in the essay collection that's coming out, you have to give the New York editors, agents, public what they expect to see. It's like Ellison's *Invisible Man*: black people, as Ellison says, are visible *only* if they are what the white world wants to see. And if they don't fit that cliché, they are invisible. That's why his narrator is invisible, has no name, and I think that's true for Indians. To be Native American in the United States you've got to conform to the stereotype, which, as Gerald Vizenor has been pointing out for years and years, was invented by the white world . . .

JP: The Invented Indian.

LO: And that's why people like Jamake Highwater are so successful, because he looked the part and wore fringe and leather, buckskin suits, did all the things and fit the images that the world expected the Indian to fit, and I think that is really central to Indian arts today, especially writing. You've got to basically write stereotypes. Basically have to construct clichés in order to be *seen* by a publisher, and that's very disheartening. That means you can't really do anything original.

JP: But that's one of the things I like about your fiction. We could go right back down the list chronologically, but say *Dark River*—you recognize that, but then you take a cliché and tweak it.

LO: One of the many things that drives me crazy today is the fact that you really have to manufacture what Charles Newman has in a book called *The Post-modern Aura* defined as "pre-sold fiction," with the huge publishing conglomerates now, and the fact that the whole industry is run by money managers, people who don't know anything about literature to start with, looking for commodities that have obvious, presold value, and as far as Indigenous writing is concerned, the value is determined by what has sold before, and the stereotypes arise from that. The people in New York don't know a damned thing about Indigenous people or much of anything beyond Manhattan, so they look for what they already know, and what they know is created by *Dances with Wolves*, *Last of the Mohicans*, Disney's *Pocahontas*, Fenimore Cooper, and Larry McMurtry's Blue Duck, all the later psychopathic breeds like in *Lonesome Dove*. And if you don't give them what they have manufactured themselves, quite frankly, they don't understand it. And if you create an anthropologist who is more Indian than the Indians, that's not what they want to see. If you have somebody who is a hair-spray addict, they think he sprays his hair all day because they don't know what's going on on reservations.

JP: Falls beyond their realm of comprehension.

LO: Exactly. And it's very frustrating. I see a number of novel manuscripts by young Indian writers that just are not going to be published in New York, and they are among the best novels I see, the most honest; they are dealing with tribal people today who are in reservation communities, or in cities, mixed-bloods, or full bloods, or whatever, but they are writing about real experience, what's happening today, which includes working on your car, or having a microwave oven, the realities of life today and not being a mystical shaman. Not to say that ceremony and traditions and spirituality are not terribly important, because they are in the communities, but what New York and Hollywood want to see are warriors, shamans, mystical medicine women, and anger, and, above all, self-destruction. Dysfunction and self-destruction are marketable commodities.

JP: A long-standing convention, right?

LO: Yeah, the new version of The Vanishing Indian; whether it's written by Indians or non-Indians, it's a way of neutralizing Native Americans because the Euro-American world looks at these books and sees Indians destroying one another and sees them as no threat. The anger is turned inward, with a lot of internal colonization going on, a lot of self-loathing, and a lot of the art depicts that, and it doesn't go beyond that, and that's the problem. Of course these things exist, and you've got to deal with them. There is dysfunction, it exists in all communities, and certainly alcoholism, and drugs, and abuse are big problems, but there's a *whole* lot more that needs to be written about, and that's survival.

JP: The center of Vizenor's canon.

LO: Yeah. I think Gerald Vizenor is a genius. I think he's the most brilliant American writer, period. And that's not to say that he's easy to understand or process as a reader, but he's way ahead of almost everybody. And his writing, I think, paradoxically, is more "traditional" than anyone else's, and I've said that in print. He's certainly writing out of a tradition of trickster stories, and what trickster is designed to do: to heal us, challenge us, and attack all our false values and stereotypes and everything that's static, and so the clichéd Indian doesn't stand a chance in Vizenor's writing, and that upsets a lot of people, both Indians and non-Indians alike. Because he doesn't leave well enough alone.

JP: Or *bad* enough alone? We were talking about Victor Masayesva's film *Imagining Indians* yesterday, and that's one of the things I like so much about it. There's that sense of clowning in it: to cure. The main character, an Indian woman in an Indian Health Service dentist's office, takes away his drill and reinscribes the lens, then tips over the camera at the end. Playful in a very profound way. That sense of attacking and taking over the mechanism, the instrument, and rewriting the image.

LO: That's wonderful, and of course it's what Victor, the director, who's in control of the camera, is doing.

JP: Exactly.

LO: And there's a lot of promise in the future with him and people like Aaron Carr, who's a great filmmaker and writer and absolutely well beyond all the clichés and stereotypes and writing brilliant stuff. And Thomas King. Tom is writing about serious issues with such wonderful humor. And he's writing about tribal people in a community who have real lives, who may be photojournalists, whatever.

JP: Well, he caught me with Harlen Bigbear; I've been a fan ever since.

LO: Harlen's a great character. I love *Medicine River*. I teach it whenever I can.

JP: That's a good direction to take this conversation. Do you know of any new writers, any young writers who may not have been published but who you see as promising?

LO: There are quite a few, a lot of promising writers who have been or are being published, like Gordon Henry . . .

JP: Oh yeah . . .

LO: *Incredible* talent that hasn't been recognized enough yet, such as Betty Bell, and here in New Mexico, Aaron Carr is going to be an artist to be reckoned with for a long time, Evilina Lucero from Isleta Pueblo, and there's a Creek, a Muskogee writer in Oklahoma named Vince Mendoza who has a lot of talent that hasn't quite been realized yet. LeAnne Howe is a wonderful, extraordinary writer. Don Birchfield. So many people who seem to be on the cusp of doing something really great. The problem is, they have to make a living, and that surely gets in the way of being an artist. So who knows if those people will finally be able to achieve the greatness they are capable of . . . but maybe.

JP: Well, I hope so.

LO: Me, too. And I see young writers all the time who are writing really wonderful works.

JP: You mentioned at the beginning that *Wolfsong* and, well, *Sharpest Sight* and *Other Destinies* are all in the Oklahoma series; that's been an influential series and one that can publish things that New York doesn't understand, and it's made money, a benefit for the press but also for this body of literature.

LO: You know, Gerald Vizenor gets the credit for creating that series.

I joined him as a coeditor pretty late in the series. It's Jerry's series, and he created it *exactly* because he felt there was a whole body of very valuable writing that would never be published in Manhattan, and of course he was right. They have nearly thirty volumes in their list now, and it's a place where writers can publish without worrying about whether they'll pay off their quarter-of-a-million-dollar advance, whatever, because unfortunately they don't get that kind of advance. It'd be nice if we all did. I think OU Press has been absolutely fantastic. They have great people. They have integrity. I don't think all the works in the series are at the same level, aesthetically, but that's always going to be the case.

I really like publishing in that series. In fact, with *Dark River* I wanted to publish it at Oklahoma from the beginning and had no plans to do otherwise, and if I write another novel it's going to come out with OU because I can write *exactly* as I want to write; I don't have to worry about what an editor in Manhattan who has never been west of the Mississippi is going to think about what I write, and I don't have to put a shamanistic warrior in it . . . so it is a tremendous liberation. So I am pleased with that series, and I think it is important; it's going to be very important historically.

JP: A lot of the small presses in this country have been carrying it for a long time. And some of them have been doing very well with it, with good reputations of doing some of the best work in American literature, period.

LO: And look at what's happening today. The midlist has virtually disappeared in the area of publishing. I know people, very successful writers, publishing with places like Knopf, for example, who aren't getting published anymore because they're midlist writers, literary writers, so they don't sell a lot of copies. Some small presses have folded over the last several years, with some notable exceptions, like Holy Cow! Press . . .

JP: Gray Wolf . . .

LO: Gray Wolf, that's the one I was trying to think of, but university presses have stepped in. Nevada is publishing people like Frank

Bergon and Gerald Haslam. University of California Press is publishing fiction now, Georgia, Colorado, Wesleyan, Minnesota, and of course Oklahoma. I think university presses are taking over.[1]

I mean, when James Joyce and people like Beckett had to go to Paris to publish—they couldn't publish in Ireland or England—today I think writers can go to university or small presses, and have to more and more, which is not to say any of us are James Joyces or Becketts, but because these presses are filling that vacuum, that void, and obviously there is some money in it because they at least break even. Writers don't make any money off the books. But it's a chance to write what you really want to write, the way you want to write it, and know you'll have an audience.

JP: Very fortunate. Glad that it is so.

LO: And I'm very proud of the books in that series . . .

JP: And hopefully there'll be some new names in the list soon.

LO: There will be. Hopefully we'll have several new Native American novels within the next couple of years. If it works out.

JP: Well, we'll keep good thoughts about that.

Owens talks about his last novel, *Dark River*, and it is an interesting book in light of this discussion. Unlike the other novels I've considered, this one moves from a conventional narrative, in many senses, through "Tribal Realism" and into the popular genres Owens mentions, concluding with a wonderful revelation of the obvious: that it *is* a novel we are holding in our hands and not a cultural artifact, not a mimetic reproduction of life as much as an imaginative linguistic stimulus. In short, it differentiates itself *as a story*, an act of the imagination, a trapdoor that has a sign on it. Within the novel as well, he investigates many of the motifs, issues, and conventions that have come to shape the critical discourse *about* Native fiction, his own included, but he then stands them on their ears. To discuss this novel I would like to blend Owens's own words with those of the critic and thus call attention to the subjective nature of both fiction and reading. As with my discussion of Vizenor's *Bearheart*, this, too, will make it personal.

In the final days of October 2002 I received a letter. It was hand-written, three pages long, and from a woman in Chicago. She was writing, she said, because she had read an article in the *Chicago Tribune* about Owens's death and had noticed in a picture on the front page of the article a woven rug hanging on Louis's office wall that resembles one she was left upon the death of her father long ago. The letter was mostly about her father and his travels and interactions with Indigenous peoples. She wanted to know if I could tell her anything about the rug's origins, since she thought hers might be quite old and valuable, and she included a photograph to help me in my task. The letter and picture sat on my desk for two months before I answered it, and for the longest time I could not understand why I was reluctant to respond.

I reread the letter and newspaper article in January 2003 in preparation for that response, and it was then that I realized what should have been obvious from the moment of the letter's arrival and my first reading of it. Her close identification of the sign "Indian" with valuable art and artifact is an old, old story, as is her complete avoidance of the significance of the article's topic: the life of a noted Native American writer. Like the author of the newspaper article itself, the letter writer was not actually interested in *the person*; she was interested in objects—the external, material adornments—of a life and not in understanding the life itself, which merely presented an opportunity to validate her own possessions, her own belongings, and her family history. The life of this author and the profound issues that concerned him were invisible or else inconsequential to her purpose.

At the best of times writers make us reflect upon our own identities and obsessions and thus allow us to reevaluate the baggage we carry through life. At the worst of times writers can have a very different effect: the reinforcement of our prejudices and obsessions, the rehashing of old plots. I believe Owens falls into the first category; the letter writer and the article writer who inspired her may inhabit the latter.

The *Tribune* reporter had interviewed me for her article. We talked on the phone for almost an hour, and one sentence of that hour-long conversation found its way into the article: simply that I had called Owens's house several times the day he died and that I was shocked to hear of his passing. However, the reporter and I had spent most of the time talking about Louis's sense of humor, his ability to look at the most tragic events and understand them in multiple ways. His knowledge of history, politics, economics, and so on was extensive, so the significance and complexity of historical events never escaped him. However, he was also able to discern irony and/or absurdity in them, so he brought many points of view and talents to bear in his writings to complicate simplistic thinking by constructing events and characters that emerge from literary and historical conventions but that satirize them.

Part of this repertoire was the humorous vein he used to highlight the sometimes paradoxical values readers hold. In essence, the *Tribune* writer paints the story of a tragic victim: his rise from poverty to success, his "sense of somehow being adrift in his own life," his "confused" identity, being caught between two worlds, and, ultimately (the article implies), his tragic inability to cope. "Owens, then, died on a travel day. But in a sense, they were all travel days; he never stopped moving, fast and far, trying to find out who he was and why he was, to separate out the variegated strands bundled in his soul" (Keller 1). This is quite sentimentally poetic and in this way perhaps a tribute to his life, or at least a mournful nod to those who knew and loved him. However, since the article is found in a newspaper of such wide circulation, it might be construed by many readers as the ultimate authority, the final evaluation of Louis's life: a public stage upon which the chorus sings the same ode, but the mask of comedy never materializes to complicate the plot. To paraphrase the grandmother once more in the concluding pages of Silko's novel *Ceremony*, I think I have heard this story many times before, only the name is different.

While I empathize with the reporter's attempt to understand why Owens died the way he did and thereby provide answers to all the unanswerable questions we have about the event, I believe that making him yet another victim to the public need for racial and economic inequity does a great disservice to his life and work, in which humor is prominent. As his friend Vizenor has said (and as he has demonstrated throughout his extensive literary canon, including his use of the French term "survivance"), humor is one way people—individuals but also cultures—transcend tragic events and learn from them for the future. In both his and Owens's writings humor leads readers into moments of productive reflection and crisis; at times satirical, at others slapstick, Owens's fiction can help us laugh at and then lighten our luggage.

In August 2002 I attended a memorial service in Louis's honor. It was held at the home of one of his "trail crew," the people he worked with in the U.S. Forest Service in the 1970s while he wrote *Wolfsong* and with whom he had kept in contact over the years. At one point, after the food and drink had been dispensed, the people present sat in a circle outside and began to tell stories of their friendship and experiences with Louis, and as the stories progressed they became increasingly funnier as the storytelling began to generate its own energy. It was a much different "reading" of his life from the one presented in the newspaper article about him. With two exceptions, the people in the circle were not academics, yet they had read his books. The dark side of his fiction, which the reporter for the *Tribune* had easily transferred into a definitive dark side of his character, was the oddity that surprised this group of old friends, who told of his practical jokes and of his trickster character but also of the times when his idealism ran afoul of his common sense and how, at these times, he was the first to laugh at himself. This is not the type of action reporters want to hear.

The use of humor in the service of social commentary is apparent throughout Owens's nonfiction writings as well, as a few chapter titles from *Mixedblood Messages* will attest: "Columbus Had It Coming," "Apocalypse at the Two-Socks Hop," "'Grinning Aboriginal Demons.'" But the line between works of fiction and nonfiction in Louis's canon is always blurred, and this includes his literary criticism. As I asked in the interviews above, "Do you see the work on fiction and criticism as a balance to one another, or do they interact in some way?" "I think . . . inevitably they will interact. They have to. The mind works as a whole, so to say while writing a piece of fiction that the ideas from reading and writing criticism don't work in somehow would be dishonest. It may not be conscious, but it has to have some effect." He does not leave what has been written and said about Native Americans alone; instead, it becomes grist for his novels—highly intertextual as they are—in which critical research and a talented, humorous imagination interact to resist and subvert and revise.

In May 2001 Louis agreed to respond to a number of questions from the students in one of my courses who had read his first novel, *Wolfsong*. The last question they asked was about the critical responses to his fiction and what he felt had not received adequate attention. His answer is the impulse behind my reading of his novel. He said: "But still, if there is one other area I'd like people to notice, critically, it's the humor. Following *Wolfsong* I've found more and more power in humor, with each novel, I think, depending increasingly on that particular tool" (personal correspondence). But his humor is always edged with its counterpart, as the later novel titles suggest: *Bone Game*, wherein one major character is a cross-dressing Indian university professor who butchers a deer in his suburban driveway, and *Nightland*, wherein a vehicle icon of drug dealers, the Land Rover, is buried beneath a corral holding the sole remaining horse on a ranch—quite an image. (Here we also find the obligatory "elder," but one who slowly fades while verbally sparring with the ghost of the man whose murder opens the novel.)[2] Struggling with that sometimes thin line between comic and tragic, readers encounter themselves.

Furthermore, as he notes in *Other Destinies*:

> Readers who fail, for example, to bring at least some knowledge of traditional Chippewa trickster tales to the fiction of Gerald Vizenor—not to mention an openness to trickster discourse—are very apt to find themselves confused and perhaps appalled. Unaware of the crucial role of play and humor in Native American cultures, readers groomed by stoic stereotypes will miss much in Vizenor and most other Indian novelists. (15)

I would suggest that these observations also hold true for Louis and that the *Tribune* reporter is but one example of readers who miss the humor in his life and works. His humor operated on subtle reversal, and if we do not engage in this flip-flop discourse, we will certainly find ourselves outside the story. In fact, I believe the title of Christopher LaLonde's book on Louis nicely encapsulates his humor pedagogy: *Grave Concerns, Trickster Turns*.

For the purpose of exploring how this trickster tells his stories I would like to focus upon some representative elements in his last novel, *Dark River*. Like the titles of the other novels, taken alone "Dark River" itself initially prepares the reader for a bleak and gloomy tale, as does the book's cover, *Honest Indian* by Bill Rabbit. However, since one of the underlying qualities of Louis's writing— fiction and nonfiction alike—is its trickster character, nothing is as it appears to be at first, and it is his task to confuse and complicate initial reading of "Indian" as victim in a tragic plot.

Owens played with names, so the title is a simple revision of the name of one of his favorite fishing streams—the Black River, a main tributary of the Salt River on Apache lands in Arizona, about which he writes often. It is a remote and rarely visited place, so it is a setting that lends itself to the imagination but also to significant and revelatory events. In fact, in *I Hear the Train* he records the experience of coming upon a deer, a doe, trying to defend her newly born fawn against an attack by a coyote on the banks of the river, a scene he presented in fictional form two years earlier in *Dark River*. In the autobiographical book, however, he pairs this story with another about how, returning to his camp from a day's fishing, he found cougar tracks in his own and realized that the cougar was in fact stalking him while he fished, oblivious to its presence.[3] The convergence of these two events in this one place leaves him pondering, on his long drive home to New Mexico from the river, the complexities of death and survivance, hunters and the hunted.

What kind of moral universe decreed that countless millions of animals must experience terror and shrieking pain in the beaks and jaws of other animals, every day, every hour, everywhere, until the natural state of the earth, it seemed, must be a single unending shriek of pain? The same god that caused the cougar, that magnificent creature of sinewy tendon and killing instincts, to contemplate me as sustenance, potential energy to drive those killing muscles. (43)

Such a moment of profound reflection is not left well enough alone, however. He concludes: "There's nothing like a sudden awakening to the fact that you are part of the food chain to cast a new light on things" (43). This humorous, brief punch line for an epiphany is characteristic of his earlier storytelling experiences on the trail crews in the mountains, where long narratives are regularly capped with similar, abrupt, one-line reversals in point of view, but also of his experiences studying other writers such as Vizenor and King. These "variegated strands [of storytelling technique are] bundled in his" sense of humor. This is, indeed, as LaLonde's title reveals, a "trickster turn."

As Louis pointed out in our conversation while the novel was in press:

> *Dark River* is very different again from what I've written before, and I'm sure it also is very similar. I wanted to overturn a lot of conventions in this novel, disrupt stereotypes in comic and violent ways, with the emphasis upon the comic. . . . There is quite a bit of violence in the novel, but I like to think it has an almost slapstick quality to it, disturbing and comic at the same time.[4]

The connection between laughter and violence—the basis of survivance Vizenor describes—is given in very condensed form in the novel through the memory of one character: an Apache World War II veteran lost in a camp of his alcoholic comrades from several wars and historic battles. "One was a Navajo code talker who'd been captured and tortured by the U.S. Marines who thought he was a Jap. He showed the scars. They all laughed about that, but it was hard laughter" (102).[5] Read one way, the phrase becomes an ironic oxymoron that is highly suggestive and reverberates throughout the novel.

The slapstick violence and humor, though, find their unique

voice in the character of Jesse, the tribal entrepreneur (aka Harold Sinseer in Vizenor's *Harold of Orange*) who sells "authentic" vision quests to those who will pay handsomely to participate in their fantasy of Indian spirituality. These include Sandrine, a French martial arts master whose quest Jesse intends to conclude with his appearance out of the dark, dressed in a wolf costume (a reversal of a wolf in sheep's clothes), to provide her with her vision of an animal helper. Sadly, though, he is shot by one of a band of paramilitary weekend warriors on an illicit training mission on the reservation who shoots to save the fair damsel (aka Red Riding Hood) from the wolf. Ironically, Jesse spends the rest of the story as her ghostly helper, sometimes appearing as a wolf, sometimes as himself, and sometimes as both, but always with an attitude. The layers of irony and humor are myriad, from the investigation of issues of white shamanism mentioned earlier, to popular "New Age" appropriations as discussed in Masayesva's movie, to "authenticity" concerns (the quest, we are told, is not an Apache tradition); the novel layers humor on them all as it addresses serious and complicated issues for contemporary Native peoples (LaLonde's "grave concerns"), asking us all the same question: What is of true and enduring value in today's societies?

For brevity's sake I would like to provide a few representative examples of the humor and "trickster turns" in *Dark River*, first with characters (who reflect then reverse the stereotypes readers may bring to Owens's novels) and then with a few situations (which take identity issues into very complicated territory).[6]

The novel is comprised of, as Louis calls it in the interview and also in *Mixedblood Messages*, "a family rainbow" of cultures and backgrounds on an Apache reservation in Arizona. The protagonist, Jacob Nashoba, is not Apache but Choctaw, and thus the tension between nations is a subject of the book. But there are also humorous characters, all of them male, who complicate even that simple Native (i.e., Apache) and non-Native (i.e., not Apache) binary. For instance, there is Shorty Luke (a figure analogous to Alexie's Thomas Builds-the-Fire), who is the local storyteller and possessor of obscure knowledge and whose birth is the genesis of an odd twist in identity deconstruction and trickster reversal. He is born one of a set of twins, and, since there is a belief that twins "were a bad sign, evidence of promiscuity or worse, even witchery," their aunt, Mrs. Edwards (whose own name derives from a short-lived marriage to the minister, John [aka Jonathan] Edwards), fixes the problem. She gives the boys names that obscure their kinship; she chooses the names arbitrarily—Shorty Luke and Domingo Perez—and then demands that each be referred to—as they are throughout their lives in the novel—as "the surviving twin" (44). That is a funny story, full of wit, but it also illustrates how communities and cultures can develop their own exclusive canon of funny stories. So, in short order, Owens starts to construct that canon and dismantle easy categorizations, including static family structures as well as the rigid classifications of stories.

However, he does not leave well enough alone. Readers' attempts to place Shorty are complicated by his years in Hollywood, where, much like the character Portland in King's *Green Grass, Running Water*, he played bit parts as "Indian" with noted Italian Americans, as Louis noted, such as Sal Mineo, where he learned Italian phrases, which he uses as he interacts with members of his community. So much for the cosmopolitan. On the reservation, in concert with his friend Avrum, he attempts to subvert a corrupt tribal official's program of providing trophy elk for rich white hunters; however, he makes his living by cutting trees for firewood using a chainsaw, and thus the ecowarrior stereotype is as difficult to pin on him as it is on any of Louis's characters.[7] Like most of the humorous characters, Shorty resists categorization by essentialist thinking, as does his friend.

Avrum Goldberg (a character mentioned in the interview) is one of the interesting non-Apache characters in the novel. A Jewish anthropologist, Goldberg forgoes the city for his romanticized idea of the West and moves to the reservation to live "a traditional lifeway." As Louis notes of the urbanite: "The anthropologist is more 'Indian' than the 'Indians.' He's done his research, and he's hell-bent on living traditionally according to a static idea two hundred years old." When Avrum and Shorty make their pitch to the tribal council, the absurdity of the situation is punctuated by the readers' laughter. Their plan to turn the reservation into an Indian theme park evokes the previous attempts to do so, from Masayesva's dentist to Walt Disney, and the culturally bound sign "Indian" that motivates them. Louis elaborates: "Well, you know, it's satire, so that stuff is always a little extreme; it's beyond reality, but it's to make a point." Readers have to laugh, and when they do, the point about essentialist discourse is made, the attitude deconstructed.

I want to make one further critical point about the humor and the intertextual, allusive nature of the novel. The novel closes with Shorty Luke and the other characters offering, and then enacting, several potential conclusions, sort of a group conversation on and revision of how the story should end. Of this ending, Louis said:

> You know, it's a strange conclusion, and some people will probably be unhappy with it, and some people may not. I like it myself. At the end of the novel I sort of wanted to deconstruct the novel, I suppose, and the whole process of storytelling. Explore what it means to say stories have no ends. And I wanted to take apart all the clichés.

Of course, readers have already written a conclusion based upon their own preferred endings for novels of violence and victimhood, an imaginative tendency that carries with it some terminal creeds. However, conventional endings are offered, then subverted and discarded, thus a comforting, "favorite" resolution is withheld. The conclusion is chosen by committee.

However, as the surviving characters hike out of the river canyon on their way home, Louis makes his nod, his final trickster turn, to his mentor in humor and survivance but also to those who may feel like they "missed much":

> Alison began walking, with the others following in a single line. Behind the surviving twin, Sam Baca said, "Does somebody want to explain what the hell's gone on here?"
>
> "Well," Shorty Luke glanced over his shoulder at Sam. "It is

said . . ." He looked back toward the treeline above them and was silent for a moment as he kept walking.

"It is said that Jacob Nashoba went home." (286)

There are several things going on here. First, one character responds to the recent events, including several deaths and a resurrection to enact a different ending, with incomprehension; much like the *Tribune* reporter, Sam is "clueless." The "insider" joke tells that trickster discourse is afoot; Coyote is present, and the story is going to take a new turn, with Shorty telling it. Also, the word "treeline" evokes Vizenor. As Louis mentioned in the interview in response to my question about his use of fishing in his novels, "you know water has always been an obsession. I guess I'm really obsessed with it. Jerry Vizenor pointed this out to me recently. You see, he's obsessed with tree lines for some reason, and for me it's water."

Finally, then, there is the sad, ominous, almost prophetic implication of Nashoba going home, for Jacob, the lone (forest) ranger who so loved the Dark River, is dead. One wonders. Is he on that dark river of the dead so clearly described in *The Sharpest Sight*? If so, I hope he has his fly rod with him, the number 7, because he's in the company of some big fish.

Dark River can be viewed in the current discussion as a compendium of the various means of differentiation employed by other Native writers and perhaps non-Native writers as well. Moreover, it brings into its stew the stock characters from popular fiction and subverts them all, Native and non-Native alike, blurring yet again the easy lines of ethnic identities. Oddly enough, in this conscious blending of critic and novelist Owens brings into being a new development in the DIAC framework, one that "deconstructs" the novel and storytelling and yet investigates and affirms contemporary Native life, sometimes by satirizing it. And finally, as for criticism today and its various supposed factions and infighting, Owens gives us his insightful and provocative essay "Coyote Story, or the Birth of a Critic" in *I Hear the Train*.

His own major work of Native criticism, *Other Destinies*, is a classic; it provides a rich resource for readers who want an expansive overview of Native fiction as well as clear and close and insightful readings of that fiction. I had published a book two years earlier, in 1990: *Word Ways: The Novels of D'Arcy McNickle*. In his book Louis also examines McNickle and his contributions. Although we met at a couple of conferences before and between these publications (the Modern Language Association's annual conference as well as the American Literature Association's), we did not discuss our readings of McNickle, nor did we visit each other's homes.

That came in 1993, when I directed a National Endowment for the Humanities Summer Seminar for School Teachers at my university: Western Washington University. The topic of the seminar was "Four Firsts," and it focused upon the first novels (and then later writings) of four Native authors. I invited Louis to visit. He accepted quickly, and when he got here I found out why.

He used to live across the street from my campus when he worked for the U.S. Forest Service in Darrington, just south of here. In a way it was a homecoming for him, and he came to talk about his first novel, *Wolfsong*, set in the landscape of the Cascade Mountain range nearby. As he mentions above, he had written the early drafts of it while he lived and worked in this place. The invitation, therefore, allowed him to get together with his Forest Service buddies, who, I would like to note once more, read everything Louis wrote.

The sixteen participants in the seminar were assigned *Other Destinies* and, in particular for Louis's visit, the chapter on McNickle, whose first novel, *The Surrounded*, was one of our central texts. I picked Louis up from his hotel, brought him to the seminar, and, after a cup of coffee, I introduced him. I noted again how valuable his book is but then also mentioned that it was sad it had not received better editing.

Louis's eyebrow went up. I called attention to his discussion of my own study of McNickle and his works, and then I read his words: "Purdy simplifies both the man and his fiction, arguing ingenuously . . ." and he then quotes a passage (72).

"It's sad to see such sloppy editing," I said, "because any good editor would have caught the misspelling of 'ingeniously.'"

We all had a good laugh, but those teachers looked from one of us to the other, a bit curious about the exchange and what it meant. By the end of the day they realized that what they had witnessed was academic discourse at work on a personal level that was also professional: we agreed to disagree. It's a good story, one with an embedded lesson about the production and publication of criticism, particularly that about Native literatures. This was "publication" of a sort very different from either of our books, oral tradition at its most immediate, laced with good humor. We kept the banter going, then and always, and then focused upon the end of the novel, which we read differently. Sharing those differences in the spirit of goodwill enriched the reading of the novel for the seminar's participants. In a letter written later Louis admitted that he was "coming closer to my reading," but I, too, was rethinking his readings into mine, as the discussion of *Dark River* demonstrates.

We talked about this event years later, and here's one point we reached: scholarship and academic writing need not be contentious. Scholarship can be accomplished with humor and goodwill and a willingness to listen intently and answer directly. The occasion for that discussion was an e-mail and, later, a telephone call from an Indian writer who was upset over an interview Louis did. Although this writer was upset by his reading of that interview, he later called Louis, I'm told, and apologized because he saw Louis on c-span and thought he looked "Indian enough" . . . to have an opinion, I guess.

Nonetheless, here is another look at *The Surrounded*, which was published over seventy years ago and provided the discourse that we shared. I wish to assess it through the ideas of DIAC, which will bring us to the point of contention Louis and I ironed out, but I wish to view the novel now through yet another lens, a blend of those of the previous chapters. I hope by providing a hybrid form of critical response that the discourse about the novel will be resurrected, like Jensen at the end of *Dark River*, so we might reconsider and reengage.

I will begin with *the* question. Despite all the attempts over the last three decades to draw lines and categorize narratives, in particular fictional narratives, is there anything inherent in them that one may point to as a truly remarkable ethnic marker, specifically in those works that are written in English for a wide, multicultural audience? In the case of the current discussion, is there anything deeper than DIAC, besides the framework itself, that marks them as "Native" and thus different from works by non-Native writers?

Now, let's reconsider Silko's provocative essay from the 1970s mentioned earlier, "An Old-Time Indian Attack." In it Silko suggests that there are significant differences between works of art produced by Native and non-Native artists. Furthermore, she argues that writers should stay within their own cultural framework when creating them:

> Since white ethnologists like Boas and Swanton first intruded into Native American communities to "collect" prayers, songs and stories, a number of implicit racist assumptions about Native American culture and literature have flourished. The first is the assumption that the white man, through some innate cultural or racial superiority, has the ability to perceive and master the essential beliefs, values and emotions of persons from Native American communities. (Hobson 211)

The conjoining of culture and text is significant, for Silko's critical eye next focuses upon two non-Native authors whose works—employing Indian "content"—won Pulitzer Prizes: Oliver LaFarge for his novel *Laughing Boy* (1930) and Gary Snyder with his poetry collection *Turtle Island* (1975). There are several issues that form the complex matrix of her argument, some of which anticipate and provide contexts for the canon and criticism debates that resonate with her broadside (and are noted above); however, despite her attempts to articulate and specify these two literary works' shortcomings, one must still ask of texts that self-differentiate as "Native," no matter who writes them, what makes them culturally representative or not on the level to which she alludes? More specifically, what in them carries and reveals "the essential beliefs, values and emotions of persons from [their respective] communities"? This would imply, in the case of LaFarge and Snyder, the beliefs, values, emotions of an Anglo community as well.

While Silko's stance on this issue may have changed over the ensuing decades as the discourse evolved, her contentions posit an intriguing dilemma for this discussion, for the differentiation observed in the novels examined thus far operates on only a few levels of understanding. They *do* allow for non-Native readers to reorient their thinking about Native cultures, and they do argue for a continuance of sovereignty and self-determination for those cultures in contemporary times, but is there another level to them that may be equally compelling in their articulation of these issues and equally forceful in the retention of that reorientation? If so, is this level ethnically driven?

Critics have wrestled with this—with varying degrees of success—over the last four decades, and I would like to offer one further consideration for the debate based upon or within the earlier discussions. To do so I would like to redirect our attention to a fairly nondescript passage in *The Surrounded*, a book that many scholars have not read. Interestingly enough, LaFarge wrote one of its first reviews, a very positive one at that, and, later in life, McNickle wrote a biography of LaFarge in which he shares some of Silko's concerns about *Laughing Boy*.

There is a passage in *The Surrounded* that intrigues me. In it Archilde, McNickle's protagonist and a member of the Montana Salish Nation, watches his mother prepare her grandson for a ceremonial dance, and he is struck by a surprisingly simple yet profound observation:

> Watching her, Archilde felt suddenly happy. She was pleased with her duties in the way that only an old art or an old way of life, long disused, can please the hand and heart returning to it. She took up the folded garments of beaded buckskin and placed them on her grandchild in a kind of devotional act that derived satisfaction from minute observances; in a matter so simple, the least part has its significance or it is all meaningless. (215)

Here, we find ourselves in one of those notable occasions in fiction where we are invited into an imaginative insight, for that is exactly what McNickle offers us in so brief a description of a character's movements, as his operative words and phrases suggest: "duties," "old art," "way of life," "devotional act," "satisfaction," "hand and heart returning." In fact, he goes further; these "minute observances" are simple yet so significant that without them "it is all meaningless." This observation provides a crucial central point for so many ideological strands of the novel, and these story lines form the helix around the binary of Archilde's mixed ancestry, his identity as either Native or non-Native, so the passage offers an intriguing access point for discussing narratives that try to differentiate between culturally determined perspectives.

I will return to this passage in greater detail later, including the "it" upon which Archilde's insight hinges, but for the moment let us consider one fundamental element of narratives, the movement discussed in the context of Welch's novels and its implications for helping readers recognize "the essential beliefs, values and emotions of persons from Native American communities." These are, of course, the core cultural elements to be affirmed *and* continued (and through) works of Native fiction.[8]

In his seminal study, *The Novel in Motion: An Approach to Modern Fiction*, Richard Pearce surveys a number of works from the Western tradition and some of its prominent innovators: Defoe, Sterne, Faulkner, Joyce, Beckett, and Pynchon, to name a few. Drawing partly upon the work of scholars such as Sergei Eisenstein, Alan Spiegel, and Roman Ingarden, Pearce develops a critical methodology that makes use of several disciplines, including film and literary studies as well as "visual thinking" psychology. It is an intriguing way of analyzing texts, but, as the subtitle asserts, Pearce is concerned with the modern novel and not necessarily the modern novel in the hands of a Native American author. *The Surrounded* was published in 1936 and, therefore, falls squarely within the traditional era of the modern novel.

Very early on Pearce makes a distinction between "the novel *of* motion" and "the novel *in* motion":

The novel *of* motion focuses on the movement of its subject; the movement is at a distance and is conveyed to us indirectly. The novel *in* motion may focus on a subject that moves fast or slowly or even stands still, but it engages us directly in the dislocations of the narrative medium. It continuously disrupts our equilibrium and imparts the sensation of motion with disturbing immediacy. (xiii)

The distinction hinges on the "narrative eye," the lens through which readers receive descriptive detail and thereby visualize scenes. As this eye "moves" (i.e., in a novel *in* motion), so moves the reader's perspective, from one detail to the next, and thus the shifting of the reader's equilibrium. It is this shifting and destabilization of perspective—the reader response—that seems relevant to the experience of McNickle's novel, as do Pearce's ideas about the differences in narrators:

> The traditional narrator, who often suppresses the act of narrative intervention, tells us what *happened* and what *was there* by covertly processing details for us. He selects them for us and arranges them to advance the story, establish a character, evoke a mood, focus the symbolism, or geometrically simplify the scene by moving from left to right, top to bottom, or near to far. But another mode of narration—established by Smollett and developed by Dickens, Conrad, Joyce, and Faulkner—engages us directly in the narrator's experience of excited perception. It does not process details but records the dynamic of the searching eye as it scans the field to discover what *is happening* and what *is there*. It causes us to feel the kinetic sensation. Modern novelists also engage us in the events of the dynamic medium and stimulate us kinetically through dislocations that jolt our mental equilibrium. We are made to experience shifting points of view, changing frames of reference, and unpredictable transformations. (xii)

At first glance, McNickle would seem to have crafted a novel *of* motion and employed a traditional narrator who supplies the distance and indirection Pearce describes. This is supported by McNickle's penchant for opening chapters with characters in motion through the landscape of the "big sky" country of Montana, or generalized overviews of place and people. However, there are two complicating factors to Pearce's binary: McNickle's protagonist and reader. Archilde is a "lens" through which scenes and events are filtered, and he is of mixed ancestry: European American and Salish. As such, he inhabits the middle terrain between two sets of beliefs/values/emotions: the potential ground for an ethically specific novel of differentiation. As he grapples with pulls in both directions (as his "searching eye . . . scans the field to discover what *is happening* and what *is there*"), his self-reflection and his observations provide the fine focus, the minute observances, that create a sense of excited perception—for Archilde and reader alike—that "jolt[s] our mental equilibrium."

This self-reflection is coupled with the expansive overviews of the turning of seasons in this land of the Salish, thus providing an oscillation between a novel *of* and *in* motion. If the ways that people move are culturally defined, so is the interpretation of an individual's movements likewise shaped by culture (see Jahner, "Cognitive Styles"). In other words, in narration as in life we read motions through a cultural lens, and this is where McNickle's narration operates on both the "traditional" and the modernist levels.[9]

Although Pearce is not using the ideas of disruption and dislocation in a cultural sense, they are the effects that McNickle achieves in his works when the "lens" supplies a contradictory view of events' and movements' significance. In other words, as the reader shifts back and forth between a "traditional-modernist" reading of signification, between the interpretive frames of the "white" and the Native communities, he or she finds that interpretive equilibrium destabilized time and time again. What this may suggest, at least in the terms Pearce conveys, is a hybrid modernist novel as well as, quite possibly, a way that McNickle found to convey those beliefs, values, and emotions in a manner that requires the reader to participate in an "excited perception."[10] It may be an innovation later writers, Welch included, discovered as well as they investigated Native points of view and affirmed them in contemporary times and into the future.

McNickle's novel employs and then subverts the Western conventions of narrative movement, and thus it is both a challenge to and an extension of Pearce's model. It does not replicate the cultural subtexts of its contemporaries, in other words, but complicates them. McNickle accomplishes this by his visualization of scenes, wherein he frames popular conventions of depictions of Native peoples and then directs our "narrative eye" to a modified visual image that subverts that popularity and its ideological underpinnings. In the terms of fiction, he moves to do what Masayesva has done in his documentary and what King has done in *Green Grass, Running Water* but without the humor and the postmodern wrinkles.

McNickle was certainly aware of previous attempts to convey the values, emotions, and beliefs of Native peoples. Almost exactly two years before the publication of his novel and while he was at work on it he wrote to noted anthropologist William Gates, whose work he greatly admired because it is "exacting, unexhibitionary, and removed from the sentimental and inept efforts that have been made in behalf of the Indian in the past and which have succeeded only in making the uplifters ridiculous and sinking the victim into deeper obscurity" (March 25, 1934). In part, he seemed concerned about the romantic stereotypes that had evolved around the sign "Indian" over the course of literary history since European colonization.

Raised on the Flathead Reservation in Montana, an adopted member of the Salish Nation, and, at the time the novel was published, an official with the Bureau of Indian Affairs (as well as an avid reader in many fields), McNickle was well versed in current conditions of Indigenous peoples and, in fact, became an activist for reform in the ways governments and individuals perceived Native cultures. It makes sense, then, that as he painted his narrative scenes, as he engaged the mise-en-scène of his mind (to explore the "map of the mind" Owens refers to in his study), he would look for points that would spark familiarity on the part of his non-Native readers—descriptive details that are, in fact, "exhibitionary"—yet provide new models of human activity that would allow for differentiation and thus the exacting reinscription of the visualizing repertoire of the reader.[11]

I would like to return now to the passage from *The Surrounded* and use these ideas about motion and movement to open it up for our consideration. To do so I would like to examine its contexts through the lens of its mise-en-scène, looking at the narrative "cuts" and the focusing of the narrative eye on movement in particular.

Chapter 24 opens in motion with a panning overview used much like an establishing shot in film. In fact, McNickle's stage directions even supply a soundtrack of sorts with the inclusion of a drumbeat, that pervasive marker of "Indian" in Hollywood tradition. The visual convention it establishes is unmistakable as it provides the image of a frontier town of the Old West and the isolated ranches that evoke that manifest history.[12]

> *De-dum, de-dum, de-dum, de-dum, de-dum...*
>
> The drum had been beating since early morning, faintly, regularly, as if the earth had begun to pulse. It was a sound to quicken the blood. People still at home, going about their daily chores, listened, and then hurried to complete what was still to do that they might be free. The throb of the drum lifted their spirits, urged them forward. It was an intoxicant. (212)

There is no ethnic marker to suggest that he describes either "settler" or Salish; the drum moves all these generalized characters. Individualization of characterization is not important yet, but the movement is, for it establishes the background of anticipation as the characters hurry their actions to respond to the draw of the festivities. This holiday spirit, soon to be bifurcated, is then drawn out to a wide-angle shot, marked by a simple paragraph break, to the expansive landscape and the scene of heightened activity on a larger scale as characters move through the land toward the hub of the town.

> Dust rose from every road leading to St. Xavier and disappeared against the cloudless sky. The sun was at white heat. People were on the move, traveling in spring wagons, in carriages, on horseback, afoot. Every roadside barn and nearly every telephone pole

was placarded with the announcement: "FOURTH OF JULY CEL-
EBRATION: BUCKING CONTESTS: HORSE RACES: BASEBALL
GAME: BIG INDIAN DANCE: DANCING AT NIGHT WITH
RAGTIME MUSIC: COME ONE! COME ALL! RIDE 'EM COW-
BOY!" (212)

The series of events listed is, of course, significant and, with the modes of transportation, helps establish the visual milieu of cowboys and Indians. Another paragraph break acts as a cut to yet another shot, but this one narrows the focus to the town itself and the activities one finds there, including the conventional image of the wild nature of the West and cowboys.

The streets are abuzz with the immediacy of impulsive actions, and this is followed by an initial individualization of the cast that draws a racial and gendered picture.

In St. Xavier groups of men stood before the poolhalls, talking and laughing. Women passed, surrounded by their children; the little girls in starched dresses and ribbons flying, the boys rigged out like baseball players.

In the dusty streets horses reared and plunged at the sound of exploding firecrackers. The riders cursed, to the amusement of the onlookers. When one rider was hurled through a store window the crowd was delighted. On the Fourth of July everybody was a little bit crazy. They shouted "Let 'er buck!"

The older boys and girls eyed each other's new clothes and made remarks. They went about in groups, the girls with arms entwined, giggling, screaming. When a group of boys went down the street, girls followed—not too near, but not far behind.

Dogs fought in the street, firecrackers exploded, babies cried, mothers were worried. Nobody above the age of twenty had a really good time, but they wouldn't have been found enjoying themselves at home for anything. Beneath all other sounds, and giving to movement as well as to sound a conscious rhythm, was the throb of the drum. . . .

Dum, de-dum . . . de-dum, de-dum, de-dum. (212–13)

In Pearce's terms, this is traditional narrative, in which the details have been selected and presented at a distance. However, there are two cultural texts at work in the narrative and its reception, one visual and one aural. The drumbeat frames these scenes and provides, literally and figuratively, the subtext to them.

The narration evokes popular images of "Independence Day" celebrations of the era and particularly in the West and in this case a "Wild West." These are generic images of the time and locale; faces and identities are not important, only character types, much like one finds in the visual imaging of Norman Rockwell and Frederic Remington. What is centered and brought into the foreground of our construction of the scene are the movements described. Also, the overall effect of the lens focusing provides a sense of compression as the dispersed farmers draw together into the crowds in the town. This generates the bedlam of dissonance and disharmony as the narrative eye flashes from action to action and thus the uncommon, contrived movements and actions such crowds create. This is not the routine of daily life movement; in McNickle's oft-repeated phrase, "something is happening." The pacing of the emotive descriptive details in the last paragraph heightens the frenetic nature of the scene: "Dogs fought in the street, firecrackers exploded, babies cried, mothers were worried." However, under it all rests the steady, rhythmic drum of the Salish, and its beat is tied as an ideological counterpoint to the movements visualized. It provides a deliberate, purposeful rhythm, unlike the movements we visualize between its inscriptions in the public space of the town's main street.

There is one more paragraph break/cut as the lens pans out and moves away from the cacophony of the streets to the Salish encampment:

The dancing ground was a mile below St. Xavier, in a grove of willows and cottonwoods near Buffalo Creek. The circle of white tepees, with their smoke-stained tops, contained more than a hundred camps. People streamed out of St. Xavier, where many had left their rigs, going toward the encampment and the sound of the drum. Dust rose chokingly from the ground. The air seemed to be turning to fire. (213)

The dissimilarity of the two villages is clear, visually and suggestively.[13] At once the scene evokes so many images popularized in film, most of which operate on ethnic and ideological binaries: modernity and "primitivism" and the conflicting images of "civilization" and pastoral ("grove, willows, creek"), all of which reside in the long history of literary—and here I include film—depictions of Natives and colonists/settlers. However, once these are evoked, McNickle complicates his audience's easy and comfortable slip into the conventional responses to the conventional images, the signs of "Indian," and a simplistic modernist and romanticist binary of "then" versus now.

The noise of the streets and crush of the crowds shift to the placidity of the encampment, with its suggestion of an equally large gathering but one with relative quiet and lack of gratuitous activity/movement. This focusing frames encampment with town as the settlers are drawn to the drum; initially, the first cut in the chapter narrowed the lens to center St. Xavier. This focusing is cued by the visual image of dust rising to a "cloudless sky," where the "sun was at white heat" (and one wonders how "white" shapes imagery) as the ranchers move toward town. However, as the lens pans out from the hectic motions in the streets and thus frames the two villages, the image of dust rising and heat oppressing again returns: "Dust rose chokingly from the ground. The air seemed to be turning to fire." The townsfolks' own movements stir the dust, and the trip to see the "Indian Dance" (framed between a baseball game and a town dance on the placard noted in the opening and thus establishing yet another sense of "surrounded") becomes unpleasant, choking, and hot. It is an ordeal for the townsfolk but not for the Salish.[14] Moreover, the description McNickle gives of the dance pavilion evokes the Sun Dance traditions and thus a very different cultural perception of the sun and heat. McNickle has told us that the dance is a symbol of endurance; for the immigrants the "air seemed to be turning to fire." One visual image evokes convocation with the creator, the other, a descent into the inferno. The same event and the same place provide two conflicting reactions, one comfortable, one not.

There is one other structuring device to the opening and chapter I need to mention, since it pertains to the cuts and shifting of the lens but also how these tie to culturally bound reactions to the images described. There is a movement from wide-angle shots to narrow focus and then back out. As I mention above, this happens quite often, for instance, from an opening panorama of Archilde riding through the spring fields to a shot of him riding into Modeste's (his uncle's) camp and then, at the end of that chapter, back out to a horse race through the valley. This pulse, in terms similar to those of the drum, is apparent in the scenes that follow, and they carry some of the destabilization and thus the cultural subtext that Archilde and reader experience: panorama, minute movements, panorama.

After the establishing shot has taken us to the encampment, the lens focuses on an individual, Archilde, and his movements through that encampment in the early morning. First, he goes into his uncle Modeste's lodge (the teepee of Hollywood's iconography) and observes preparations there. He is motionless, the panning narrative eye describing, first, his uncle: "He found the old man sitting with his hands in his lap, in an attitude of contemplation, calling to mind the sweet peace of the past; his lips moved, his eyelids fluttered; in different dress he might have been taken for a priest preparing himself for some ceremony" (214).[15] One wonders, Whose mind? The brief clause, "calling to mind the sweet peace of the past," can operate in two directions: either as a movement into the old man's mind and the image that is evoked therein—an earlier world—or as the visualization of the old man himself from Archilde's point of view, the way that he evokes a timeless image of peace and tranquility.

Furthermore, the evocation of "priest" directs attention to the subjective nature of this lens and thus marks the "traditional" narration Pearce describes. However, it also is the "hinge" upon which the scene opens into the modernist tradition. There is no dialogue, only images as the lens pans and the narrative commentary cues the reader. The movements in the mise-en-scène open up the subtext to be found in it; moving lips and fluttering eyelids carry signification. As our focus narrows to these minute movements, we experience Archilde's dawning awareness of the devotion he witnesses and the cosmology it implies and therefore the dislocation of the reader's understanding from Modeste as priest to Modeste as holy man. The call on the "emotions" Silko raises is a Native one. This excites the revelation that Modeste is no longer an artifact but instead a practitioner of ancient devotions. Bodily movements of the characters become the locus of discovery and the evolving vision Archilde experiences in the chapter and his emotional evolution. First, though, as he watches his aunt paint Mike's (Archilde's nephew) face for the ceremony, the paintings signify nothing other than "an old woman's fancy." There is a tension, a conflict, between the lens as an objective window into events and its own interpretation of the movements found therein.

Mike's participation in the ceremony, however, is to cure him of the "sickness" of fear instilled in him by the Catholic priests. At once the narration constructs Anglo metaphors to mark the significance of actions—"if Modeste was a priest, Mike was his altar boy, and each was absorbed in the part"—while reconfiguring the metaphors subtly through the focusing of the lens: Archilde.

> Mike was quiet, but not dull, as he had been too much of late. Archilde watched him closely. His eyes were active, examining the old woman's paint pots and following her agile fingers. At odd times, he looked guardedly at Modeste, revealing a shyness which expressed his awe of the old man and his excitement at the drama he was to have a part in. (214)

There is no element of fancy here, however. The lens records those movements that prepare us for insight. The sense of anticipation and "drama" begins to deconstruct an old conventional image of American Indians as "The Vanishing Indians" whose cultures are on the brink of extinction: the old man and the peace of the past. The lens itself records the rebuttal in the movements of characters and the unspoken subtext they imply: the "active" practice of culture in the "present," across generations. The old woman's fingers are agile, Mike's eyes are busy, and Archilde's next action underscores the importance of what lies below the surface of the scene and determines his own actions.

Archilde did not wait for them to quit the lodge. Occasions of that sort, he knew, required a *decent* privacy. Intruders were not wanted, strange voices were unkind. The old man with the boy leading him would move across the prairie in their own *dignity*, and anyone would show them small *respect* who sought to share the *honor* with them. (214–15, emphasis mine)

There is a brief cut from this private space to another as the lens moves to his mother's, Catharine's, lodge and her hands in motion. Once again:

Watching her, Archilde felt suddenly happy. She was pleased with her duties in the way that only an old art or an old way of life, long disused, can please the hand and heart returning to it. She took up the folded garments of beaded buckskin and placed them on her grandchild in a kind of devotional act that derived satisfaction from minute observances; in a matter so simple, the least part has its significance or it is all meaningless. (215)

This is followed by an extension of the intuitive awareness that centers on hands (including those of Modeste's wife) and their minute movements.

Archilde could see that for his mother this was a real thing, and he had felt the same way a moment before in Modeste's lodge. For these old people it was real, almost real enough to make it seem like a spirit come from the grave. Watching his mother's experienced hands, he could guess how she had lived, what she had thought about in her childhood. A great deal had happened since those hands were young, but in making them work in this way, in the way she had been taught, it was a little bit as if the intervening happenings [the coming of the priests and subsequent colonial history] had never been. He watched the hands move and thought these things. For a moment, almost, he was not an outsider, so close did he feel to those ministering hands. (215)

This series of scenes has a distinct progression. Within the relative solitude of the two lodges the narrative eye pans and then focuses upon individual movements. With the narrator/Archilde's commentary, we are provided a movement from our first images of relics of the past—a tableau that reminds us of a museum display or any number of Hollywood representations—to a recognition of an ongoing cultural lifeway. This lifeway is not described in any significant detail, but it is said to reside in the ways people move, the actions they perform.[16] The tighter the focus, the closer Archilde comes to his people, to belonging to the community. It also marks a shifting in the audience's interpretive lens, for we are curiously situated for translating Archilde's intuitive recording of these actions and their signification.

Archilde's attention to his mother's motions acknowledges and "validates" an event of which he has no knowledge; the evening before, his mother renounced her Catholicism of sixty years and returned the tribe to a "traditional Salish" lifeway. Privy to this event and its genesis, the reader is at once more knowledgeable than the protagonist (the observer/lens) and therefore more closely aligned with the participants being described. The reenactment of a pre-colonized and culturally rich lifeway is affirmed here *by the reader* through the recognition that "minute observances" can reorient us with a whole cosmology by simply changing the motions we make. Our initial sign "Indian" as relic of and locked into the past has come to live in the present with its own agency, a destabilization of perception as we focus on a visual image of movements.

Our lens leaves Catherine's lodge and goes to the dance ground, positioning him, significantly, with the Anglo audience surrounding the dancers. The narration provides his shift back to that audience's orientation: "There was nothing real in the scene he came upon" (216). There are, however, several movements that draw his/ our attention, marked once more by rising dust. This time, however, the dancers' movements generate it. Modeste opens the ceremony with an utterance now deepened with Archilde's observations in the lodges. "Ho! Let it be as it was in old times," and the "dancers went forward like actors in a play and lost themselves in their game" (217).

Our lens is physically and metaphorically on the margins gazing in at a public space become private; simultaneously, he records a lifeway that is perceived as a hollow relic ("actors," "play," and "game") and devalued through the derision the white spectators heap upon the actions themselves and the people performing them, but in the private space it is alive and dynamic.

The audience is comprised of "intruders [who] were not wanted, strange voices [that are] unkind," and they certainly show no respect. There is much of Hollywood in the visual imagery and audience's response, at least initially: the dancers "echoed the war cry from time to time and made threatening gestures with a feathered carpenter's hatchet, which was fierce enough to cause a white woman to grow pale and draw back" (217). The red savage/white female victim binary, dating from colonial captivity narratives and James Fenimore Cooper, inheres in the scene, but this, nonetheless, is a "small matter." When the lens refocuses, however, from those distracting movements, the spatial and philosophical distances diminish as McNickle paints the details of the dance movements in his mise-en-scène.

Mike appears out of the cloud of dust, dancing. "And then he came forward with a slow, weaving, muscular movement that was inexplicably graceful—a detached element of rhythm, moving unhindered through space" (218). Modeste appears in the background, dancing slowly, and the two come to within two feet, we are told, of Archilde as they pass around the circle. The physical proximity in this scene is symbolic (the diminishment of the individual and time through the closing of three generations of the family as all focus upon the movements of the dance and their curative effect), but it also fulfills the structural function of drawing the lens into the center and away from the disruptive actions and orientation of the audience on the margins.

> For a moment he felt everything Mike felt—the rhythmic movement, the body's delight in a sinuous thrusting of arms and legs, the wild music of the drum and dancing bells, and best of all, the majesty of the dancers. It really seemed, for a moment, as if they were unconquerable and as if they might move the world were they to set their strength to it. (218)

The disrespect of the surrounding culture defuses the potential for romanticizing the "exhibition," but McNickle goes further. The kinetic quality Pearce describes moves from eye to body. With this shift McNickle accomplishes the "shifting points of view, changing frames of reference, and unpredictable transformations" Pearce notes of the modern novel; as an audience imaginatively inhabits Mike's body, it moves from the margins into the center, and the two locations cannot be reconciled. The townsfolk—the caricatures—who surround the dancers do not offer a viable lens or interpretation of movements. While I do not suggest that a non-Native audience can, as a result of this dislocation, now fully comprehend, or "master," in Silko's terms, the beliefs, values, and emotions of the Salish community, I would argue that it does open up a revised conceptualization of cultural performance in which minute motions gain greater significance and, in this case, a sense of continuity with ancient lifeways, despite the weak qualifiers McNickle offers: "seemed," "might," "for a moment."[17]

This momentary revelation is brought into an abrupt crisis as the laughter of the crowd rises in volume. The lens pans back out, but not before it reveals one significant image, the old man at whom the laughter is directed and upon whose movements the lens focuses: "an old man, too weak to move in the circle, who stood in one place and bobbed himself up and down. His face showed his inner contentment and he was oblivious of the laughter at his expense" (219). In the context of the preceding visual imagery this centering of a character also accomplishes, I would argue, much of what Silko contends is lost in LaFarge's and Snyder's books: if not the beliefs in specific detail, then at least the values and emotions of this Salish community embodied in the old man's movements (and Mike's and Modeste's as well as Archilde's/the reader's empathic response). It does this by once again destabilizing the audience's orientation. In this image of a "relic" of the past, the binary of strength/weakness inherent in the colonial paradigm (white/red, modernity/past, civilized/savage) is deconstructed. The townsfolk's perspective, shaped by the circus (Hollywood) atmosphere it self-generates, is revealed once more as foolish, mean-spirited, and wrong.

Significantly, the chapter ends in the solitude of his mother's lodge with Archilde once more in the center, and the lens is now external and focused upon him and his emotions. Outside, riders circle the camp, and the sound of the bells on their horses is rendered as "ca-ring, ca-ring." Archilde is motionless as the narration brings home the point: "Archilde sat quietly and felt those people move in his blood. . . . It was all quite near, quite a part of him; it was his necessity, for the first time" (222). And this takes us to the pronoun once more.

What could the antecedent be for "it" but the culture itself, "the essential beliefs, values and emotions" of the community in which he belongs? McNickle describes very little of the Salish material lifeways; he provides, instead, through the movements of his characters, the emotive power they possess and thus a vitality in conflict with the image of their inevitable demise in modern times. Through the crafting of the scenes and imagery in this chapter McNickle has brought the audience to moments of excited perception focused upon characters' movements, which in turn provide a re-visioned interpretive lens through which subsequent movements/actions are assessed. These are also the images we carry with us, since they are the ones the camera has "zoomed" in upon for emphasis and critical assessment.

Interestingly, as McNickle's first novel was going to print, he was at work on another. However, *Wind from an Enemy Sky* was printed in 1978, a year after his death, so in a way it reflects his lifelong fascination with this subject. Once again employing the cross-cultural shift in point of view, McNickle takes his readers into the observations of the Anglo Indian agent, Rafferty, the narrative eye who continually focuses upon the differences he sees between his own culture and that of his charges:

Rafferty watched The Boy's [a tribal police officer] deft movements as he worked on the fire—the delicate touch of the large hands, the ease of the crouch—and he could see the fitness of the man in his situation. What a man [*sic*] learned, and it was all he learned in a lifetime, was a degree of fitness for the things he had to do. (125)

Later in the novel Rafferty's initial curiosity reaches the point of insight:

Quite suddenly, and effortlessly it now seemed, he had begun to get the feel of their perceptive world. It had something to do with motion, with the way they gestured, their facial movements, and the way they walked—he had a glimpse of it for the first time the day he watched The Boy mending the fire, and only partially absorbed it. Later it grew large in his mind. But there seemed to be a still larger aspect, and this he did not yet understand. It had to do with their way of *talking*, and that followed habits *bred in the senses* themselves and *made the world the way it is* to a seeing and hearing and feeling man. (176, emphasis mine)

McNickle's elemental definition of Native identity is expanded here. The dislocation for the reader comes from the point of view employed: a non-Native's inward gaze with which the reader aligns. Rafferty's observations unite three elements of human experience McNickle's audience may not see as interrelated: perception, motion, and articulation. All types of movements reveal culture, for they have emerged from place, from "situation," and evolved over a long period of time until they have become ingrained, endemic to all aspects of culture: customs, senses, ceremonies, gestures, language itself.

One wonders. What of the other side of the ethnic binary, what of LaFarge's and Snyder's own cultural communities and thus the orientations they carry with them? I would now like to provide briefly a few scenes from other works that may take this discussion beyond one novel produced in the 1930s and carry it into contemporary times and texts. Although I do not examine them in detail as with *The Surrounded*, I would hope that offering them provokes an extension of the methodology to other ethnically/culturally defined works and extends our critical discourse accordingly.

Consider Henry David Thoreau, who made an "American" psyche the subject of his studies and who was mentioned in our conversation above. His travelogues—*A Week on the Concord and Merrimack Rivers*, *Cape Cod*, and in particular *The Maine Woods*—can be read as quests to understand Indigenous patterns of movement in the specific landscapes of "New England" and thereby to enact a new sense of individuality that follows Emerson's dictate to "beware the courtly muses of Europe." However, even in his opposition to them he may have replicated them.[18]

For example, *The Maine Woods*, published from notebooks edited after his death, reveals Thoreau's idealistic imaging of Indigenous ways of moving, yet these clash harshly with his judgmental assessment of the "real" movements he observes and records. In other words, as he describes his Penobscot guides' movements he lapses into the schizophrenic literary conventions of the times, at once valorizing Native Americans' fitness for effective movements across their "stage" while feeling threatened or repulsed by them. Consider two passages:

> He [Joe Aitteon, one of the guides] proceeded rapidly up the bank and through the woods, with a peculiar, elastic, noiseless, and stealthy tread, looking to right and left on the ground, and stepping in the faint tracks of the wounded moose, now and then pointing in silence to a single drop of blood. . . . I followed, watching his motions more than the trail of the moose. . . . At another time, when he heard a slight crackling of twigs and he landed [the canoe] to reconnoitre, he stepped lightly and gracefully, stealing through the bushes with the least possible noise, in a way in which no white man does,—as it were, finding a place for his foot each time. (146)

There seems to be no ethnic marker in the scene that differentiates from Rafferty's own impressions about Indians and movements. Here, though, the words "stealth" and "stealthy" match movements to military connotations, reinforced by "reconnoitre" and "stealing," and one wonders why the scene is crafted imaginatively with these prompts. Later, the results of such motions are dealt with in language that at once creates a pastoral mise-en-scène and performs an ideology within it.

Here, just at the head of the murmuring rapids, Joe now proceeded to skin the moose with a pocket-knife, while I looked on; and a tragical business it was,—to see that still warm and palpitating body pierced with a knife, to see the ghastly naked red carcass appearing from within its seemly robe, which was made to hide it. . . . In the bed of this narrow, wild, and rocky stream, between two lofty walls of spruce and firs, a mere cleft in the forest which the stream had made, this work went on. (151)

The description of these movements is heavily loaded; "tragical," "pierced," "ghastly," "naked," and "robed" convey more than a descriptive chronicle of actions. They provide the interpretative notations for the reader to visualize the scene and then evaluate the Indian guide's movements accordingly. We thus construct an image that resonates with the popular stereotype of "savage" along with that motif's military subtexts. It is not the *action* itself that holds the ideology, it is in the linguistic construction of it and the ways we are directed to create a scene imaginatively.

Now consider another moose story. This one is from Erdrich's *Tracks*. As the old, starving storyteller Nanapush waits for his kinsman Eli to return with much-needed meat, he provides a lens into the hunt:

I began to sing slowly, calling on my helpers, until the words came from my mouth but were not mine, until the rattle started, the song sang itself, and there, in the deep bright drifts I saw the tracks of Eli's snowshoes clearly. . . .

He had seen the tracks before, down near a frozen shallow slough. So he went there, knowing a moose is dull and has no imagination, although its hearing is particularly keen. He walked carefully around the rim of the depression. Now, he was thinking. His vision had cleared and right away he saw the trail leading over the ice and back into the brush and overgrowth. Immediately, he stepped downwind and branched away, walked parallel and then looped back to find the animal's trail. He tracked like that, never right behind it, always careful of the wind, cautious on the harsh ground. (101)

As is Thoreau's guide, Eli is successful, although it is not simply through stealth but through movements guided by supranatural connections. The scene that follows extends this:

> He used a tree limb to roll it on its back and then with his knife, cut the line down the middle. . . . To gain strength for the hard work ahead he carefully removed the liver, sliced off a bit. With a strip of cloth torn from the hem of his shirt, he wrapped that piece, sprinkled it with tobacco, and buried it under a handful of snow. Half of the rest, he ate. The other he saved for me. . . . He put his jacket right side out again, smeared it with tallow from a packet in his shirt, then quickly cut off warm slabs of meat and bound them to his body with sinew so that they would mold to fit him as they froze. He secured jagged ovals of haunch meat to his thighs, then fitted smaller rectangles down his legs, below the knees. He pressed himself a new body, red and steaming. . . . Last of all, he wrapped new muscles, wide and thick, around each forearm and past his elbows. What he could not pack, he covered with snow and branches, or hoisted laboriously into the boughs of an ash tree. (103)

The cultural contexts of Eli's movements are provided, ones that Thoreau does not see or does not create for his readers; Thoreau's actions are devoid of Native philosophical, cultural subtexts. This is not so with Erdrich, whose passage suggests the cosmological differentiation through its suggestive language and description of ritual. This is a convention of other Native American authors as well, although, like any convention, there are those who construct hybrid visualizations that overturn simplistic binaries, thus calling to attention the images that have shaped them. Sometimes this is masterfully laced with humor.

I wish to present a long passage mentioned above from Owens's *Bone Game*. It offers its own distinct variation on the theme, one no doubt enlightened by Owens's extensive understanding of American and Native American literatures. I quote at length to provide this author's satirical voice by way of conclusion. On the campus of the University of California, Santa Cruz, the motif enters the world of the literary critic and the trickster. As Owens mentions above, the place was scary, but this humor balances the bleak nature of that landscape.

When he parked his truck at the faculty complex, he saw a crowd gathered near one of the townhouse units. The vice chancellor, flanked by a campus cop, rushed toward Cole as soon as he stepped out of the pickup.

"He can't do this," Spanner said, his voice taut with desperation, and Cole noticed that the thin-shouldered vice chancellor was actually wringing his hands.

"It's a violation of state game laws as well as university regulations. I've told him this, but he won't stop. He just ignores me."

"I said we ought to just haul his ass in." As she spoke, the cop glared at Cole, her mouth a grim line, right hand on the butt of her pistol. Her buzzcut hair was so blond it seemed no color at all, and through the open leather jacket he could see that her breasts strained at the uniform shirt. At the same moment it occurred to him that the women of Santa Cruz were absolutely right. Here he was, in a critical situation, obsessed with the breasts of a campus cop. Even her anger had an erotic edge to it, and he wondered if it was just him, her, both of them, or the whole world. Or had he simply been alone too long?

"I thought you could talk to him," the vice chancellor added, the corners of his mouth twitching.

"Skin to Skin?" Cole turned from the cop to the administrator for a moment before he pushed his way through the two dozen gaping academics, spouses, and pale children.

The field-dressed carcass of a deer hung by its hind feet from an ornamental mulberry tree. A steaming pile of entrails lay on the manicured lawn beneath the two-point buck, and the smell of blood was warm and rich on the sea air. A dark, wiry young man with a long black ponytail, wearing only a black pleated skirt and running shoes with no socks, was skinning the animal, laying the hide off expertly with a large, curved knife.

Cole watched the man with the knife work, admiring the precise skill and trying to remember the last time he'd field dressed a buck. It had been twenty years, and it had been in the coast range to the south on a cold morning with his father.

He stepped close, watching the rapid movements of the knife and the sharp flexing of the skinner's hard muscles. "They seem to be upset," he said.

The young Indian looked up with a quick, gap-toothed grin, and the nearly black eyes, long face, and gaunt cheeks reminded Cole of a laughing predator, a fox or coyote or perhaps a scrawny prairie wolf. "Yes. I've gathered as much," the man said as he pulled the skin down over the deer's head like a sweat shirt and began to cut through the neck. Over his shoulder he said loudly, "One of these women came out screaming, 'He's killed his wife. He's killed his wife.'" Mimicking the words with a falsetto, he glanced up again and grinned the wide grin. "Too bad the liver and heart are on that grass. I wasn't thinking. I should have put a tarp or something down first. They use herbicides and pesticides on the lawn here, so now they're ruined. This place is poisoned."

"They say you can't hunt on campus," Cole explained.

"Oh, I know that." He made a final cut, and the head fell onto the entrails, the pale inside of the hide dropping to cover both. The audience gasped. He smiled and looked at the carcass. "He's a good one. Probably a hundred and twenty dressed out like this. That wouldn't be much for a mule deer, but it's pretty big for one of these coastal bucks." Dropping the knife, he dipped his cupped hand into the chest cavity, and it came out filled with blood. With an index finger he drew two slashes of blood down each cheek and another across his forehead. Then he made full, bloody handprints on each breast. He looked directly at Cole, and one eye winked. He began to do a shuffling dance around the headless carcass, singing a nasal "*hey-ah-nah, hey-ah-nah*," over and over until he had completed seven rounds.

"Explain to him that it's against both state and university regulations," the vice chancellor said desperately at Cole's shoulder.

"You look Navajo," Cole said, turning away from Spanner. "Is that a skirt you're wearing?"

"Alex Yazzie. Salt Clan, Born-for-Water. Chinle." He extended a bloody hand and then looked down at the hand and took it back with a shrug. "It's an Evan Picone. You think it's too short, too daring?"

"Cole McCurtain. Choctaw-Cherokee-Irish-Cajun, Mississippi and Oklahoma by way of New Mexico and California. Looks the right length to me."

"They seem a bit nonplussed, don't they?" Alex Yazzie grinned. "This fine animal gave himself to me. I was driving up the hill over there, just going along you know like I always do, when he jumped in front of my truck. I didn't see him till it was too late. Luckily, I had pollen with me. You see, I need some sinew for a special project and I figured I might as well also make some venison stew; maybe even turn out a little jerky in my townhouse and offer some to my colleagues." He glanced at the crowd and then looked down at the skirt. "Unfortunately, I stained my new skirt. As you can see, however, I had enough foresight to remove my blouse and jacket. Also my heels. You ever tried to field dress a buck in heels?" (24–26)

It is impossible to conceive of a definition of culture that does not have at its center the fundamental kernel of narrative. We are—as individuals and as cultures—the stories we tell of ourselves. And the stories change as cultures change, or vice versa. Historical events, shifts in philosophical orientation, conflicts based upon ethnicity, traumatic reactions to war and/or colonialism, all elements of human endeavor can have the profound formative power of shaping cultures because, as we engage these endeavors in language by telling about them and the effects they have had upon people (in other words, by crafting an imaginative mise-en-scène about them), we reshape those events.

The same can be said for individual authors, our storytellers, our storiers. It is revealing that the attempt to portray and thus convey Indigenous patterns of movement—however perceived and presented—continues to this day and is increasing in popularity. Celebrities such as the New Age idol Lynn Andrews, quasi visionary Carlos

Castaneda, not to mention Kevin Costner (*Dances with Wolves*), all engage and enact their own visions of movements that serve to situate individual and place in a relationship they perceive as distinct from the one that came to the North American continent from Europe. However, these attempts must not go unquestioned.

The texts imaginatively dramatize movements, but we must carefully assess these movements in light of the historical and literary contexts of previous attempts to do so and ultimately in relation to alternative narratives to that impetus: in the narratives that emerge from within communities marked by long-term, ethnic, and culturally defined points of view. This contemporary reenvisioning of the cultural core of literary movement and thus identity may in fact reflect an evolutionary moment, a time when cultures productively interact because the ways we craft our stories of ourselves change to reflect a more astute understanding of ourselves and each other. It is also one agenda that Native authors share, no matter how they situate themselves within the community of authors that has developed over the last three decades: to acknowledge their cultural roots (differentiation); to investigate those roots as they inform identity in contemporary times; to (re)affirm the beliefs, values, and emotions of Native communities; and to call for their continuation into the future.

We come to books down and from a variety of avenues, of backgrounds and experiences. Mine do not replicate yours; however, we do, as humans, often share points of connectivity in the things we have seen and experienced: not always, but often enough that we can each reach an understanding of the same novel—not the same understanding, always, to be sure—and appreciation of its merits, accomplishments, and art. Thus with criticism in general. As the stories in chapter 4 illustrate, there are points where—despite the rhetoric and posturing—critics are closer in readings than they often allow. Such is the life, as Owens says, of tenure, and promotion, and publication, and academics in general.

These conversations in and about Native fiction are, therefore, an attempt to provoke yet more "voices" in the new millennium scholarly discourse, voices shaped by and emergent from the past that call for us to read, reread, and reappreciate the stories as stories, as provisional locations of imaginative interaction. Are they divorced from lived experience? Of course not. However, like all literary, fictional constructions, they belong to an odd, surreal realm beyond that "real-world" experience and those of both writer and reader: Vizenor's imitation, not representation. "This ain't just real estate," to be sure, but the "bottom line" at the center of the ideas offered in this book—mine and those of the people interviewed—is this: how does the thing we call "Native American fiction" shape our present and our world? There is such great diversity—and here I will note that "great" has many senses to it—in the "canon" of Native literatures that we always look for a point in common, a "middle." I admire the work of those writers mentioned here, discussed here, interviewed here, and implied here. The wide array of their styles and approaches is truly remarkable, and I would hope that recognizing their overarching connections—the DIAC—complements and compliments this community of writers and calls upon the considerable creativity that it possesses to continue into the next seven generations that same sense of purpose and direction. The world needs it, some people more than others.

Years ago as a "new" PhD I taught as an adjunct faculty member at the University of Oregon. One of the courses I taught was English 240, Introduction to American Indian Literatures, created originally by Barre Toelken. My class had an enrollment of sixty plus. It was an introduction, indeed. From that first time through it I have three vivid and distinct memories.

One is of the first day of class. After the introductory maneuverings were completed and class was dismissed, one woman came forward to tell her story, to share her background in Indian literatures: she carried a book by Lynn Andrews. She was a convert to the New Age movement through the works of this author. I kept my mouth shut, and then, later in the quarter, I encouraged her to do her term project on Andrews's canon. An element of that project was a class presentation to share her readings and conclusions. When her turn came, she spent thirty minutes castigating New Age appropriation of Indigenous worldviews, ceremonies, and identities, using excerpts from Andrews's texts to demonstrate the danger of so doing. The stories and poems we read together had rewritten her universe: a conversion of matter. She had found Paula Gunn Allen's work, and it saved her. Surprise. The best critics are chosen and willing to rethink.

The second memory is of Michael. Bright, articulate, a senior in prelaw, he approached me after the fourth week to tell me his story. It is a story I have watched develop many times since, names changing like seasons. Nez Perce by birth, he grew up far from his grandparents after his father shut the door on past and family. Like many second generations, his dad wanted to save him the pain of conforming to the "mainstream." Moving away meant beginning anew; success came from blanching the color out of their lives.

There were bits of information that survived: his grandfather was a Dreamer who, at the end of his life, drove his pickup into the heartland of the Wallowa Mountains, locked it, placed the keys on the front right tire, and walked into the mountains, never to be seen again. The door seemed not only shut but locked forever. Unlike the third-generation characters in the stories we read—Archilde in *The Surrounded*, Leon Burnt Horn in Roxy Gordon's "Pilgrims," the unnamed protagonist in *Winter in the Blood*—the path back seemed irretrievably lost. By reading these, though, we know better.

Michael's presentation of his project was supposed to last five to eight minutes, but it took sixty-two. The class was to last only fifty; near the end of it, students enrolled in the course that met in the room after ours tried to get into the room only to be kept outside that shut door, held closed by Michael's classmates until he had had his say. Sixty-two minutes of complete absorption, his the only voice, the only sound.

His project? A pasticcio of self. Like the larvae of the caddis fly in the McKenzie and Willamette rivers (less than a mile from his voice) that piece together their outward skins from pebbles, sand, fir needles, and sticks, the detritus of their environment, Michael presented a spoken text that patched together bits of treaties, novels, newspapers, poems, congressional acts, television commercials, his own journal, and popular songs. This was his song of self composed with fragments of the printed past woven into a new linguistic construction. In one utterance he had moved issues of identity from a description of prescriptive criteria to an illustration of its true adaptive nature: a fluid, ever-evolving imaginative process, referential to but not solely determined by the past. Was he a "victim" in the sense of some novels? Yes. Was he powerless to revise that victimhood? No.

My third vivid memory of that class is of its last meeting. For the occasion I had invited my former professor, Montana Richards Walking Bull, and her husband, Gilbert. They drove down from Monmouth—sixty-five miles north of Eugene—to have lunch and then talk to the class.

I have often wondered what Montana thought when we first met, years prior to this visit. That was in a "methods course" she taught entitled Teaching the Novel. She was born of a minister father and Cherokee mother; she had taught for years in public schools herself, moving here and there around the country, ending up in Oregon a college professor, one who trains teachers, a writer, a scholar. Now, before her, there sat yet another batch, a new generation of white faces looking back and one looking sorely out of place. I was a "nontraditional" student.

I was back from Vietnam and trying to decide between a career in corrections or philosophy, and at one point in my search for an image of me in the future I stood knee-deep in Mom's bathroom, my feet in the crawl space, replacing the subfloor, rotten from water that had seeped through cracked caulking for a long time. The tub sat out on the back lawn while I sliced out the offending wood with my mother's Swedish carpenter father's saw. Mother cried in the living room; I chuckled under my breath. On the television she was watching Richard Nixon resign as president of the United States. The saw sighed through the foundation. Political institutions are of our own making, as is socioacupuncture.

Montana drew us through *Snow Country* and Faulkner, *Hunger* and Hemingway, and somewhere between Filipino narrative styles and French plot structures I converted. As I mentioned earlier in the conversation with Vizenor, *When the Legends Die* surprised me.

So, several presidents later, she and Gilbert came to talk to students once more. We ate in the University Club. We had sandwiches, soup, soft drinks. Over lunch she surveyed me closely. I had invited students: two fans from the course and two graduate students. It was a small gathering. Gilbert told a funny story. We ate well, and she watched. I think she was wondering who or what I had become. I wondered, too.

I introduced Montana and Gilbert to a packed classroom. I was left sandwiched up against a window, far away from the door but close to the podium. Outside the window there are huge firs and the oldest buildings on campus, the stone memories of early immigrant days in the Willamette Valley. Montana spoke first. She asked what the students thought about Indian literatures. They responded. She told them her own story: growing up in Oklahoma, going to school, moving around the country, coming to Oregon, becoming a professor. And then she stepped to the podium to read some of her own poetry, but then, from a spiral binder, a manuscript in progress about Native American women poets. By that time I was watching the students. They were respectfully attentive.

When she finished, Gilbert reached into his bag and pulled out his drum. He walked over toward the window, looking out at those buildings and the old-growth firs that surround them, tapping the drumhead lightly, singing and humming under his breath. The tune in order, he hit a quick, loud song and took it to the rafters. The next was softer, then rose. Gilbert had a wonderful voice and a deep repertoire of songs from his Sioux folks back home. Within ten minutes both doors to the classroom had been flung open, and lines of students from other classes stretched as far, and farther, than I could see in either direction. The next class in the room was canceled, since we went long over our scheduled time, once again. Gilbert sang on. Montana's manuscript was, unfortunately, never published; she passed on a few months later. He, a few years ago.

They were happily married, Montana and Gilbert. They had very different personal stories, as different in their configurations of self as two people could get, identifying as Cherokee scholar and Sioux singer; however, the two halves, the plots, entwined. Evidently, there was room for both in the home they built together. Taken together, their lives enriched the world.

This book is for them, and for those whose works continue to inspire: D'Arcy, James, Paula, Louis. It is for all those whose art, like that of the authors discussed, brings us closer, allows us to touch across barriers that are immaterial, and asks us to converse with respect, and dignity, through all our relations.

Source Acknowledgments

Interview transcripts and portions of the author's essays, revised for this volume, originally appeared in the following publications.

"'No one ever did this to me before': Contemporary American Indian Texts in the Classroom" originally appeared in *American Indian Quarterly* 16, no. 1 (Winter 1992): 53–61, and is reprinted by permission of the University of Nebraska Press. Copyright © 1992.

"'perspective, proportion, design': The Moral Lesson of *House Made of Dawn*" originally appeared in *N. Scott Momaday and "House Made of Dawn,"* ed. Bernadette Regal-Cellard (Paris: Éditions Ellipses, 1997), 34–41, and is reprinted by permission of Éditions Ellipses.

"Bha'a and *The Death of Jim Loney*" originally appeared in *Studies in American Indian Literatures* 11, no. 1 (Winter 1987): 17–25, and is reprinted by permission of the author.

"The Transformation: Tayo's Genealogy in *Ceremony*" originally appeared in *Studies in American Indian Literatures* 10, no. 3 (Winter 1986): 121–33, and is reprinted by permission of the author.

"He Was Going Along: Motion in the Novels of James Welch" originally appeared in *American Indian Quarterly* 14, no. 2 (Spring 1990): 133–47, and is reprinted by permission of the University of Nebraska Press. Copyright © 1990.

"Against All Odds: Games of Chance in the Novels of Louise Erdrich" originally appeared in *The Chippewa Landscape of Louise Erdrich*, ed. Allan Chavkin (Tuscaloosa: University of Alabama Press, 1999), 8–35, and is reprinted by permission of the University of Alabama Press. Copyright © 1999.

"Building Bridges: Crossing the Waters to a Love Medicine" originally appeared in *Teaching American Ethnic Literatures*, ed. John R. Maitino and David Peck (Albuquerque: University of New Mexico Press, 1996), 83–100, and is reprinted by permission of the University of New Mexico Press.

"Agents of Agitation in Vizenor's *The Heirship Chronicles*" appears in revised form in *Gerald Vizenor: Litterateur at Large*, ed. Simone Pellerin (University Press of Montpellier, forthcoming), 181–91, and is used by permission of Presses Universitaires de la Méditerranée.

"Tricksters of the Trade: 'Remagining' the Filmic Image of Native Americans" originally appeared in *Native American Representations: First Encounters, Distorted Images, and Literary Appropriations*, ed. Gretchen M. Bataille (Lincoln: University of Nebraska Press, 2001), 100–118, and is reprinted by permission of the University of Nebraska Press. © 2001 by the University of Nebraska Press.

"Grafting Film and Fiction: A Reading of *Green Grass, Running Water*" originally appeared in *Imaginary (Re-)Locations: Tradition, Modernity, and the Market in Contemporary Native American Literature and Culture*, ed. Helmbrecht Breinig (Tübingen: Stauffenburg Verlag, 2003), 185–99, and is reprinted by permission of Stauffenburg Verlag.

"Hard Laughter: Humor and Survivance in Louis Owens' Novels" originally appeared in *Indian Stories, Indian Histories*, ed. Fedora Giordano and Enrico Comba (Torino: Otto Editore, 2004), 59–67, and is reprinted by permission.

"Moving Stories: Visualizations, Mise-en-scène, and Native American Fiction" originally appeared in *Western American Literature* 41, no. 2 (Summer 2006): 177–200, and is reprinted by permission of the author.

"A Conversation with Simon Ortiz" originally appeared in *Studies in American Indian Literatures* 12, no. 4 (Winter 2000): 1–14, and is reprinted by permission of the author.

"Clear Waters: A Conversation with Louis Owens" originally appeared in *Studies in American Indian Literatures* 10, no. 2 (Summer 1998): 6–22, and is reprinted by permission of the author.

"Crossroads: A Conversation with Sherman Alexie" originally appeared in *Studies in American Indian Literatures* 9, no. 4 (Winter 1997): 1–18, and is reprinted by permission of the author.

"'And then, twenty years later . . .': A Conversation with Paula Gunn Allen" originally appeared in *Studies in American Indian Literatures* 9, no. 3 (Fall 1997): 5–16, and is reprinted by permission of the author.

"The Future of Print Narratives and Comic Holotropes: A Conversation with Gerald Vizenor" originally appeared in *American Indian Quarterly* 29, nos. 1 & 2 (Winter–Spring 2005): 212–25, and is reprinted by permission of the University of Nebraska Press. Copyright © 2005 by the University of Nebraska Press.

Notes

INTRODUCTIONS

1. In an oddly ironic way, others challenge the ethnicity of the author, who is Sicilian. How, it is contended, could someone other than a Native person critique colonialism and the texts it produces? Given the multiple colonial forces that have occupied Sicily, one wonders.
2. There are texts that complicate this, and for these I would add one other marker: by its relationship to other works by the same author. Consider D'Arcy McNickle's short story "The Hawk Is Hungry." Read alone, it would not seem "Indian" (as if it needs to be if read alone), but in relation to his other stories one can see its Indigenous critique of Manifest Destiny and colonial attitudes. One could make a similar case after comparing *Gorky Park* and *Stallion Gate* by Martin Cruz Smith.

1. THE 1970S

1. This is an approach regaining popularity with the works of David Treuer and James Cox, mentioned in the introduction. The interviews speak to the current critical productions of Native scholars and scholars of Native literatures. Therefore, I defer to the insights of those interviewed in these chapters.
2. And this is the purpose of this book: to offer ways to "open up" texts.
3. The ways that the Indigenous peoples of the Southwest incorporated non-Indigenous elements into their own ceremonies are evident in Silko's "The Man to Send Rain Clouds" and the Deer Dances of the Yaqui.
4. In this concern about alienation Momaday's novel reflects the literary conventions of its time; in the 1960s much of "mainstream" American literature was devoted to an exploration of the apparent unraveling of society: the concerns about the disintegration of "the

nuclear family," the various "counterculture" movements, and the novel of alienation itself.

5. This power is represented in numerous books and films, including Hopi filmmaker Victor Masayesva's movie *Itam Hakim, Hopiit*. In the story of the Bow Clan's migration we are told that the village chief at Oraibi greets the clan and asks three questions: "What power do you have to keep your children happy? What power do you move with? Do you have a dance or a song to bring into the village?" The conjunctions of these imperatives—power, song and dance, movement, children's happiness—are all relevant for the Pueblo people Momaday depicts as well.

6. Interestingly, as he runs at the end of the book, it begins to rain; he is, after all, a rain maker and eagle hunter.

7. As Helen Jaskoski points out, however, Abel should go through a ceremony for returning warriors, and since he does not, this may be one explanation why he is unable to reintegrate and becomes violent.

8. It has not always been a cordial landscape, as the advertisement of the National Association of Scholars denotes. In the 1970s one colleague who teaches Native American literatures and participated in the Flagstaff conference endured the harassment of his colleagues, who termed the canon "shit lit" (see Roemer).

2. THE 1980S

1. This is part of the point that Michael Dorris made in the late 1970s, using it to argue for a "reading" of Native stories from within the framework of the culture that produced it.

2. The critics surveyed in the introduction certainly moved the discourse in this direction, and writer-scholars such as Elizabeth Cook-Lynn formed writing groups that composed in Native languages.

3. I will come back to this idea in chapter 4 as a means of bringing this observation into the new millennium.

4. Interestingly, the only highway alternate is the proposed trip with the Airplane Man north into Canada, and this never happens.

5. This and all subsequent references are to the 1993 edition.

6. Although Trump argued against Native casinos and then in favor of their regulation and taxing, in 1993 he flew to New Zealand and, meeting the matriarch of an *iwi* near Auckland, noted how wonder-

ful it was to go into partnership in a casino with the Indigenous people of that country.

7. It is interesting to consider Gerald Vizenor's (Anishinaabe) stories in this context, particularly the scene in *Darkness in Saint Louis Bearheart* where the pilgrims face the Evil Gambler, who has grown up on the nation's interstates, and the short story "The Moccasin Game," in which the people face the *wiindigoo* who wants to win their children.

8. Since the new edition of *Love Medicine* almost coincides with the publication of *The Bingo Palace*, it is therefore a revised conceptualization, in a way, of the whole early tetralogy. With the publication of *Tales of Burning Love*, June's story and the subsequent nature of "chance" have been extended dramatically.

9. Furthermore, in her story and indeed in the stories of all Erdrich's characters we find a fundamental questioning of our immediate readings of events: Is there such a thing as chance, coincidence, destiny? A contrived plot? If one considers these questions in an historical context, they lead to others: Is the continuation of colonial domination of Indigenous communities inevitable? Is it "meant to be"? If one believes so, the communities—and in this one instance June—become tragic victims and their "fate" inescapable. Obviously, for someone at a gambling table playing for the future of generations, this question is important; the working out of an answer becomes a test of knowledge, and faith.

10. It is interesting to note that, in a televised interview with Paul Bailey for the BBC, Erdrich revealed that *Tracks* was written first, as early as 1980. Gambling is central to the text, as I discuss later. To have it play such an overt role so early in Erdrich's fiction lends further support to its centrality not only in *Love Medicine* but also in the less obvious *The Beet Queen*.

11. In this context it is curious to consider the Latin roots of the words "rival" and "river" and their variations, for example, *rïvus* for "stream."

12. In an interesting narrative ploy Erdrich calls to question any attempts to dismiss this event as the mere dream of an unreliable narrator. Later, we see Lulu's shoes return to the narrative in such a way that the veracity of the land of the dead scene is reinforced.

13. The nature of the afterlife Pauline describes is curious. It is obviously not exclusionary, for the Europeans are here, since they also

inhabit "the real world" of the living, one assumes. Also, unlike Argus, here Pauline is visible. The disfigured, dismembered people she sees reflect her own vision of reality, bleak as it is.

14. Luck in gambling is synonymous with luck in other aspects of life and vice versa. Although it may be a bit too playful to suggest it, this luck may also relate to success in a literary sense. In fact, it is interesting to review the various inscriptions to the five novels, each of which includes Michael Dorris, Erdrich's spouse-collaborator. The dedications in the last three published novels are particularly interesting: in *Tracks*: "Michael, / The story comes up different / every time and has no ending / but always begins with you"; in *The Bingo Palace*: "To Michael, / U R lucky 4 me"; and in *Tales of Burning Love*: "To Michael" followed by a heart symbol and the letter Q, a heart, and the letter J, the queen and jack of hearts.

15. Tellingly, Lipsha outlines the road of the dead, as June has walked it to return to him. Once again the road is found in her novels, and once again it is tied to gambling. Here Lipsha takes the return as a sign of her concern for him or at least of the importance of what she is conveying. Her potential concern is, of course, qualified by June's reclaiming her car.

16. In terms of the water metaphor Erdrich employs at the conclusion of *Love Medicine*, the (cash) flow always remains the same: toward the house. One needs to recognize this reality and play in those eddies where flow direction changes, in the whorls, and turn the current to one's benefit, as Fleur does in Argus. However, one may also turn the flow to tribal benefit over the long term, and thus the Indian casino is born. At the novel's end Fleur gives up her "house" for the building of a casino.

17. Erdrich's use of English is wonderfully playful at times. "Real estate" carries the obvious in the sense of land or home ownership and the "dealers" and "agents" who help people sell or buy it. "Real" could mean reality; "estate" evokes the legal sense, of something that is left for future generations. Also, the phrase could be read as "the casino ain't nothing real" (substantial) to leave for the next generations. There are other possibilities, such as Fleur's land is not for "sale."

3. THE 1990S

1. In fact, since the publication of Alexie's novel *Flight* with its experimental style, one wonders even more.

2. This and all references are to the unpublished personal correspondence of May 5, 2005.
3. This wonderful line is from William Stafford's poem "At the Bomb Testing Site."
4. He examines elements of story fully in his wonderfully insightful book *The Truth about Stories*. As with all King's writing, this is a remarkable read.
5. I am using the term "graft" from botany that describes the process by which hybridity is accomplished. The metaphor is particularly suited for King's methodology and for use in a discussion of the 1990s, which saw the use of the term "hybrid" increase in critical circles.
6. The ways that television became central to the popular mythology of the Kennedy era are an interesting study. Consider the first televised tour of the White House by the first lady; also consider the highly publicized refusal to allow Nikita Khrushchev to visit the recently constructed Disneyland, where Disney's dream of imagination management became a physical reality through which people moved.
7. As one character, Portland, puts it late in the novel after he plays the role of savage in a burlesque theater's rendering of the Pocahontas myth: "It's a dumb routine, . . . [b]ut that's acting" (239).
8. I will come back to this idea in chapter 4 and blend it with the earlier discussion of "motion" in Welch's works in order to experiment with yet one more critical approach/lens for discussing DIAC.
9. I love this title, for it smacks of *The Mysterious Stranger*, the book project that marked Mark Twain's later years and vision, the satirist's cutting commentary on American society.
10. This ties once more the ideas of movies and food, of consumption that becomes a part of us. Also, there is the implicit idea that Christian rules are being applied again, this time as the character "Christian" manipulates his siblings' actions using the stimulus of food.
11. In fact, in my article on the 1950s I do a close reading of the scene in Disney's *Peter Pan* where the Lost Boys spar with the "Blackfoot," whose chief matches my image of Portland with a fake nose.
12. In an earlier essay I explore this naming in greater detail, particularly the role of "the hero" in audience participation. For these fictional characters, in other words, there is little doubt in the audience's mind of who is "the master."

13. It is interesting to note as well that none of the female characters, Alberta included, seems as attracted to the genre as the male characters. Moreover, the male characters respond to it in a spectrum of ways based upon their own backgrounds. Charlie, for instance, "sees" it through the personal lens of his father's career in Hollywood.

14. Some critics think of this as the difference between comedy and tragedy in a classical sense, with the former developing a trickster edge.

15. The war genre includes a scene in which Gary Cooper and his cavalry troops withstand an attack by the Cheyenne, who charge the troops' position down a shallow river, which, as noted above, is almost identical to the charge found in several places in King's novel.

16. I should note here that I am drawing material from two sources, the screenplay and the movie. There are distinct variations in the two that I will note as necessary.

17. This is from the screenplay and is slightly different from the film, in which New Crows' first response is simply "Which way?" This opens the possibility for the board member to question the answering question, which could mean "which way do you want me to think?"

18. It is attractive to paraphrase Vizenor's words during the softball game: "Remember what American writers said our ancestors did."

19. In a comic exchange between two board members the nature of this revolution is once more outlined:

ANDREW: Kingsley, tell me, is he serious?
KINGSLEY: Harold insists that he is a trickster . . .
ANDREW: A confidence man?
KINGSLEY: No, a tribal trickster is not the same . . . He is rather sincere, even innocent, artless at times . . . He believes that he can stop time and change the world through the imagination.

Andrew is nonplussed; he pulls his ear and frowns.

ANDREW: With a foundation grant of course . . .
KINGSLEY: Of course . . . Who could change the world without a foundation grant?

The primacy of the imagination, coupled with wordplay focused on "foundation grants," carries much of Vizenor's humor forward.

4. THE NEW MILLENNIUM AND ITS ORIGINS

1. I would add to the list the University of Nebraska Press, which currently has a series coedited by Vizenor and Diane Glancy.
2. One should note here how this ghost motif is so prevalent in Louis's work. It reaches its humorous fruition, though, in *Dark River*, where the spirit-quest entrepreneur, Jesse, is killed only to return to the story as a trickster/animal helper/smartass.
3. It is difficult to read this story without evoking the episode in Silko's *Ceremony* where Tayo encounters a cougar on Mount Taylor. Tayo's epiphany from that event is equally profound.
4. One also must consider Sherwood Anderson's novel *Dark Laughter* in this context.
5. The mistaken identity is, once again, intertextual: in *Ceremony* Tayo is debilitated when he is told to fire upon a group of Japanese soldiers who have surrendered because he sees the face of his uncle on one of them. This is a moment of destabilized identity when nationalism confronts older, more intimate connections.
6. I use the term "territory" here for a purpose. In Santa Fe in 1993 I attended a workshop in which Vizenor and Owens presented (as did several others). Owens's presentation was on the nature of "territory" in American literature and Native American literatures. It was a term that met with some resistance from a few participants but one that he "reversed" by considering "territory" as the frontiers of Indigenous lands.
7. In fact, ecological issues are central to his first novel, *Wolfsong*. The protagonist, Tom Joseph, precipitates an act of ecoterrorism, killing a local developer. However, Louis notes that it was not intentional but the result of a "trickster turn."
8. The movements of people are so fundamental to life that the term itself would seem devoid of meaning. However, if we isolate them and examine them in detail, we find even slight movements can indeed reveal significant insights into culture. Several disciplines do just that: study movements. For example, the "reading" of "body language" is a popular science for revealing preconscious subtexts. Moreover, in dance, theater, and film the movements of participants are carefully orchestrated because of their crucial importance for the construction of meaning. I suggest that the same holds true for other means of human expression: from the slight bodily readjustments of people on an elevator to accommodate the arrival of

another passenger, to the ways that authors conceive of and employ language to represent the motions of characters on the printed page. In this latter sense the term "movement" implies more than the limited critical traditions of "action" or "plot." By movements I mean primarily those *dramatized imaginatively* and thus visualized by writer and reader alike as each focuses on text: the working out of a story, a narrative, in relation to shared or differing concepts of this human universal.

9. There have been several worthwhile studies of motion besides Pearce's. However, critics such as Robert James Butler and Carol E. Henderson focus on movement in its larger sense (e.g., the journey motif), although Shannon Russell does consider the potential connection between movement or perception of movement and a spiritual revelation. Even those who focus primarily upon ethnicity follow the same overarching patterns for examination (see Bruce-Nova; Baker).

10. This is where recent "postcolonial" scholarship may come closer to McNickle's purpose. Bakhtin's ideas of double voicing and hybridity in texts are certainly relevant, but perhaps more specifically Homi Bhabha's sense of hybrid texts that "estrange" colonial discourse.

11. It is interesting to note that concurrent with the publication of the novel Hollywood directors were reimprinting the popular images and actions of Indians on a new generation. *The Last of the Mohicans* was produced again, with Randolph Scott in the starring role of Natty Bumppo/Hawkeye. In fact, McNickle's agent was also in negotiations with film producers to make a movie of his novel.

12. McNickle evokes this connection in many ways throughout the novel, establishing the setting at a historical moment of transitions for this land and people. However, there are many "residual" elements of the old days, including a Hollywood favorite: an old sheriff who relishes his role as a tie to the Old West and costumes himself accordingly.

13. Earlier in the novel McNickle—once again in the opening pages of a chapter—offers a close description of St. Xavier, the new town of the Anglos as well as the "old town" of the Salish. The comparison very subtly draws a cultural distinction about senses of "order" in which the immigrants' perception is devalued. In other words, the Anglos are incapable of recognizing the significance of Salish homes being centered on the church. This lack of understanding, ironically,

"saves" the Salish from the incursion of the Anglos. This, in fact, may be one instance of the difference in values to which Silko refers.

14. In a short story from the same era, "Snowfall," McNickle creates a similar scene wherein a wind arises as a medicine man calls it forth and lashes dust into the faces of frightened townsfolk who have come to see an "Indian Show," a Native ceremony.

15. Although the mannerism is similar, this action is not that of Bill Bursum in King's *Green Grass*.

16. This would certainly reflect McNickle's other activities in 1936; as a budding cultural anthropologist, he focused upon manifestations of culture, one of which is the material lifeway of a people. Fundamental to this is the behavior of individuals at moments: their bodily movements. Another element is the ways genders interact, so a comparison of the movements of women in the two villages could be very revealing.

17. In fact, I argue in *Word Ways* that Archilde's education is based upon his recognition of this survival of cultural values and that his maturity comes when he begins to align his behavior with them.

18. As the story goes, on his deathbed Thoreau was purported to have said "Moose, Indian" with his dying breath. Be that as it may, we do know that he had accumulated two thousand pages of material on Native Americans, so his interest was genuine, even if the interpretative methodology he employed was ethnocentric.

Works Cited

Alabaster, Carol. "Indian Voices Flow Together to Indict Tribal Life." *Arizona Republic*, February 10, 1985.

Alexie, Sherman. *The Business of Fancydancing*. Brooklyn: Hanging Loose Press, 1992.

———. *Flight: A Novel*. New York: Grove/Atlantic, 2007.

———. *The Lone Ranger and Tonto Fistfight in Heaven*. New York: Atlantic Monthly Press, 1993.

———. *Reservation Blues*. New York: Atlantic Monthly Press, 1995.

———. *Smoke Signals: A Screenplay*. New York: Hyperion, 1998.

———. *The Summer of Black Widows*. Brooklyn: Hanging Loose Press, 1996.

Allen, Paula Gunn. *Grandmothers of the Light: A Medicine Woman's Sourcebook*. Boston: Beacon Press, 1991.

———. *Life Is a Fatal Disease: Collected Poems 1962–1995*. Albuquerque: West End Press, 1997.

———. *Off the Reservation: Reflections on Boundary-Busting, Border-Crossing Loose Canons*. Boston: Beacon Press, 1998.

———. *The Sacred Hoop: Recovering the Feminine in American Indian Traditions*. Boston: Beacon Press, 1986.

———. *Song of the Turtle: American Indian Literature, 1974–1994*. New York: Ballantine Books, 1996.

———. *Spider Woman's Granddaughters: Traditional Tales and Contemporary Writing by Native American Women*. Boston: Beacon Press, 1989.

———. *Studies in American Indian Literature: Critical Essays and Course Designs*. New York: MLA, 1983.

Allen, Paula Gunn, and Patricia Clark Smith. *As Long as the Rivers Flow: The Stories of Nine Native Americans*. New York: Scholastic, 2001.

American Indian Quarterly 29.1–2 (2005).

Baker, Houston A. "To Move without Moving: An Analysis of Creativity and Commerce in Ralph Ellison's Trueblood Episode." *Close Reading: The Reader*. Ed. Frank Lentricchia. Durham NC: Duke University Press, 2003. 337–65.

Bevis, Bill. "Dialogue with James Welch." *Northwest Review* 20.2–3 (1982): 162–85.

———. "Native American Novels: Homing In." *Recovering the Word: Essays on Native American Literature*. Ed. Brian Swann and Arnold Krupat. Berkeley: University of California Press, 1987. 580–620.

Bhabha, Homi K. *The Location of Culture*. London: Routledge, 1994.

Blaeser, Kimberly M. *Gerald Vizenor: Writing in the Oral Tradition*. Norman: University of Oklahoma Press, 1996.

Boas, Franz. *Keresan Texts*. New York: American Ethnological Society, 1925.

Borland, Hal. *When the Legends Die*. New York: Lippincott, 1963.

Bruce-Nova, Juan. "Judith Ortiz Cofer's Rituals of Movement." *Americas Review* 19.3–4 (1991): 88–99.

Bruchac, Joseph, ed. *Songs from This Earth on Turtle's Back: Contemporary American Indian Poetry*. Greenfield Center NY: Greenfield Review Press, 1983.

———. "Whatever Is Really Yours: An Interview with Louise Erdrich." *Survival This Way: Interviews with American Indian Poets*. Ed. Joseph Bruchac. Tucson: University of Arizona Press, 1987. 73–86.

Bullchild, Percy. *The Sun Came Down: The History of the World as My Blackfeet Elders Told It*. San Francisco: Harper & Row, 1985.

Butler, Robert James. "The American Quest for Pure Movement in Dos Passos' *U.S.A.*" *Twentieth Century Literature: A Scholarly and Critical Journal* 30.1 (1984): 80–99.

Canton, Jeffrey. "Coyote Lives: Thomas King." *The Power to Bend Spoons: Interviews with Canadian Novelists*. Toronto: Mercury, 1998. 90–97.

Carr, A. A. *Eye Killers*. Norman: University of Oklahoma Press, 1995.

Coltelli, Laura. "Louise Erdrich and Michael Dorris." *Winged Words: American Indian Writers Speak*. Lincoln: University of Nebraska Press, 1990. 41–52.

Cox, James H. *Muting White Noise: Native American and European American Novel Traditions*. Norman: University of Oklahoma Press, 2006.

Dorris, Michael. "Native American Literature in an Ethnohistorical Context." *College English* 41.2 (1979): 147–62.

Erdrich, Louise. *The Beet Queen*. New York: Henry Holt and Company, 1986.

———. *The Bingo Palace*. New York: HarperCollins, 1994.

———. *Love Medicine*. New York: Holt, Rinehart, and Winston, 1984.

———. *Love Medicine: New and Expanded Version*. New York: Henry Holt and Company, 1993.

———. *Tales of Burning Love*. New York, HarperCollins, 1996.

———. *Tracks*. New York: Henry Holt and Company, 1988.

Evers, Larry. Video interview with James Welch. *Words and Places*.

Flannery, Regina. *The Gros Ventres of Montana*. Washington: Catholic University of America Press, 1953–57.

Grinnell, George Bird. *Blackfoot Lodge Tales: The Story of a Prairie People*. Lincoln: University of Nebraska Press, 1962.

Gunn, John M. *Schat-chen: History, Traditions, and Narratives of the Queres Indians of Laguna and Acoma*. Albuquerque: Albright & Anderson, 1917.

Harrod, Howard. *Mission among the Blackfeet*. Norman: University of Oklahoma Press, 1971.

Henderson, Carol E. "Freedom to Self-Create: Identity and the Politics of Movement in Contemporary African American Fiction." MFS: *Modern Fiction Studies* 46.4 (2000): 998–1003.

Hobson, Geary, ed. *The Remembered Earth: An Anthology of Contemporary Native American Literature*. Albuquerque: University of New Mexico Press, 1979.

———. "The Rise of the White Shaman as a New Version of Cultural Imperialism." *The Remembered Earth: An Anthology of Contemporary Native American Literature*. Ed. Geary Hobson. Albuquerque: University of New Mexico Press, 1979. 100–108.

Jahner, Elaine. "An Act of Attention: Event Structure in *Ceremony*." *American Indian Quarterly* 5.1 (1979): 37–46.

———. "Cognitive Styles in Oral Literatures." *Language and Style: An International Journal* 16.1 (1983): 32–51.

———. "Language Change and Cultural Dynamics: A Study of Lakota Verbs of Movement." *Languages in Conflict: Linguistic Acculturation on the Great Plains*. Ed. Paul Schach. Lincoln: University of Nebraska Press, 1980. 129–47.

Jaskoski, Helen. "Beauty before Me: Notes on *House Made of Dawn*." *Teaching American Ethnic Literatures*. Ed. John R. Maitino and David R. Peck. Albuquerque: University of New Mexico Press, 1996. 37–54.

Keller, Julia. 2002. "The Life He Left Behind." *Chicago Tribune* October 11, 2002, Tempo sec.: 1.

Kesey, Ken. *One Flew over the Cuckoo's Nest*. 1962; New York: Viking, 1973.

King, Thomas. *Green Grass, Running Water*. New York: Bantam Books, 1993.

———. *Medicine River*. New York: Viking, 1990.

———. *The Truth about Stories: A Native Narrative*. Minneapolis: University of Minnesota Press, 2005.

Kunstler, James Howard. *The Long Emergency*. Boston: Atlantic Monthly Press, 2006.

LaLonde, Christopher A. *Grave Concerns, Trickster Turns: The Novels of Louis Owens*. Norman: University of Oklahoma Press, 2002.

Larson, Charles R. *American Indian Fiction*. Albuquerque: University of New Mexico Press, 1978.

Lincoln, Kenneth. *Native American Renaissance*. Berkeley: University of California Press, 1983.

Littlefield, Daniel F., Jr., and James W. Parins. *A Bibliography of Native American Writers, 1772–1924*. Metuchen NJ: Scarecrow Press, 1981.

Lyons, Gene. "In Indian Territory." *Newsweek* February 11, 1985: 70–71.

Masayesva, Victor, Jr. *Imagining Indians*. Videocassette. Isis Productions, 1993.

———. *Itam Hakim, Hopiit*. Intermedia Arts, 1984.

McClintock, Walter. *Old Indian Trails*. New York: Houghton Mifflin, 1923.

———. *Old North Trail: Life, Legends and Religion of the Blackfeet Indians*. Lincoln: University of Nebraska Press, 1968.

McFarland, Ron. "An Interview with James Welch." *James Welch*. Ed. Ron McFarland. Lewiston ID: Confluence Press, 1986. 1–19.

McNickle, D'Arcy. *Indian Man: A Life of Oliver LaFarge*. Bloomington: Indiana University Press, 1971.

———. Letter, March 25, 1934. D'Arcy McNickle Papers, 1913–1986, Newberry Library, Chicago.

———. *Runner in the Sun: A Story of Indian Maize*. Albuquerque: University of New Mexico Press, 1987.

———. *The Surrounded*. New York: Dodd & Mead, 1936; repr., Albuquerque: University of New Mexico Press, 1977.

———. *Wind from an Enemy Sky*. Albuquerque: University of New Mexico Press, 1978.

Momaday, N. Scott. "An American Land Ethic." *Sierra Club Bulletin* 55 (February 1970): 8–11.

——. *The Ancient Child*. New York: Doubleday, 1989.

——. *House Made of Dawn*. New York: Harper & Row, 1968.

——. *The Way to Rainy Mountain*. Albuquerque: University of New Mexico Press, 1969.

Morris, Irvin. *From the Glittering World: A Navajo Story*. Norman: University of Oklahoma Press, 1997.

Nash, Roderick. *Wilderness and the American Mind*. New Haven: Yale University Press, 1967.

Nelson, Robert M. *Place and Vision: The Function of Landscape in Native American Fiction*. New York: P. Lang, 1993.

O'Connell, Nicholas, ed. *At the Field's End: Interviews with 20 Pacific Northwest Writers*. Seattle: Madrona Publishers, 1987.

Ortiz, Simon, ed. *Earth Power Coming: Short Fiction in Native American Literature*. Tsaile NM: Navajo Community College Press, 1983.

Owens, Louis. *Bone Game*. Norman: University of Oklahoma Press, 1994.

——. *Dark River*. Norman: University of Oklahoma Press, 1999.

——. *I Hear the Train: Reflections, Inventions, Refractions*. Norman: University of Oklahoma Press, 2001.

——. *Mixedblood Messages: Literature, Film, Family, Place*. Norman: University of Oklahoma Press, 1998.

——. *Nightland*. Norman: University of Oklahoma Press, 2001.

——. *Other Destinies: Understanding the American Indian Novel*. Norman: University of Oklahoma Press, 1992.

——. *The Sharpest Sight*. Norman: University of Oklahoma Press, 1992.

——. *Wolfsong*. Albuquerque: West End Press, 1991.

Parker, Dorothy R. *Singing and Indian Song: A Biography of D'Arcy McNickle*. Lincoln: University of Nebraska Press, 1992.

Parsons, Elsie Clews. *Pueblo Indian Religion*. Chicago: University of Chicago Press, 1939.

——. *The Pueblo of Jemez*. New Haven: Yale University Press, 1925.

Pearce, Richard. *The Novel in Motion: An Approach to Modern Fiction*. Columbus: Ohio State University Press, 1983.

Pulitano, Elvira. *Toward a Native American Critical Theory*. Lincoln: University of Nebraska Press, 2003.

Purdy, John. "The Babyboom Generation and the Reception of Native

American Literatures: D'Arcy McNickle's *Runner in the Sun.*" *Western American Literature* 43 (Fall 2008): 233–57.

———. *The Legacy of D'Arcy McNickle: Writer, Historian, Activist.* Norman: University of Oklahoma Press, 1996.

———. "'perspective, proportion, design': The Moral Lesson of *House Made of Dawn.*" *N. Scott Momaday and "House Made of Dawn.*" Ed. Bernadette Regal-Cellard. Paris: Éditions Ellipses, 1997. 34–41.

———. *Word Ways: The Novels of D'Arcy McNickle.* Tucson: University of Arizona Press, 1990.

Rekow, Alec. "Telling about Bear in N. Scott Momaday's *The Ancient Child.*" *Wicazo Sa Review* 12.1 (1997): 149–69.

Roemer, Kenneth. "A Retro-Prospective on Audience, Oral Literatures and Ignorance." *Studies in American Indian Literature* 9 (Fall 1997): 17–25.

Rosen, Kenneth. *The Man to Send Rain Clouds: Contemporary Stories by American Indians.* New York: Viking, 1974.

Ruppert, James. "Mediation and Multiple Narrative in *Love Medicine.*" *North Dakota Quarterly* 59.4 (1991): 229–41.

———. *Mediation in Contemporary Native American Fiction.* Norman: University of Oklahoma Press, 1995.

Russell, Shannon. "Space and Movement through Space in *Everything That Rises Must Converge*: A Consideration of Flannery O'Connor's Imaginative Vision." *Southern Literary Journal* 22.2 (1988): 81–98.

Said, Edward W. *Culture and Imperialism.* New York: Vintage, 1994.

Sands, Kathleen Mullen. "*The Death of Jim Loney*: Indian or Not?" *Studies in American Indian Literatures* 7.1 (1980): 61–78.

Scarberry-Garcia, Susan. *Landmarks of Healing: A Study of "House Made of Dawn.*" Albuquerque: University of New Mexico Press, 1990.

Silko, Leslie Marmon. *Almanac of the Dead.* New York: Simon and Schuster, 1991.

———. *Ceremony.* New York: Viking, 1977.

———. "The Man to Send Rain Clouds." *The Man to Send Rain Clouds: Contemporary Stories by American Indians.* Ed. Kenneth Rosen. New York: Viking, 1974. 3–8.

———. "An Old-Time Indian Attack Conducted in Two Parts: Part One: Imitation 'Indian' Poems; Part Two: Gary Snyder's *Turtle Island.*" *The Remembered Earth: An Anthology of Contemporary Native American Literature.* Ed. Geary Hobson. Albuquerque: University of New Mexico Press, 1981. 211–16.

———. *Storyteller*. New York: Arcade Publishing, 1981.

Stafford, William. *Stories That Could Be True*. New York: Harper & Row, 1978.

Studies in American Indian Literature 19.4 (2007).

Thoreau, Henry David. *The Maine Woods*. New York: Thomas Y. Crowell, 1961.

Treuer, David. *Native American Fiction: A User's Manual*. St. Paul MN: Graywolf Press, 2006.

Velie, Alan R. *Four American Indian Literary Masters: N. Scott Momaday, James Welch, Leslie Marmon Silko and Gerald Vizenor*. Norman: University of Oklahoma Press, 1982.

Vizenor, Gerald. *Bearheart: The Heirship Chronicles*. Minneapolis: University of Minnesota Press, 1990.

———. *Bear Island: The War at Sugar Point*. Minneapolis: University of Minnesota Press, 2006.

———. *Chancers*. Norman: University of Oklahoma Press, 2000.

———. *Darkness in Saint Louis Bearheart*. Repr. as *Bearheart: The Heirship Chronicles*. Minneapolis: University of Minnesota Press, 1990.

———. *Griever: An American Monkey King in China*. Minneapolis: University of Minnesota Press, 1987.

———. *Harold of Orange*. Screenplay. *Studies in American Indian Literatures* 5.3 (1993): 53–88.

———. *Hiroshima Bugi: Atomu 57*. Lincoln: University of Nebraska Press, 2003.

———. *Hotline Healers*. Hanover: Wesleyan University Press, 1997.

———. *Interior Landscapes: Autobiographical Myths and Metaphors*. Minneapolis: University of Minnesota Press, 1990.

———, ed. *Narrative Chance: Post Modern Discourse on Native American Indian Literatures*. Albuquerque: University of New Mexico Press, 1989.

Warrior, Robert Allen. *Tribal Secrets: Recovering American Indian Intellectual Traditions*. Minneapolis: University of Minnesota Press, 1995.

Weaver, Jace. *That the People Might Live: Native American Literatures and Native American Community*. New York: Oxford University Press, 1997.

Welch, James. *The Death of Jim Loney*. New York: Harper & Row, 1979.

———. *Fools Crow*. New York: Viking, 1986.

———. *Riding the Earthboy 40*. 1971; New York: Harper & Row, 1976.

————. *Winter in the Blood*. San Francisco: Harper & Row, 1974.

Wild, Peter. *James Welch*. Boise ID: Boise State University Press, 1983.

Wissler, Clark, and D. C. Duvall. *Mythology of the Blackfoot Indians*. New York: American Museum of Natural History, 1908.

Womack, Craig S. *Red on Red: Native American Literary Separatism*. Minneapolis: University of Minnesota Press, 1999.

Index

201–02, 217; commercial notions of, 114–15; death in, 23–25, 26, 33, 75, 80; different traditions in, 6; evil in, 23–27, 36; families in, 83–85; gambling in, 87–89, 92–93, 97–110, 256n6; gender in, 9–11; identity in, 137–38, 239; Indigenous language and, 48–49; and influence on narrative viewpoint, 238–46; language in, 48–53, 57–59; Manifest Destiny and, 60, 71, 170, 174; movement and, 224–27, 261n8, 262n9; music and singing in, 133–34, 251; orientation and Native text reading, xi–xv; popular images of, 13; portrayed in film and television, 162, 164, 166–76, 199–200, 259n11, 260n15; revenge against whites and, 22, 23–24; sexuality in, 80, 82; spiritual systems in, 12–13, 20–22; stereotypes of, 78, 204, 206, 217, 240–41, 262n11; worldview in, 61–62. *See also* literature, Native

Dances with Wolves (film), 154, 178, 185, 199–200, 205, 246
Dark Laughter (Anderson), 261n4
Darkness in Saint Louis Bearheart (Vizenor), 45; animals in, 152–58; audience of, 150–51; women in, 158–60. See also *Bearheart: The Heirship Chronicles* (Vizenor); Vizenor, Gerald
Dark River (Owens), 154, 178, 196–97, 202, 204, 208–09, 214–19, 261n2
The Dark Wind (film), 176–77
Davis, Miles, 111

death, 23–25, 26, 33, 75, 80
The Death of Jim Loney (Welch), 1, 28–34, 61, 71
decolonizing strategies, 47–48, 52, 86
The Deer Hunter (film), 171
Deloria, Vine, Jr., 146
DeMille, Cecil B., 173
differentiation, xiv, xvi, 2, 59–60, 81, 86
Disney Co. and Walt Disney, 162, 164, 182, 186, 205, 218, 259n6, 259n11
dogs, 152–58
Dorris, Michael, viii, 3, 76, 83, 129, 256n1, 258n14
Dostoyevsky, Fyodor, 55
Dubliners (Joyce), 119
Duvall, D. C., 61

Earth Power Coming (Ortiz), 46
Eastwood, Clint, 186
Edmo, Ed, 135
Eisenstein, Sergei, 224
Eliot, T. S., 122
Ellison, Ralph, 28, 202, 204
empowerment, 97–99, 105–06
Erdrich, Louise, 1, 18, 45, 55, 75, 130; *The Beet Queen* by, 87, 94, 95, 96–97, 257n10; *The Bingo Palace* by, 87, 92, 100–108, 257n8, 258n14; encounters with chance portrayed by, 95–96, 257n9; first-person narrative used by, 77, 257n12; gambling portrayed by, 87–89, 92–93, 97–101; on Indian culture blended with others, 81–82; *Love Medicine* by, 76–94, 107–10, 257n8, 257n10; Simon

Midge, Tiffany, 13, 135, 139
Miles, Ella, 131
Million, Dian, 135
Mineo, Sal, 198, 217
Mix, Tom, 186
Mixedblood Messages (Owens), 199, 212, 216–17
Moby Dick (Melville), 119
modernist novels, 226–27, 232–33
Momaday, N. Scott, 45, 46, 55, 60, 67, 74, 146, 202, 255n4; evil explored by, 23–27; *House Made of Dawn* by, 1, 5, 17–27, 67, 79, 138; narrative point of view of, 17–18; Paula Gunn Allen on, 3, 5, 12; Simon Ortiz on, 56
Morris, Irvin, 139
Morrison, Marion Michael, 167
movement and culture, 224–27, 261n8, 262n9
movies. *See* filmmaking
music and singing, 133–34, 251
Muting White Noise (Cox), viii
The Mysterious Warrior (film), 168–71, 177, 259n9
Mythology of the Blackfoot Indians (Wissler), 61

Narrative Chance (Vizenor, ed.), 116, 137
narratives: abduction, 6; modernist, 226–27, 232–33; viewpoint, 238–46
National Association of Scholars, xi, 152
Native American Fiction (Treuer), viii
"Native American Literature in an Ethnohistorical Context" (Dorris), viii

Native American Renaissance (Lincoln), 1
Native literature. *See* literature, Native
Nelson, Robert, 19
Newman, Charles, 204–05
"New Shoes" (Hogan), xiii
The New York Review of Books, xi
The New York Times, 4
Ngugi, James (Ngũgĩ wa Thiong'o), 47–49, 52
Nightland (Owens), 194–96, 213
Nixon, Richard, 250
No-No Boy (Okada), 16
Northern Exposure (TV series), 131
North of Sixty (TV series), 131
The Novel in Motion (Pearce), 224
novel writing, 14, 59–60, 191, 224–27, 232–33. *See also specific novels*

Occum, Samson, x
Off the Reservation (Allen), 13
O'Hara, Maureen, 168
Okada, John, 16
"An Old-Time Indian Attack" (Silko) 222–23
Ong, Walter, 122
Ortiz, Simon, xiii, 46, 64, 72, 77; on Anglo-American literature, 54–57; on decolonizing strategies, 47–48, 52, 86; on language, 48–53, 57–59; on poetry, 54–55
Other Destinies (Owens), 26, 189, 191, 192, 207–08, 213, 219–20
Owens, Louis, ix, 18, 111, 130, 137, 187, 247; on anthropologists, 202–03, 217–18; *Bone Game* by, 192–94, 200–201, 213, 242–45; on book-publishing industry, 204–05,

Vizenor, Gerald (*cont.*)